UNITED COUNTIES BUSES

A FLEET HISTORY, 1921–2014

UNITED COUNTIES BUSES

A FLEET HISTORY, 1921–2014

DAVID BEDDALL

Pen & Sword
TRANSPORT
AN IMPRINT OF PEN & SWORD BOOKS LTD.
YORKSHIRE - PHILADELPHIA

First published in Great Britain in 2020 by
Pen and Sword Transport
An imprint of
Pen & Sword Books Ltd
Yorkshire - Philadelphia

Copyright © David Beddall, 2020

ISBN 978 1 52675 554 4

The right of David Beddall to be identified as Author of this work has been asserted by him in accordance with the Copyright, Designs and Patents Act 1988.

A CIP catalogue record for this book is available from the British Library.

All rights reserved. No part of this book may be reproduced or transmitted in any form or by any means, electronic or mechanical including photocopying, recording or by any information storage and retrieval system, without permission from the Publisher in writing.

Typeset by Aura Technology and Software Services, India

Printed and bound in India by Replika Press Pvt. Ltd.

Pen & Sword Books Ltd incorporates the Imprints of Pen & Sword Books Archaeology, Atlas, Aviation, Battleground, Discovery, Family History, History, Maritime, Military, Naval, Politics, Railways, Select, Transport, True Crime, Fiction, Frontline Books, Leo Cooper, Praetorian Press, Seaforth Publishing, Wharncliffe and White Owl.

For a complete list of Pen & Sword titles please contact

PEN & SWORD BOOKS LIMITED
47 Church Street, Barnsley, South Yorkshire, S70 2AS, England
E-mail: enquiries@pen-and-sword.co.uk
Website: www.pen-and-sword.co.uk

or

PEN AND SWORD BOOKS
1950 Lawrence Rd, Havertown, PA 19083, USA
E-mail: Uspen-and-sword@casematepublishers.com
Website: www.penandswordbooks.com

CONTENTS

Acknowledgements 6
Introduction 7
1921–1929 18
1930–1939 26
1940–1949 38
1950–1959 44
1960–1969 67
1970–1979 84
1980–1989 116
1990–1999 145
2000–2009 172
The Final Years: 2010–2014 205
Index 220

ACKNOWLEDGEMENTS

First and foremost, I would like to thank my wife Helen for encouraging me to contact Pen and Sword about this project. A big thank you also goes to Roger Warwick; without his excellent series on United Counties, this book would not have been possible, for allowing me to use information from this series, and providing much needed assistance with photographs. Steve Loveridge and Gary Seamarks for taking the time to proofread my work and providing photographs. Lastly, my thanks go to Liam Farrer-Beddall, David Hancock, Simon Butler, the 794 Preservation Group, Graham Smith, Bruce Pyne, Thomas Knowles and Tony Burgoyne for providing additional photographs for this project.

INTRODUCTION

In its heyday, United Counties Omnibus Company Limited had an operating area covering the counties of Northamptonshire, Bedfordshire, Buckinghamshire and Huntingdonshire, as well as a garage in the north Hertfordshire town of Hitchin. Services reached into neighbouring Lincolnshire, Leicestershire, Oxfordshire, Cambridgeshire and Rutland, with express services between London, Leicester and Nottingham.

The focus of this book is on the vehicles operated by this company, rather than the day to day running. A brief history of the company's expansion is included within this introduction, with a look at the independent operators acquired by United Counties over the years. Not all of these led to the acquisition of vehicles and, where this did happen, they are listed under the appropriate years later in the book.

Before we start looking at how United Counties expanded over the years, it would be wrong to exclude a brief history of the company's predecessor, the Wellingborough Motor Omnibus Company Limited (WMOC). WMOC was formed in 1913 and built the foundations of what was to become the United Counties Omnibus and Road Transport Company Limited. Interest in Wellingborough was drawn by Mr William Benjamin Richardson who, prior to 1913, worked for the London Central Motor Omnibus Co. Ltd. The company had a garage in nearby Bedford, from which a driver and conductor would hire a bus and ply for hire in the town. Mr Richardson saw potential in this and had the bus followed to see the response to this service. This led to him sending a bus crew to Wellingborough to operate a service connecting Wellingborough to Finedon, Irthlingborough, Higham Ferrers and Rushden. The success of this initial operation led to a second vehicle being sent to Wellingborough from Bedford. On 3 May 1913, the Wellingborough Motor Omnibus Company Limited was formed, with a head office located at 1 High Street, Wellingborough. By June, the company was operating six buses on circular services. Expansion began in June when a new service was introduced running to Kettering, with a service to Northampton soon following. Construction of a garage facility at Finedon Road, Irthlingborough, started in September 1913 to house eleven vehicles, opening for use in January 1914.

By June 1914, the company was operating six services serving smaller towns and villages in close proximity to Wellingborough, as well as Northampton, Kettering and Desborough. The outbreak of war saw the number of services operated reduced. A small number of vehicles continued to enter service with WMOC over the war period. By the summer of 1919, normal service had resumed on those that had been withdrawn during the war. Expansion by the company saw a need for the garage facility in Irthlingborough to be extended. This took place in August 1919, doubling the size of the garage. 1919 also saw the introduction of route numbers by the company. By 1921, WMOC was operating the following services which were later acquired by United Counties:

1. Irthlingborough – Finedon – Wellingborough – Irchester Turn – Rushden
2. Wellingborough – Wilby – Earls Barton – Ecton – Northampton
3. Rushden – Higham Ferrers – Irthlingborough – Finedon – Burton Latimer – Kettering – Rothwell – Desborough
4. Wellingborough – Irchester Turn – Rushden – Higham Ferrers – Stanwick – Raunds
5. Finedon – Wellingborough – Irchester Turn – Wollaston
6. Kettering – Broughton – Moulton Turn – Northampton
7. Wellingborough – Great Harrowden – Little Harrowden – Isham – Kettering – Rothwell - Desborough

The company sought to expand their operations into Kettering and Northampton. For this purpose, land in both towns was purchased. Premises in Northall Street and Upper Field Street, Kettering, were purchased in April 1921, whilst land in Houghton Road, Northampton, was acquired in May 1921. However, WMOC was under-capitalised to support the expansion plans, so a decision was made by the directors to sell the company to the United Counties Omnibus and Road Transport Company Limited, one of the shareholders of WMOC. This took place on 1 September 1921, when the United Counties Omnibus and Road Transport Company was officially formed. The opening fleet stood at a total of thirty-seven omnibuses, and five service vehicles. Two omnibuses were also in construction and were also included in the sale, along with the garage facility in the small town of Irthlingborough. Head office for the company remained at 1 High Street, Wellingborough.

It was not long before a second garage was established, located in Havelock Street, Kettering. Opening on 3 February 1922, it had the capacity to house ten vehicles. The garage was constructed in the grounds of Rockingham House and remained operational for around thirteen years. A third garage commenced construction in June 1922; taking over a year to construct, it opened the following September. It was located on Bedford Road, Northampton, and eventually became the head office and main works for the company. Due to the small capacity of the Kettering garage, a decision was soon taken to establish another garage in nearby Desborough, this opening in 1925 with the capability to hold thirty-two vehicles.

Between 1928 and 1938, United Counties acquired no less than fifty-nine independent operators in Northamptonshire, Lincolnshire, Leicestershire and Buckinghamshire, expanding the operating territory significantly. To simplify these acquisitions, a table lists them below, noting how many vehicles were acquired and the significant towns and villages added to the United Counties operating area. Some of the companies will be explored in more depth after this table.

Operator	Year	No. of Vehicles	Area Covered
Summerly Bros., Desborough	05/03/28	2	Desborough, Kettering
Northampton Omnibus Co. Ltd	20/07/28	5	Northampton, Daventry, Stony Stratford
A.J. & A. York, Irchester	12/07/28	1	Irchester, Wellingborough
T.W. Smith & H. Roughton, Brigstock	25/03/29	0	Kettering, Geddington, Thrapston
Shakespeare Omnibus Co., N'hampton	29/09/29	0	Northampton, Duston
F.J. Crick & F.J. Compton, D'borough	02/12/29	1	Desborough, Rothwell, Kettering
Bagshaw & Sons, Kettering	20/01/30	1	Thrapston, Raunds, Ringstead
Clarke Bros., Weedon	29/12/30	4	Upper Weedon, Northampton, Daventry
W. & A. Ayres, Hardingstone	19/03/31	0	Northampton, Hardingstone, Wootton
J. Smith (Blue Fly Services), Creaton	26/03/31	6	Northampton, Creaton, Market Harborough
T.J. Miller, Welford	01/09/31	2	Welford, Northampton, Market Harborough
H.J. Newman, Rushden	24/09/31	0	Rushden, Kimbolton, St Neots
H.M. Spruel, Scaldwell	17/10/31	0	Brixworth, Old, Kettering
G.W. Frisby, Broughton	16/11/31	1	Kettering, Northampton
A.O. Clarke, Moulton	16/11/31	4	Moulton, Northampton
J.H. White, Brixworth	25/03/32	2	Brixworth, Northampton
G.E. Richardson: W.A. Nightingale	01/04/32	0	Northampton, Roade, Hanslope, Wolverton
J.C. Abram, Earls Barton	04/04/32	4	Northampton, Earls Barton Wellingborough
W.N. Colver, South Kilworth (Leics)	30/05/32	0	Husbands Bosworth, Market Harborough
W. Jackson, Brixworth	01/07/32	0	Northampton, Brixworth
C.E. Bundy, Oakham	30/07/32	0	Oakham, Stamford, Exton
H. Phillips, Long Buckby	31/07/32	5	Long Buckby, Northampton, Daventry
G. Blundell, Spratton	01/08/32	0	Spratton, Northampton
J.G. Ambrose Smith, Creaton	01/10/32	0	Cottesbrooke, Northampton
R.W. & H.J. Leathersich, Walgrave	01/01/33	0	Old, Northampton, Walgrave, Wellingborough
W.G. Gibson, Walgrave	01/01/33	0	Old, Northampton
F. Story, Tinwell	21/03/33	5	Stamford, Edith Weston, Kings Cliffe
B.W. H. & F. O. M. Davis, Lavendon	25/03/33	2	Olney, Bozeat, Wollaston, Wellingborough
Drage Bros., Bozeat	25/03/33	0	Rushden, Harrold, Wellingborough, Bozeat
H.G. Wright, Irchester	25/03/33	2	Wellingborough, Rushden, Irchester
R. Bagshaw & Sons, Kettering	01/07/33	6	Irthlingborough, Wellingborough, Kettering
A. Roberts, Gayton	18/10/33	0	Gayton, Blisworth, Northampton

Operator	Year	No. of Vehicles	Area Covered
Eastern National, Stony Stratford	01/12/33	11	Stony Stratford, Wolverton
Aylesbury Omnibus Co. Ltd	01/12/33	4	Aylesbury, Buckingham
Allchin & Sons, Northampton	01/12/33	31	Express services
G.E. Drage, Bozeat	17/12/33	0	Bozeat, Rushden
W.C. Nutt, Harpole	29/01/34	0	Harpole, Northampton
W.A. Nightingale	05/02/34	16	Northampton, Blisworth, Towcester
S. Kingston, Silverstone	05/02/34	0	Northampton, Towcester, Syresham
Dunkley, Buckingham	19/02/34	1	Buckingham, Northampton, Towcester
Tibbetts, Akeley	19/02/34	1	Buckingham, Towcester, Stony Stratford
A.J. & A.G. Varney, Buckingham	19/02/34	0	Buckingham, Aylesbury, Northampton
M. E. Jelley	26/02/34	4	Cosgrove, Stony Stratford, Leighton Buzzard
J.H. Bates, Wolverton	26/02/34	3	Stony Stratford, Wolverton, Stantonbury
Varsity Express, Oxford	22/04/34	6	Oxford, London Express service
R. J.E. Humphrey	08/10/34	3	Stony Stratford, Woburn, Fenny Stratford
Frosts Motors, Kettering	28/10/34	13	Corby, Kettering, Burton Latimer
W.M. Rice, Wollaston	28/10/34	1	Wollaston, Wellingborough
W.F. Pack, Brigstock	01/02/35	2	Kettering, Stanion, Brigstock, Thrapston
A.R. Surridge, Harpole	22/04/35	0	Northampton, Harpole
L. Timson & Son, Burton Latimer	08/03/36	5	Kettering, Finedon, Burton Latimer
H. Buckby & Son, Rothwell	27/09/36	0	Kettering, Market Harborough
R.L. Seamarks & Son, Higham Ferrers	24/01/37	5	Rushden, Sharnbrook, Higham Ferrers
C. Eglesfield, Wolverton	01/05/38	4	Stony Stratford, Wolverton, Stantonbury
S. Smith, Irthlingborough	03/05/38	1	Excursion & Tours Licence
G. Keeber, Wellingborough	22/06/38	0	Excursion licence (from Wellingborough)
F. Abbot, Great Doddington	26/06/38	0	Great Doddington, Wellingborough
F. Beeden, Northampton	26/06/38	18	Northampton, Newport Pagnell, Towcester
J. Meadows & Son, Barton Seagrave	04/12/38	8	Kettering, Old, Barton Seagrave, Thrapston

Out of the above operators, perhaps one of the most important acquisitions in the history of United Counties was that of the Northampton Omnibus Company. It greatly increased the presence of the company in Northampton, in particular in the north, south and west of the town. It extended services out to areas such as Daventry, Weedon, Yardley Hastings and Lavendon. The latter point provided onward journeys to Bedford with the National Omnibus Company. Smaller villages bordering Northampton such as West Haddon, Harlestone, Wootton and Roade were also encompassed.

July 1933 saw the next significant operator taken over. R. Bagshaw & Sons of Kettering allowed United Counties to expand further in the Kettering, Thrapston,

Raunds and Wellingborough areas. The main service taken over ran between Irthlingborough, Wellingborough and Northampton.

Later that year, Eastern National transferred the Stony Stratford garage of the Aylesbury Omnibus Co. Limited to the control of United Counties. A number of services in the Stony Stratford area were taken over, expanding the company's operating area into North Buckinghamshire, this taking place in December 1933. Services centred more on Aylesbury were redistributed between Eastern National, London Transport, Thames Valley and the City of Oxford Motors.

In the same month, United Counties also took control of Allchin & Sons of Northampton. With this acquisition came an extensive network of express services, primarily centring on Nottingham, Leicester, Northampton, London, Coventry, Birmingham and Oxford. Other such services also travelled as far as north Devon, Eastbourne, Brighton, Hastings, Great Yarmouth and Lowestoft. All services ran through Northampton at some point. A large fleet of thirty-one coaches was acquired from this company to run these services.

An unusual acquisition took place in April 1934 when Eastern Counties took control of the Varsity Express service. As well as a garage at Cambridge, another was established at Oxford which was a distance from the Eastern Counties operating area. United Counties was the nearest Tilling Group company to Oxford, so therefore, the garage was transferred to them. The route ran from Oxford to London via High Wycombe, Uxbridge, Southall and Shepherds Bush. A dedicated garage was established in the city.

Moving north again, the Kettering area operations were expanded further when the company acquired the business of Frost Motors (Kettering) Limited. A principal route running between Burton Latimer and Kettering was operated, as well as numerous work services in the industrial town of Corby, giving United Counties a bigger presence there too.

The final significant operator of the above list to be acquired was J. Meadows & Sons of Barton Seagrave. They operated two Kettering town services along with a circular in Thrapston. In addition to these services, another was operated between Kettering, Thrapston and Huntingdon. The latter town was in the Eastern National operating area. Due to this, the Thrapston circular and Thrapston to Huntingdon area services were transferred across to Eastern National, whilst the Kettering area services were retained. The longer Kettering to Huntingdon service became jointly operated by the two companies.

Thomas Tilling Limited of Westminster acquired the business of United Counties in July 1931. Under the new owners, United Counties continued to flourish, acquiring many more independent operators. Just prior to the takeover by Tilling, United Counties acquired the operations of Wallace and Amy Ayres, Hardingstone, on 19 March. The company operated services along the Northampton, Hardingstone and Wootton corridor. The acquisition of the Blue Fly Service in March 1931 increased the capacity of the Northampton to Market Harborough service. September 1931 saw a garage established in the small village of Welford. This was the former premises of Thomas J. Miller, a small independent which United Counties acquired on 1 September. Two routes were taken over centred on this town, running to Northampton and Market Harborough respectively.

The expansion in the Kettering and Thrapston areas called for the need of a new garaging facility. Located in Northampton Road, Kettering, the new garage was constructed to replace the small facility in the town, and the building was able to house 100 vehicles.

Head office of the United Counties Omnibus Company Limited was transferred from Irthlingborough to Houghton Road, Northampton. On this site, a new office block and garage was constructed, located in close proximity to the Derngate Coach Station.

The ageing garage in Irthlingborough was replaced in 1938 by garages in Wellingborough and Rushden. Construction of the former garage commenced in 1938. Two areas in Rushden were purchased, the first being in Skinners Hill located in the town centre, this housing an open-air parking ground. The second was in Newton Road, Rushden, where a garage building was erected, Both garage buildings opened in November, whilst the Skinners Hill facility opened in August.

1939 saw the outbreak of war, and therefore no operators were acquired between the period of 1939 to 1945. United Counties assisted with the war effort in various ways. Limited to the number of new vehicles that were taken into stock, the fleet began to suffer. This resulted in a large number of vehicles being hired by the company, which will be looked at in later sections.

After the war ended, United Counties slowly began getting back to normal. The first sign of this was the establishment of a small garage in the town of Olney, north Buckinghamshire. This was in the form of a small shed which was used to accommodate two double-decks used on a service between the town and Wellingborough.

Daventry was the next town to see the construction of a small garage. Construction commenced in 1948, several years after the land was purchased. However, it was only built to accommodate four vehicles. The increased presence of United Counties in the town of Corby led to the need for a garage to be built in the town. A site on Station Road, adjacent to the town's railway station, was acquired, where a small garage was constructed.

After the war, United Counties was trying to save as much money as possible when it came to the operation of certain services in their portfolio. This had already been shown with the purchase of the depot in Olney. The company set out to establish a small garage in the town of Market Harborough, where they were successful in finding accommodation to house a solitary single-deck used on more lightly-trafficked routes in the local area.

The rapid expansion of services in the Corby area called for the expansion of the original garaging facility in the town. A need arose to house ten vehicles in the town, rather than the original four.

The following years remained rather quiet, with no significant goings on to note. One of the most notable events in the history of United Counties, however, was the doubling in size of the fleet on 1 May 1952. This was the date that the Midland area of the Eastern National Omnibus Company Limited was transferred. Eastern National had two operating areas, which were split from each other. The more traditional operating area was centred on Essex. The Midland area had garages in Bedford, Biggleswade, Luton, Huntingdon, Hitchin and Aylesbury. In January 1949, the Tilling Group had lost its interests in the bus industry to the British Transport Commission, which took the decision to transfer the Midland operation from Eastern National to the more logical control of United Counties. The agreement was reached for this transfer in December 1951 and took effect from the above date. This added 247 vehicles to the United Counties fleet.

On a smaller scale, 1952 also saw the acquisition of the business of M. Knight of Northampton. This operator ran a service between Northampton and Brixworth, enhancing United Counties' existing services on this corridor.

The allocation at the newly acquired Biggleswade garage was enhanced with the takeover of O.A. Bartle of Potton in June 1953. The operations included a number of routes centred on the village, running out to Biggleswade, Bedford, St Neots and Royston, along with a number of school contracts.

The expansion of services in Stony Stratford led to a new, larger garage facility being constructed, replacing the two original garages in the town. Construction commenced in 1954, and the garage opened its doors in July 1955. Staying with garages, the facilities acquired from Eastern National at Biggleswade were in a poor state by the mid-1950s. This led to United Counties demolishing the original buildings over the course of 1956, with new buildings being constructed, along with a new parking area. Construction of these facilities was completed during 1957.

Another small Bedfordshire independent was added to United Counties during 1960. The operations of Keysoe based Keysonian Coaches were acquired in May. With this came three services, operating between Bedford and north Bedfordshire villages, and Keysoe and St Neots.

The small outstation at Long Buckby was closed in January 1960, the work from this depot being redistributed between Northampton and Daventry. Bedford was the recipient of a new bus station in December 1960, built after a redevelopment of the town centre area. Yet another garage was constructed and opened this time at Bletchley. This garage replaced the small outstation at nearby Fenny Stratford.

Next to be acquired was the operations of Pytchley-based Royal Blue Coach & Transport Company. Services were centred on the Kettering area. These were taken over by the company, whilst the tour business was sold to Shelton-Osborn of Wollaston along with eight vehicles.

1968 saw a new garaging facility open in the Lincolnshire town of Stamford. There was a need for this new facility as United Counties was made to vacate the original premises in the town.

Ownership of United Counties changed in 1969 from the British Transport Commission to the newly formed National Bus Company. Under this ownership, the green livery was retained by the vehicles.

Two significant takeovers took place over the course of 1969 and 1970. Firstly, the bus operations of Birch Bros. Limited was acquired on 14 September 1969. Twelve vehicles were acquired and soon repainted into United Counties livery. The vehicles concerned were all allocated to Rushden garage. The second acquisition was of the fleet of Luton Corporation on 4 January 1970. The takeover added a further seventy-seven vehicles to the United Counties fleet, making the company the dominating concern in the town.

1971 saw the construction of the new town of Milton Keynes commence. The developers required United Counties to provide a number of services around the new town. A handful of services were introduced over the coming years, operating from Bletchley and Stony Stratford garages.

Two sites were in operation in Aylesbury, both acquired from Eastern National. The smaller of the two premises, at Walton Street, was required by the local council. In exchange, land adjacent to the Buckingham Street depot was acquired by United Counties, and the site was expanded to accommodate the fleet.

The expansion of the Bletchley fleet called for an extension to the existing garage facility. Land next to the garage was acquired and was subsequently doubled in size during 1973. Corby received a new under-cover bus station in Anne Street on the edge of the town centre during 1973.

The operations and vehicles of Court Line Coaches were purchased by United Counties in 1974. The company operated a small set of services centred on the Luton,

Dunstable and Hemel Hempstead areas. The existing garage at Luton Airport was not acquired by United Counties as it was repossessed by the local council. This led to the overcrowding of Castle Street garage, and a temporary arrangement was made with Luton Borough Council to house a number of the vehicles.

In 1975, United Counties acquired a number of services from Yorks Bros. of Cogenhoe, running two services between Northampton and Wollaston, via a number of villages en-route.

Due to the considerable expansion of the Luton fleet, the garage was doubled in size, opening in 1975. The new facilities included a new inspection pit area, as well as an office block and canteen. The new facilities catered well for the sizeable fleet of well over 100 vehicles allocated to Luton at the time.

By 1976, the number of services operated in the new Milton Keynes area had reached twenty. The majority of them were centred on Bletchley, with others serving Stony Stratford and Wolverton. Central Milton Keynes Shopping Centre was later opened in 1979 and a large network of services was established to serve this new facility. United Counties also submitted plans for a new garage facility to replace the garages at Bletchley and Stony Stratford.

The long-serving Derngate Coach Station in Northampton was replaced by a new bus station facility in the town centre. The infamous Greyfriars Bus Station was opened on 2 May 1976.

A third town in the United Counties area also received a new bus station in 1976. Luton received a more permanent site at Bute Street, replacing the temporary bus station. It was located next to the town's Midland Road train station. Like Northampton's new facility, the bus station was under-cover. Huntingdon followed suit the following year when a modernised bus station was opened in the town; however, this facility was open to the elements.

Major service cuts in the Northamptonshire area in 1978 led to the closure of Daventry garage. A solitary vehicle was still out-stationed within the town. In the same year, Rushden garage was also closed, with the vehicles and services passing to nearby Wellingborough and Kettering garages.

Two further garages closed their doors over the course of 1980 and 1981. First to close was Stamford in 1980, this virtually removing United Counties from the Lincolnshire area. A year later, the Desborough garage was also closed. As well as this, United Counties sold off a lot of properties that they owned during the year.

In 1980, it was the turn of Bedford and Wellingborough garages to be modernised. The former garage had its existing inspection pits enlarged, a new store building was constructed along with a new workshop area. The pit area was expanded, a rolling road being installed. The site was also used as an MOT testing centre for PSVs. The engineering facilities at Wellingborough were also improved. The inspection pits were updated and new fuelling facilities were installed along with a new bus wash.

Work on a new central bus garage commenced in March 1981 in the Winterhill area of Milton Keynes. The new facility was handed over to United Counties two years later. The new facility had the capacity to garage 125 vehicles, instead of the proposed 250. The garage officially opened on 27 May 1983, replacing Stony Stratford and Bletchley garages. A new bus station was also opened in the town close to the railway station.

A decision was made in September 1985 to split United Counties into three operating companies. The United Counties name would be retained for one operating concern, taking control of garages at Northampton, Kettering, Corby, Wellingborough, Bedford and Huntingdon. Luton & District was another subsidiary set up to take control of the Luton, Hitchin and Aylesbury garages. The final new company formed was Milton

Keynes Citybus. These changes took effect from 1 January 1986, when three different liveries were introduced. The division of the company was done in readiness for the National Bus Company to be sold off to private operators. Dividing the larger companies into smaller ones would make it easier for them to be sold.

The garage in Wellingborough only remained operational until April 1986 before being closed by United Counties. The vehicles and services were distributed between Northampton and Kettering garages respectively.

United Counties introduced a new coaching network in May 1986 when they launched the Coachlinks network. Vehicles operating these services were painted into a white and blue livery, making them stand out from the service fleet. The brand continued for many years, being adopted by Stagecoach until the early 2000s.

The growth of the Cambridgeshire town of St Neots led United Counties to launch another new brand of bus, this time the 'Street Shuttle', being operated by a small fleet of minibuses to replace double-deck vehicles on town services. This brand became successful and was used initially in the town but was later rolled out in Bedford, Corby and Kettering. Again, this brand lasted into the 2000s with Stagecoach.

United Counties was purchased in 1987 by the Stagecoach Group Ltd of Perth. Ownership of the company passed from the National Bus Company to Stagecoach on 18 November 1987. The sale brought about a number of changes to the company, including a livery change to the infamous stripes.

The competition between United Counties and Yorks Travel of Cogenhoe led Stagecoach to purchase two services, the first between Northampton, Irthlinborough and Wellingborough and the second between Northampton and Nether Heyford from Yorks, along with two vehicles.

The Biggleswade garage in Shortmead Street was sold to a development company which then leased it back to United Counties for a short period of time before the site was vacated in September 1989. An alternative location was sourced to house the fleet, with a site being found at the former Charles Cook coach company in Langford Road, Biggleswade. This site was later downgraded to an outstation of Bedford in August 1991, with the site remaining in use by Stagecoach until it closed in 2018.

Corby had suffered with high competition from the taxis within the town. The introduction of Routemasters in 1988 saw the number of passengers carried by United Counties' increase significantly. 1990 saw the company compete further with the local taxis by introducing the new 'Corby Magic Mini' minibus operation, along with a new black and gold livery too. Like the Routemaster initiative, the Magic Mini network was a big success.

During the mid-1990s, Stagecoach Holdings expanded further in the Cambridgeshire area, purchasing the operations of Cambus and Viscount. The Cambus operations also included a garage in Milton Keynes. It was deemed by the Competition Commission that Stagecoach had a large presence in the area, owning United Counties, Cambus and Viscount. It was suggested that the company should sell some of its garages. The chosen ones were the Milton Keynes garage of Cambus, and United Counties' Huntingdon garage. The sale took place on 2 May 1997, when the Huntingdon allocation passed to a new company trading as MK Metro, with the fleet name Premier Buses being applied to the Huntingdon vehicles.

2001 saw a new identity given to the Stagecoach UK Bus operations, introducing a new corporate livery to the company's vehicles, as well as new local identities. United Counties gained the names of 'Stagecoach in Bedford' and 'Stagecoach in Northants' respectively. Further developments saw the amalgamation of the Cambus, United Counties and Viscount operations under the common name of Stagecoach East, introducing a single fleet numbering system for all three operators. This was short lived, being replaced by the introduction of a national fleet numbering scheme in January 2003.

No significant events took place between 2003 and 2010 in terms of the day to day running of the company. This changed in August 2010 when control of Bedford garage transferred to Cambus Ltd, Cambridge. However, vehicles remained operating on the United Counties licence until March 2013 when the fleet, along with Viscount and Stagecoach in the Fens, was officially transferred to the Cambus licence.

The United Counties story concludes in October 2014 when the vehicles operating from three garages at Northampton, Kettering and Corby were transferred onto the Midland Red South operators' licence. Control for the Northamptonshire and Warwickshire garages were all placed onto the new licence, and the new Stagecoach Midlands group was formed, being controlled from the new Far Cotton, Northampton garage.

David Beddall
Wollaston, 2020

United Counties rebodied a number of its Bristol JO5G models during the 1950s to give the vehicles a more modern appearance. An example of this is 451 – VV5697 which is seen after its career with United Counties as a non-PSV vehicle. *794 Preservation Group*

Just before we start looking at the fleet history of United Counties, the following two photographs are worthy of a place at this point in the book. Two preserved vehicles from the opening years of the company are now in preservation with the Shuttleworth Collection in Bedfordshire. Perhaps the oldest vehicle is former Wellingborough Motor Omnibus Company Leyland ST LF9967. It is seen at Wellingborough Museum in 2013 showing off the original colours of the WMOC.
Liam Farrer-Beddall

Another preserved vehicle is BD209 (B15). This vehicle represents the Leyland 36HP model, one that United Counties acquired a number from WMOC. Originally bodied by Dodson, United Counties fitted one of its own bodies to this vehicle in May 1927. The original green livery worn by the company was lighter than that worn by vehicles under National Bus Company control. It is seen attending the Showbus 2015 event at Woburn Abbey.
Liam Farrer-Beddall

1921–1929

1921

The United Counties Omnibus and Road Transport Company was formed on 24 September 1921, when the business of the Wellingborough Motor Omnibus Company Ltd. was acquired. The opening fleet comprised thirty-seven operational buses of Leyland manufacture, along with two vehicles that were under construction. Broken down, the fleet acquired was made up of twenty-nine double-deck machines and eight saloons. They retained their original Wellingborough fleet numbers of A1 to A17; B1 to B14 and S2 to S7 respectively. The two vehicles that were still being built when the takeover took place were delivered in November 1921. These vehicles were registered BD257 and BD481, numbered S8 and S9. United Counties fitted their own bodies to these two vehicles which were based on the Leyland RAF chassis, which were reconditioned chassis dating back to the First World War. The first new vehicle orders placed by the company called for twelve Leyland chassis for delivery in 1922.

Vehicles were garaged in the small Northamptonshire town of Irthlingborough whilst the head office was in Wellingborough. Services operated at this time were focused on the Wellingborough, Rushden, Irthlingborough, Raunds and Kettering areas, serving nearby villages, with one service reaching Northampton.

It is worth noting at this point that United Counties applied a fleet number to both the chassis and bodywork. These were generally allocated to the vehicles when they were taken into stock by the company, hence some vehicles being numbered out of sequence. Over the coming chapters, the chassis number is displayed first, followed by the body numbers in brackets. In the list below, the body number is shown after the chassis number.

The opening fleet was as follows:

A1	1	LN329	A14	14	BD4147	B3	33	BD513
A2	2	LF9876	A15	15	BD4580	B4	34	BD557
A3	3	LF9967	A16	16	BD5049	B5	35	BD588
A4	4	LF9969	A17	17	BD5844	B6	36	BD948
A5	5	LF9970	S1	22	BD3890	B7	37	BD1128
A6	6	LH8633	S2	23	BD1642	B8	38	BD1130
A7	7	LH8651	S3	24	BD2038	B9	39	BD1709
A8	8	LF9877	S4	25	BD3039	B10	40	BD2321
A9	9	LH8721	S5	26	BD3042	B11	41	BD3488
A10	10	LH8893	S6	27	BD986	B12	42	BD3870
A11	11	LH8933	S7	28	BD3056	B13	43	BD4414
A12	12	LH8934	B1	31	BD476	B14	44	BD5845
A13	13	BD3218	B2	32	BD491			

1922

Delivery of the above-mentioned order for twelve Leyland chassis was completed between February and May 1922 and were again of the Leyland RAF model. These were numbered S10 to S20 (45/6/53/47/57/54/48/55/6/8/9) in the United Counties fleet. Like the previous order, United Counties constructed their own bodywork for the first five, whilst S15-S20 were given single-deck bodies constructed by Dodson. Registration marks BD3476, 6240, 6388/9, 6676, 6391, 6390, 6392, 6499, 6500/1 were carried by these vehicles. The twelfth vehicle was numbered C1 (60) - BD7049 and was also bodied by the company. This vehicle was unique in that it was built to carry sixty passengers, a capacity that was not seen on another United Counties vehicle until the mid-1950s.

Three further Leyland chassis were purchased in February 1922. Two of these were bodied as lorries, whilst the third one, A20, gained a United Counties double-deck body in May 1922. Ancillary vehicle S1 donated its lorry body to one of these new chassis, in return being bodied as a double-deck bus.

The first second-hand vehicle to be acquired by the company entered the fleet in April 1922. BD209 originated with Luck & Andrews of Kettering and was numbered B15 (49) upon entry into the fleet.

1923

Vehicle orders for 1923 called for seven Leyland GH7 chassis which were ordered alongside four Dodson single-deck bodies. Rolling stock numbers C3 to C9 (63-69) were allocated to this batch. The first three were taken into stock during August 1923, the balance being delivered the following year. The four Dodson saloon bodies were fitted to C3 to C6. C3-5 were the only ones to arrive in 1923, with these vehicles being registered BD8208, 8216, 8219.

United Counties also purchased a former demonstration vehicle registered TC2128. The vehicle was taken into stock in May 1923 and preceded the new vehicles, being allocated rolling stock number C2 (61) by the company.

1924

Other than the outstanding vehicles from 1923, no new vehicles entered the fleet during 1924. C6 was the first of these to be delivered, arriving in January registered BD8618. The remaining three, C7-9, arrived during April and were uniformly registered BD9104-6 respectively.

Six vehicles were rebodied during the year. B3, B4 and B10 gained new body work constructed by the company, with the bodies being donated to A2, A9 and A16.

1925

A new Leyland chassis was introduced in 1925, this being the Leyland Z5. Five of this new chassis type were purchased by United Counties. Four were bodied by Dodson with twenty-seat saloon bodies and were numbered Z2-5 (72-75) – RP457/8, 580, 674. The other example, numbered Z1 (71) – RP976, was the first saloon body to be constructed by United Counties themselves.

A further six new vehicles entered the United Counties fleet in August; the company ordered six Leyland C7 chassis along with an equal number of Dodson single-deck bodies. Fitted with pneumatic tyres, these vehicles were numbered D1-D6 (76-81) by the company and carried registrations RP1540-5.

The re-bodying of older vehicles in the fleet continued during 1925 when United Counties built two bodies and mounted them on to chassis A3 and A15, the two vehicles being re-registered to RP977 and RP978 respectively. At the same time, the body and registration (BD4580) from A15 was transferred to the chassis of A7.

1926

Vehicle orders for 1926 called for six Leyland chassis. However, eight Leyland chassis were delivered to United Counties over the course of 1926. The original order for six materialised in May and June 1926 numbered C10-15 (85-90) and were built on the Leyland SG11 model. These vehicles gained bodywork by Dodson and were registered RP2789/7, 2864-7. The two additional chassis were again built by Leyland, this time the SG7 model. These two were numbered B16 and B17 (83/4) by the company. United Counties constructed the two double-deck bodies fitted to these machines. Registrations RP2710 and RP2788 were allotted to B16 and B17.

A further three older vehicles in the fleet were treated to a re-body. First was double-deck A13 which had a new single-deck body fitted. However, unlike similar vehicles already in stock, United Counties did not build the body for this vehicle; instead a new Dodson saloon body was purchased and mounted on the chassis. Sister vehicle A14 had its original saloon body replaced by one built by United Counties. The final vehicle to be treated to a re-body during 1926 was single-deck S2, which was converted from a single-deck vehicle to a double-deck machine.

1927

1927 saw a large batch of eighteen single-deck vehicles delivered to the company. This introduced the Leyland Lion chassis to the fleet. They were appropriately allocated rolling stock numbers L1-18 (97-123). The Leyland Lion itself was one of the earliest buses that was specifically designed for passenger-carrying purposes. The first six, L1-6 – RP4520-2, 4633-5, carried Dodson bodies, whilst the remainder of the batch were bodied by Shorts of Rochester under contract to Leyland Motors Ltd. After the introduction of this batch of vehicles, the fleet total stood at 97 vehicles. L7-18 were registered RP5003-8, 5190/1, RP5202/3/5 and RP5236.

A further nine vehicles were placed through the re-bodying programme during 1927. A2/4/5/7/11/12 and B15 were rebodied using United Counties own-built bus bodies. The final two, S3 and S4, had their original Hora saloon bodies replaced with United Counties built double-deck bodies.

1928

1928 saw three independent operators purchased by United Counties. The first company concerned was that of Desborough-based Summerly Bros. The acquisition included a pair of Lancia single-deck vehicles, which became numbered LA1/2 (114/5) in the United Counties fleet, carrying registrations RP264, 4091.

One of the most important acquisitions made by United Counties was of the Northampton Omnibus Co. Ltd. The takeover allowed United Counties to expand its operating territory to the south, north and west of the town. In order for the company to be able to operate the newly acquired services, a fleet of twenty-five Leyland Lion saloons were soon purchased. These vehicles followed on from the original batch, being numbered L19-L43 (127-151) and were all bodied by Shorts, seating thirty-five passengers. The first twelve materialised in May; the next four in June and the remaining nine in July. These vehicles were registered RP5970-81, 6104/2/3, 6156, 6196/7, 6225-8, 6242/4/3.

Five of the original Northampton Omnibus vehicles were taken into stock by United Counties, all in the form of Daimler Y machines; two carrying Strachan bodies, two with Grose bodywork and the final one a Brown body. These vehicles were allocated body numbers 116-120 by the company, but no chassis numbers were allocated. These lasted only a few months, being displaced by a batch of Leyland Lion saloons mentioned below. Various registration plates were carried, NH4819, XF9423, NH6327, 5618 and 5423.

The final operator to be acquired was A.J. and A. York of Irchester in July. Included in this sale was a two-year-old 20-seat Thornycroft A1 saloon bus registered RP2138, and numbered T1 (126) by United Counties. This acquisition allowed United Counties to increase its services between the village and near-by Wellingborough.

During 1928, thirteen Leyland Lion saloons were purchased by United Counties. However, not all arrived during 1928, with delivery being completed in January 1929. Seven were delivered to the company in December numbered L44-51 (152-159) – RP6715-22. These carried body work constructed by Short, similar to previous deliveries of the type. They displaced a similar number of older vehicles from the fleet.

1929

The outstanding Leyland Lions arrived during January, numbered L52-6 (160-4), registered RP6723-6, 6805. The first three were again bodied by Short, whilst the final pair were bodied by Leyland. In addition to these outstanding vehicles, a further twenty-two were ordered for 1929 delivery. The batch was numbered L57 to L78 (165-186) and all carried thirty-five-seat rear-entrance Leyland bodies. Delivery of this sizeable batch was spread between January and March 1929 respectively, registered RP6806-8, 6861, 6913/4, 6946-9, 7114-25. The influx of these new vehicles saw the withdrawal of seventeen older vehicles; ten A-type saloons; an S-type saloon and six double-deck machines.

A solitary vehicle was acquired from Desborough-based independent Crick & Compton, when the company was acquired by United Counties in December 1929. The vehicle in question was a Reo saloon which seated eighteen. Registered RP1192, it was allotted fleet number 190. This small vehicle did not last long with United Counties and was withdrawn the following year.

United Counties took on loan a Leyland Titan demonstration vehicle from Leyland Motors Ltd. This vehicle carried a 51-seat Leyland body and was numbered TN1 (191) - TE9626 by United Counties. The vehicle remained on loan for a three-month period before being officially acquired by the company in January 1930. This led to the order of eight similar vehicles for 1930 delivery.

Irthlingborough Cross finds Leyland ST LF9876 in May 1913. This vehicle was one of the first to operate with the Wellingborough Motor Omnibus Company Limited. Originally numbered C, it later gained fleet number A2. It passed to United Counties in 1921. *Roger Warwick Collection*

Another shot here of LF9967 which featured in the introduction. It is seen standing at the George and Dragon, Raunds, in this 1914 shot. The vehicle originally carried the letter H, later being renumbered to A3. It clearly shows the Birch body style, built on the Leyland 36HP chassis. *Roger Warwick Collection*

The original garage for the Wellingborough Motor Omnibus Company Limited was located in the small Northamptonshire town of Irthlingborough. This photograph shows Leyland ST A4 (LF9969) leaving the garage in January 1914. This was another vehicle acquired by United Counties in 1921. *Roger Warwick Collection*

Representing the small number of single-deck vehicles acquired from WMOC is LH8934. This vehicle took up rolling stock number A12 and is another example of the Leyland ST model. It is seen passing through Broughton destined for Northampton, contrary to the destination board. *Roger Warwick Collection*

The George and Dragon, Raunds, provides the backdrop to Leyland 36HP B9 (BD1709). This vehicle was new to the Wellingborough Motor Omnibus Company in July 1919, the same year that this photograph was taken. BD1709 was one of a number of vehicles to pass to United Counties in 1921. *Roger Warwick Collection*

During the early 1920s, United Counties Omnibus and Road Transport Co. Ltd took stock of a number of Leyland RAF chassis. S10 – BD3476 was new in February 1922 and is seen carrying a body constructed by United Counties themselves. *Roger Warwick Collection*

The Leyland Lion was the first significant type of single-decker taken into stock by United Counties. Eighty-nine were purchased by the company between 1927 and 1930, and all gained fleet numbers beginning with 'L'. Here we see two fine examples of the type, L68 – RP7115 (above) and L73 – RP7120 (below). They are both photographed at Skegness whilst on private hire duties. *G. H. F. Atkins Archive/S. J. Butler Collection*

1930–1939

1930

During 1929, ten Leyland Lion saloons were ordered for 1930 delivery. These vehicles duly arrived during March 1930, numbered L80 to L89 (193-202) and were registered RP8552-8561. The intake again led to more elderly buses being withdrawn from service, which saw the last of the A-type saloons leave the fleet, along with four S-type double-deck machines, four S-type saloons and two Z-type machines, along with recently acquired Reo 190.

The order for eight Leyland Titan machines was reduced to seven when the demonstration vehicle was retained by the company. The first five arrived in the designated year, whilst the remaining two found their way to the company the following year. Stock numbers TN2 to TN6 (203-207) were taken up by these vehicles along with registrations RP8562-6.

An order was placed at the close of 1930 for five Leyland Lion saloons and ten Leyland Titan double-decks for delivery during 1931.

An additional Leyland Lion saloon was acquired by United Counties from Kettering based Bagshaw & Sons in January. As this vehicle was purchased prior to the new Lions entering the fleet, it was numbered as L79 (192) (RP5440), bridging the gap between the 1929 and 1930 deliveries.

The second acquisition of the year came from Clarke Bros. of Weedon, from which United Counties acquired four vehicles. These comprised three Tilling-Stevens saloons and a solitary Maudslay saloon. The latter vehicle was registered RP6839 and was numbered M1 (208). The three Tilling-Stevens machines carried registrations UP218, RP6142 and RP3609, and were numbered X1-3 (209-211). The bodywork of the last of the trio was in poor shape and only lasted six months before it was rebodied by United Counties with a Dodson body donated by withdrawn S26.

1931

The first two new vehicles to be taken into stock during 1931 were the two outstanding Leyland Titan machines, TN7 and TN8 (212/3). These were shortly followed by TN9-18 (214/5, 224-231). TN7-10 arrived during March 1931, whilst TN11-18 came to the company between May and July 1931 respectively. The batch was registered NV7-10, NV233/78-82, 495/6 respectively.

The vehicles of three independent operators were added to the United Counties fleet during 1931. The first six came in the form of six Reo saloons from A.E. Smith of Creaton. Four of the six vehicles were in such a poor condition that they did not see service with United Counties. The remaining two were quickly overhauled by the company and pressed into service. No chassis numbers were allocated to these vehicles, instead body numbers 217-222 were carried. They were registered BD9550, RP204, 713, 3124, 5469 and 5715.

Next came two Reo saloons from T.J. Miller of Welford. The acquisition took place on 1 September 1931 and saw a small garage established in the village. Chassis numbers R3/R4 (232/3) were allotted to these vehicles which were registered RP6047 and RP3540.

November saw the final second-hand vehicles acquired by the company. This time the business of A.O. Clarke of Moulton was acquired, which added a GMC saloon and three Chevrolet machines to the fleet. Again, these vehicles were only allotted body numbers 234 to 237. The GMC gained the first number and was registered RP6514, whilst the Chevrolet machines were registered RP5842, 7956 and 9905.

1932

1932 was a busy year for vehicles entering the United Counties fleet. The first new vehicles to enter the fleet came in the form of sixteen new Leyland Titan TD2 double-decks which were spread across the year. They took up stock numbers TN19 to TN34 (242-257). The first arrived during February 1932, when TN19-29 entered the fleet. TN30 to TN34 arrived during March 1932 and completed the batch. Registrations NV1038-46, 1105/6, 1157-9, 1257/8 were allocated to this batch.

The first two second-hand vehicles to enter the fleet in 1932 came from J.H. White of Brixworth in March 1932. RP7357 was a Dennis G saloon, numbered 239 by United Counties. This vehicle lasted three months with the company before it was withdrawn. The second vehicle was a Bedford WLG with a Willowbrook body registered NV258, numbered 240. This vehicle fared a little better, lasting longer than its sister vehicle.

April 1932 saw the acquisition of J.C. Abram of Earls Barton. With this acquisition came four vehicles; three of them being variants of Thornycroft machines, the fourth a Commer Invader. The Thornycroft machines were registered RP665, RP3537, RP6417 and carried body numbers 258 to 260, with 259/260 gaining chassis numbers TH1/2 (259/60). 258 was withdrawn soon after acquisition. The Commer machine was numbered 261 by the company.

The final five vehicles to enter the fleet during 1932 came from Long Buckby based H. Phillips. The operation was acquired in July 1932 and involved two Reo saloons, a Star B, a Chevrolet LO and an ADC machine. The two Reo machines were registered RP5540 (a Reo Sprinter); and NF5444 (a Reo Pullman). The Star B was registered RA4044. RY6495 was the identity carried by the Chevrolet LO machine, whilst the ADC saloon was identified as VF2871. Collectively, these five vehicles were numbered 264 to 268 by United Counties.

1933

The name of the company was changed on 20 September 1933, when the Road Transport part of the original name was dropped, the company simply becoming known as the United Counties Omnibus Company Limited. The introduction of this name also saw the introduction of a new livery, a green and cream livery adorned the buses in the fleet after this date, replacing the original blue and white livery.

1933 saw the delivery of eighteen Leyland Titan TD2 machines to the company. These vehicles carried the Eastern Counties body style. Delivery of this batch was completed over the months of March and April 1933, when they were numbered TN35 to TN49 (269-283). Consecutive registrations from NV2268 to NV2282 were carried by these vehicles. These vehicles were the last to be allocated both chassis and body numbers.

The vehicles of four independents were acquired over the course of 1933. First to be acquired was of F. Story of Tinwell, which added five vehicles to the fleet. All five vehicles were of a different type, these being a Chevrolet, a Lancia, a Dennis, a Reo and finally a Federal. Fleet numbers 284 to 288 were allotted to these vehicles.

Two vehicles came from Lavendon based B.W.H. & F.O.M. Davis and were numbered 289 and 290. The former vehicle was registered VV877 and carried a Bedford WLB chassis. The latter vehicle was a Reo saloon registered PP5205.

H.G. Wright of Irchester was acquired in March 1933, from which came VX3821 and RP8420. These were numbered 291 and 292, these being a Duple bodied Gilford saloon (291) and a Commer P5 saloon with Willowbrook bodywork (292).

Further vehicles were acquired from R. Bagshaw & Sons of Kettering in July 1933. These vehicles were numbered 294 to 299 and again added a variety of chassis to the company.

The closing three months of 1933 saw no less than forty-two second hand vehicles taken into stock from various independents taken over by United Counties. The first such vehicles came from the acquisition of the Stony Stratford garage of Eastern National. Eastern National had acquired this depot from the Aylesbury Omnibus Co. Ltd. in May 1933, shortly before it was handed over to United Counties. The takeover of this garage duly took place on 1 December 1933, when the route and vehicles transferred to United Counties. The vehicles taken into stock by United Counties consisted of three Leyland Titan TD1 double-decks, numbered 309 to 311 by the company; two Leyland Lion saloons which preceded these vehicles and were numbered 307 and 308 respectively. Two A.D.C. saloons were also acquired numbered 305 and 306. To make up numbers, four Duple bodied Leyland Tiger TS3 coaches were also acquired and gained rolling stock numbers 312-315.

The remaining second-hand vehicles were acquired from Northampton based Allchin & Sons on 1 December 1933. The acquisition of this business brought with it a large express service network and thirty-one coaches to operate the routes. These vehicles took up the fleet number block 316 to 346. Broken down, this batch was made up of three Duple bodied Leyland Tigers; a similar number of Duple bodied A.E.C. Regal machines; sixteen Daimler CF6 coaches; seven Reo Pullmans and two Brockways.

Vehicle orders placed in 1933 called for five Dennis Lancet saloons for 1934 delivery.

1934

The delivery of the new Dennis Lancet saloons was over-shadowed by the acquisition of fifty second-hand vehicles from the numerous operators acquired by United Counties during the year.

The first sixteen second-hand machines came from Nightingales of Northampton on 5 February 1934. The vehicles acquired from this operator were of various types. Three Maudslay coaches were taken into stock, numbered 347 to 349; a similar number of Gilford coaches were acquired, numbered 350 to 352. Fleet numbers 353 to 355 were allocated to three Studebaker charabancs. Three Brockway charabancs became 356 to 358. Guy B chassis carried 359 and 360. The final two vehicles were a G.M.C. machine and a Reo, and these two vehicles were numbered 361 and 362 respectively.

Nightingales jointly operated a service between Northampton and the village of Syresham via Towcester with an S. Kingston of Silverstone. United Counties also acquired this business at the same time as the former operator. This acquisition added two saloons to the fleet, a Guy B which became United Counties 364, and a Gilford saloon which was numbered 363.

A trio of operators was acquired on 19 February 1934 in the Buckingham area. These were Dunkley of Buckingham; Tibbetts of Akeley; and Varney of Buckingham respectively. The first operator provided United Counties with a Morris Viceroy saloon which became numbered 365. A Chevrolet saloon registered KX5207 was acquired from Tibbetts and was allotted fleet number 366. However, United Counties did not acquire any vehicles from Varney.

The Stony Stratford operations were strengthened on 26 February 1934 when United Counties acquired the operations of M.E. Jelley of Cosgrove. With this acquisition came four vehicles. Allocated fleet numbers 367 to 370 by United Counties, these vehicles consisted of an A.J.S. Pilot, a Crossley Alpha and two different Reo machines.

On the same date, the operations of Bates, Wolverton, was sold to Eastern National which then quickly disposed of it to United Counties. Three vehicles passed to United Counties which continued the fleet number sequence from 371 to 373. As was common during 1934, the vehicles acquired were all different from one another.

Varsity Express Motors Ltd of Cambridge operated a number of express services between Cambridge and London, and Oxford and London. This business was acquired by Eastern Counties Omnibus Co. Ltd in 1933. The Oxford to London service was a fair distance away from the traditional Eastern Counties operating area and was subsequently passed over to the nearest Tilling operator, which happened to be United Counties. This brought in four A.E.C. Regal coaches which carried Duple and Dodson bodywork. Allotted rolling stock numbers 374 to 379, these vehicles were garaged at the former Varsity premises in the city.

Three vehicles, a Leyland Lioness, a Leyland Cub and a Chevrolet LO, were acquired from the business of R.J.E. Humphrey of Old Stratford. Registered PP9925, NV1156 and KX2221, these vehicles were numbered 383 to 385 by United Counties.

The company's presence in the town of Kettering was greatly increased when the operations of Frosts Motors (Kettering) Ltd was acquired on 28 October 1934. Routes from this operator were centred on Kettering, Corby, Rushden and Burton Latimer. Thirteen vehicles were acquired along with the services operated by this company. The vehicles acquired were manufactured by Guy, Lancia, Reo, Tilling-Stevens and Vulcan which took up stock numbers 386 to 399.

The final vehicle to enter the fleet came from Wollaston based W.M. Rice on the same date as the above operator. Registered NV1491, this vehicle was a twenty-seat Bedford WLB saloon which was numbered 400 by United Counties.

Vehicle orders for 1935 delivery called for seven Leyland Titan double-deck machines and five Leyland Tiger coaches, all bodied by Eastern Counties.

1935

The small batch of Leyland Titan machines ordered the previous year put in an appearance in May 1935. These Leyland Titan TD4 machines carried fifty-four-seat Eastern Counties double-deck bodies and were given rolling stock numbers 406 to 412. Northampton garage was chosen to house these vehicles.

Delivery of the five Leyland Tiger TS7 coaches commenced in May and was complete in June. Fitted with luxury Eastern Counties coach bodies, these five vehicles were numbered 401 to 405 by United Counties and wore the new cream with green relief livery.

1935 was a quiet year for the intake of second-hand vehicles into the fleet. A nominal three vehicles were taken into stock during the year from Pack of Brigstock, two

Bedford saloons and a Gilford. Registered NV727, RH3421 and NV1916, these vehicles became 414 to 416 in the United Counties fleet.

New orders for 1936 delivery called for eight vehicles. The order was split into two, with four being Burlingham bodied Leyland Tiger coaches, the second being similar bodied Bristol J-type saloons.

1936

1936 started with the cancellation of the four Burlingham bodied Leyland Tiger coaches ordered the previous year in favour of four additional Bristol J saloons, this time bodied by Eastern Counties. Before the vehicles were delivered, the body building part of Eastern Counties was renamed Eastern Coach Works (ECW) and therefore the new saloons carried this new body type.

The original order for four Burlingham-bodied Bristol J saloons was delivered to the company in March 1936, numbered 423 to 426 respectively. The new order arrived with the company during July when they took up rolling stock numbers 427 to 430 inclusively. The introduction of the Bristol/ECW combination began a good relationship between United Counties and these manufacturers, and the fleet slowly became standardised to this type, ending with the cessation of Bristol Motors in the early 1980s.

Five second-hand machines were also taken into stock during the year. These all came from the same operator, L. Timson & Son of Burton Latimer. On 8 March 1936, two Gilford saloons, two Commer Centaurs and a solitary Reo Pullman were added to the United Counties rolling stock, numbered 431-435.

The intake of these thirteen vehicles in no way made up for the forty-one older vehicles withdrawn from the company's rolling stock. Orders for 1937 delivery called for seven Bristol J05G saloons.

1937

The new vehicles arrived during March and carried ECW bodywork. These vehicles were registered NV8666/7, VV5693-7 and were numbered 445 to 451. An order for a further eighteen of these vehicles was soon placed in March, along with an order for eight Bristol K5G double-deck machines. The saloons were delivered to United Counties between August and September. The first twelve were higher capacity than the remainder of the batch. 459 to 470 carried the larger 35-seat ECW body, whilst 471 to 476 the slightly smaller thirty-one.

The eight double-deck machines were delivered in December. Following on from the Bristol saloons delivered the same year, these vehicles were numbered 477 to 484, and carried registration plates NV9817/8, VV6347 to VV6352.

Four coach bodies were ordered from Mumford Ltd of Plymouth. These arrived between March and April 1937 and replaced the bodies of three Leyland Tiger TS3 coaches and an A.E.C. Regal, all acquired from Allchin & Sons. The vehicles treated to these new bodies were 316 to 318 and 321.

Again, a small number of second-hand vehicles were acquired during 1937, this time from Higham Ferrers based L. Seamarks & Son. This acquisition brought five additional vehicles into the fleet. The vehicles taken over comprised a Maudslay Mentor ML7 registered EV3403; an A.E.C. Regent registered RM7328, and three Gilford saloons registered VX5346, UE8526 and JN256. The vehicles were allotted rolling stock numbers 440 to 445.

1938

Orders for 1938 delivery were not placed until halfway through the year, when nineteen Bristol L saloons were ordered, again complete with ECW bodies, although these were ordered a couple of months later than the chassis themselves. Two Burlingham bodies were also ordered and were to be fixed to older chassis. July saw an order placed for four Leyland Tiger TS8 chassis and a duo of Dennis Ace chassis. The Dennis saloons were to carry ECW bodies, whilst the Leyland Tiger coaches the more luxurious Burlingham coach body.

First out of this order to arrive were the two Burlingham bodies, arriving in June 1938. These were fitted to two of the acquired A.E.C. Regal coaches from Varsity in Oxford. Due to restrictions imposed by the war effort, these two vehicles saw little service during the rest of their lives.

The large batch of nineteen Bristol L5G saloons were delivered to the company during 1938. They were given rolling stock numbers 485 to 503, and were registered in two registration series, VV7250-7255 and ANV411-423.

October also saw delivery commence of the four Leyland Tiger TS8 coaches, being completed in November. All four were allocated to the company's Oxford garage, from where they operated express services into London for the majority of their lives.

The vehicles of three independents were taken into stock during 1938. The first operator to be assumed by United Counties was that of Eglesfield of Stony Stratford. This acquisition bought with it four vehicles which took up stock numbers 513 through to 516. The deal was complete in early May. Also in May came the business of Stan Smith of Irthlingborough. This added a Leyland Cub coach to the fleet numbered 510.

The most significant operator to be acquired by the company in 1938 was that of F. Beeden of Northampton. This operator was the last of the large independent operators of service work in the town. Services acquired by the company operated to the south of the town, the furthest reaching Newport Pagnell in Buckinghamshire. With the acquisition came eighteen buses and coaches of various A.E.C., Gilford, Lancia and Tilling-Stevens models, all being sold by United Counties by the close of the following year. Rolling stock numbers 517 to 534 were adopted by these vehicles.

The final acquisition of the year was of J. Meadows & Son of Barton Seagrave. 4 December 1938 was the takeover date which saw eight buses in total arrive with United Counties. Fleet numbers 538 to 545 were given to this group of buses, which was made up of a trio of Bedford saloons, two Leyland Lions, a similar number of Dennis Lancets and a solitary GMC machine. This operator ran a couple of services into the Huntingdon area, which was in Eastern National territory. Therefore, a service between Thrapston and Huntingdon was passed to the latter company, whilst the two companies operated the service running between Kettering and Huntingdon.

1939

The two outstanding Dennis Ace saloons from 1938 were the first vehicles to be taken into stock by United Counties in January 1939 numbered 504 and 505. The delay to delivery of these two vehicles, registered VV7278/9, was down to a swap in body manufacture from ECW to Mumford. Northampton and Kettering garages were the recipients of these two vehicles.

The vehicle order for 1939 was placed in March and called for a quartet of Bristol double-decks and a dozen Bristol saloons, along with four semi-coach ECW bodies.

GK441 was acquired by United Counties when the company acquired the Stony Stratford operations of Eastern National. A small batch of Leyland Tiger TS3 coaches were acquired at this time depicted by the vehicle below. They were originally bodied by Duple but were rebodied by ECW in 1939. GK441 was numbered 312 by United Counties.
*ECW Archive/
S.J. Butler Collection*

The outbreak of war luckily did not hinder the delivery of these vehicles, and the first arrived in November when the four Bristol double-deckers put in an appearance. They were registered VV8250-3, numbered 546 to 549.

Delivery of the twelve Bristol saloons began in November and concluded in December. The batch took up the rolling stock number block 550 to 561, and were split into two registration sequences, VV8254-9 and BBD122-7 respectively.

Four Leyland Tiger TS3 coaches that the company had acquired from the Aylesbury Omnibus Company received the four ECW semi-coach bodies to replace their original, ageing bodies.

As mentioned above, war had broken out on 3 September 1939. United Counties helped with the war effort of the duration of the conflict in a number of ways. Five withdrawn Leyland Lion saloons were converted to emergency ambulances. For this they had their seats removed, and a set of doors fitted to the rear of the vehicles. The vehicles involved in this conversion were 104 to 108, RP5003-7. They were garaged at Northampton, Kettering, Wellingborough, with Stony Stratford gaining two.

The company also began to experiment with vehicles running on producer gas as an alternative to petrol. The first vehicle to be trialled on this new form of power was 459 – VV6257, which had the gas unit built into the rear of the vehicle. This vehicle was garaged at Northampton from where it operated in this state for two years. Leyland Lion 110 – RP5190 was similarly converted to this source of power during 1940. Trailers were also used with producer gas and a special area for refuelling these vehicles was built at the rear of Wellingborough garage. The building remained until the closure of Wellingborough garage, and was known as 'The Gas House'.

Orders were placed during late 1939 for the delivery of seventeen Bristol L5G saloons and five Bristol K5G double-deck machines for 1940 delivery.

1930–1939 • 33

The Leyland Titan became the first bulk-purchase made by United Counties during the 1930s. These vehicles featured various different body styles and the chassis varied slightly from each other, being of the TD1 and TD2 models. Above we see TN35 (269) – NV2268, a Leyland Titan TD2 model bodied by Eastern Counties, later known as Eastern Coach Works (ECW). *ECW Archives/ S.J. Butler Collection*

In their early years, United Counties favoured the Leyland Titan chassis for its double-deck vehicles. 273 (NV2272) was one of the TD2 models bodied by ECOC. This vehicle was rebodied by ECW in January 1949 as shown in this photograph where it is seen on its final approach to Northampton's Derngate Bus and Coach station. *794 Preservation Group*

Above and below: Here we have views of ECOC bodied Leyland Tiger coaches 403 (VV3773 above seen in Nottingham) and 404 (VV3774 below seen in Leicester). Both arrived with United Counties in June 1935 to operate the express service between Nottingham, Leicester, Northampton and London. The coaches carried appropriate branding for the service which can be clearly seen. Two different liveries were worn by the coaches as can be seen. They lasted in service with United Counties until 1951 when they departed the fleet. *G.H.F. Atkins Archive/S.J. Butler Collection*

Another Bristol JO5G model is seen here in service with United Counties. New to the company in September 1937, 471 – VV6251 was rebodied twice by the company, once in 1946, the second in April 1951. It is seen about to enter Derngate Bus and Coach Station, Northampton. *794 Preservation Group*

A batch of twenty-five ECW bodied Bristol JO5G saloons was purchased by United Counties and delivered during 1937. Representing the batch is 476 (VV6256). The entire batch were rebodied at least once during their careers with United Counties, some of them being rebodied for a third time. *ECW Archive/ S.J. Butler Collection*

The mid-1930s saw United Counties change to purchasing vehicles of the Bristol/ECW combination. December 1937 saw the arrival of eight ECW bodied Bristol K5G double-deck machines, the first new double-decks to enter the fleet since 1935. VV6348 was one of the eight, gaining fleet number 480. *ECW Archive/ S.J. Butler Collection*

483 – VV6351 was new to United Counties in December 1937. It was the first generation of Bristol K models, being the K5G model. They were the first Bristol double-deck machines to be taken into stock by the company, and also the first to be bodied by Eastern Coach Works (ECW). *794 Preservation Group*

1930–1939 • **37**

In 1939, a number of ECW bodied Bristol L5G saloons were taken into stock by United Counties. Some of the batch were the last registered in the two letters and four numbers registration series. 550 – VV8254 was one such vehicle arriving with the company in December 1939, and is seen above. *ECW Archive/S.J. Butler Collection*

A new registration system was introduced in 1939, changing from two letters and four numbers, to three letters and three numbers. One of the first United Counties vehicles to carry this style registration was BBD126, numbered 560 by the company. It was an ECW bodied Bristol L5G saloon, delivered in December 1939. *794 Preservation Group*

1940–1949

1940

The early 1940s saw few new vehicles enter the fleet due to restrictions imposed by the Government due to the on-going war. United Counties was successful in purchasing a small number of new vehicles, whilst some second-hand vehicles were also sourced, along with several vehicles that came on loan from various sources.

January 1940 saw the purchase of a set of ECW saloon bodies to be fitted to the seventeen Bristol saloons. March saw an order for bodies produced by Roe rather than the standard ECW, these being for four Bristol K-types.

The double-deck machines were the first to be delivered to United Counties. Registered BBD811-815, these vehicles arrived in May 1940 numbered 567-571. All were allocated to Northampton depot. The seventeen saloons were next to arrive. Delivery was spread between May and July 1940, when registrations BBD788-96 and VV8459-66 were allocated to them. They carried on the company's numbering system on from 572 to 588.

Three open staircase double-deck machines were still in active service in 1940 and were due to be withdrawn. However, 191, 309 and 310 were spared as they were required for service. This resulted in the open stair cases being enclosed.

Six Leyland Lions, 109, 111-3, 128 and 192, were acquired by the war department for various uses. All but 113 and 192 returned to the company during the following years.

The Bristol factory ceased manufacturing bus chassis during the war, the manufacturing changing to parts for aircraft. This meant that the order of thirteen Bristol double-deck machines and seven saloons was not fulfilled.

The London Passenger Transport Board were suffering a severe shortage of vehicles in the capital due to the number being lost due to enemy action. United Counties loaned a number of buses to this operator over the war period. The first vehicles to go on loan were four Tilling Stevens saloons, 300/1/3/4 – NV3145/6/8/9. Placed on loan in October 1940, these vehicles served the capital until February 1941 when they returned.

1941

The United Counties fleet began to show its age in 1941. A programme was embarked on at the close of 1940 to recondition a number of older Leyland Titan machines at Irthlingborough, which was in use by ECW. No less than twenty-two of these machines were treated to this, which included an increase in seating capacity to fifty-three. A further seventeen were upgraded to fifty-five-seaters without undergoing the reconditioning programme. The company's single-deck fleet also had their seating capacity increased during the year with the fitting of perimeter seats. Twenty-five vehicles, 193-202; 300-4/12-4, 401-5 and 575/6, were the vehicles treated to this.

Four Leyland Lion saloons were again taken by the Military Authorities. The first one went in April, the vehicle concerned being 145 – RP6225. The remaining three – 129, 130 and 140 – were acquired in August. 129/30 returned to United Counties by the beginning of 1943, with 140 and 145 not returning at all.

Sister Tilling company Brighton, Hove & District hired some of their vehicles to United Counties to assist them with vehicle shortages. The first three arrived in February 1941 when a trio of Dennis Lance machines were taken on loan. A further seven vehicles were hired from Brighton in September when three Bristol G05Gs and four A.E.C. Regents, all bodied by Tilling, came on loan. These vehicles remained on loan to United Counties for the duration of the war. The details of the hired vehicles are listed below:

H1	NJ5975	Dennis Lance	H8	ANJ832	Bristol G05G
H2	NJ5976	Dennis Lance	H9	ANJ833	Bristol G05G
H3	NJ5978	Dennis Lance	H10	GJ2002	A.E.C. Regent
H4	NJ5979	Dennis Lance	H11	GJ2010	A.E.C. Regent
H5	NJ5974	Dennis Lance	H12	GJ2008	A.E.C. Regent
H6	NJ5977	Dennis Lance	H13	GJ2007	A.E.C. Regent
H7	ANJ831	Bristol G05G			

The company placed an order for six Burlingham coach bodies to replace older coach bodies on a fleet of A.E.C. Regal coaches. The vehicles treated to this upgrade were 319/20 – VV694/5 and 376-9 – VE3033/440/1/4852.

United Counties converted Commer saloon 434 – NV4404 to a fire tender during 1941. The vehicle hauled a trailer pump whilst in use in this capacity.

1942

In 1942, the company received four new vehicles, a rarity at the time. The first two machines put in an appearance in January 1942, when a pair of Bristol K double-deck machines entered the fleet. These vehicles were bodied by Duple and carried registrations BRP232/3 and stock numbers 614/5.

March saw an order for two Guy Arab chassis to be built and delivered to United Counties. These were supplied to the company registered BRP787/8. Carrying bodywork by Brush of Loughborough, these vehicles entered service as 617/8. A further three Guy chassis were ordered by United Counties but this order was cancelled the following year. The chassis that had been ordered were diverted to Enterprise of Scunthorpe and two to London Transport.

A further five Leyland Tiger coaches were converted to operate on producer gas during 1942. The vehicles concerned were VV3771-5 (401-5), all of which being allocated to the company's Wellingborough garage.

1943

The remaining five Leyland Titan TD2 machines were up-seated during 1943 to increase the capacity on these vehicles. Similar TD4 machine 407 – NV5138 was given an additional two seats, with the rest of the batch following suit.

1943 was another year when no new buses entered the fleet. Six A.E.C. Regent double-deck machines were acquired from Brighton, Hove & District, all having open staircases. Five of the six were placed into service numbered 623 to 627. The sixth vehicle was numbered 629, but this vehicle was purchased for cannibalisation purposes.

London Transport loaned three A.E.C. Regent machines to United Counties during 1943. These were from a pool of 140 vehicles of this type made available by London Transport for provincial operators. Entering service from Northampton garage in March 1943, the trio remained on loan to the company for around eighteen months.

A seventh vehicle was converted to operate on gas during 1943. The vehicle chosen was Leyland Titan TD1 191 – TE9626, the first of the type purchased by the company. It was also the first double-deck machine to be converted to such power. By the end of the year, the number of gas buses had reached fifteen. 315 – GN5143 was converted in March 1943, with sister vehicles 312-4 swiftly following. Three additional double-deck machines were converted, these being 203 to 205.

1944

United Counties was permitted to order three Bristol K double-deck vehicles in July 1944. The trio of vehicles was delivered to the company during November. Fitted with a Stratchan body, these vehicles were registered CBD762 to CBD764, they were allocated fleet numbers 630 to 632.

The previously mentioned batch of six A.E.C. Regents acquired from Brighton in 1943 were overhauled and had their existing bodywork replaced by new ECW 53-seat bodies during the early part of 1944.

1945

The lack of availability of new vehicles to the bus industry saw many companies recondition their existing fleet. United Counties undertook this work on twelve of its elderly Leyland Lion saloons which gained new Willowbrook bodies during 1945. This programme significantly changed the appearance of these early vehicles.

United Counties was successful in acquiring six Leyland Titan machines that originated with Plymouth Corporation during March 1945. A solitary TD2 model was acquired registered DR9856, and took up stock number 633. The remaining five were registered DR7404/6, 9066/8/70. Following on from the TD2s, these Titan TD1 machines were numbered 634 to 638 by the company. 635 was chosen to be cannibalised to keep the remaining examples in service.

Two elderly Leyland Lion saloons were purchased from West Yorkshire Road Car for the purpose of cannibalisation. Registered VY956/7, these vehicles were purchased for a nominal fee.

The company introduced allocation plates to help identify where vehicles were from during 1945. Northampton had a green background with the letter 'N' in the foreground. Kettering was a yellow background with a 'K'; Wellingborough red with a 'W'; Stony Stratford on a blue background with 'S' and Oxford had the pleasure of a black background with an 'O'.

1946

1946 saw an order for eight Bristol K double-decks and seven Bedford OBs. The Bristols were to be bodied by ECW, whilst the Bedfords by Beadle. However, none of these vehicles materialised during 1946.

A further eighteen Leyland Lion saloons were rebodied by Willowbrook over the course of March and December 1946. In addition, United Counties reconditioned a number of Bristol J type saloons themselves. The bodies were removed from the chassis, which were quicker to complete, and bodies were not matched to their original chassis. Subsequently 424 (NV6639) became 471; 425 (VV4563) became 476; 471 (VV6251) to 472; 472 (VV6252) to 475; 473 (VV6253) to 474; 474 (VV6254) to 424; 475 (VV6255) to 425 and 476 (VV6256) to 473. A similar vehicle, 446 – NV8667, was up-seated to thirty-five seats during the year.

1947

By 1947, the United Counties fleet was coming under strain from the lack of investment due to the war. Since the turn of the decade, only seventeen vehicles had entered service with the company, ten of these being acquired from other operators.

United Counties was successful in receiving some new buses during 1947; however, the intake only totalled three vehicles, carrying ECW double-deck bodies on the Bristol K5G chassis. Registered DBD980-2, they took up rolling stock numbers 639-641 respectively.

1947 saw the placement of orders of new vehicles up until 1950. Twelve Bristol K double-decks and fourteen Bristol L saloons were ordered for 1948 delivery; a further nineteen double-decks and nine single-decks for 1949 and twenty-eight vehicles for 1950, split between ten saloons and the balance consisting of double-deck machines.

1948

1948 saw a more sizeable delivery of new vehicles to the fleet. Firstly, five ECW bodied Bristol K machines that were outstanding from the 1946 order finally arrived in May when they were numbered 642 to 646, and carried on the registration system from the previous batch as DBD983 to DBD987 respectively.

Other outstanding vehicles were seven Bedford OB saloons, of which only six materialised with United Counties. These machines were bodied by Beadle, and were given stock numbers 101 to 106, registered DBD936-941.

Orders placed the previous year for 1948 delivery called for fourteen Bristol saloons and twelve Bristol double-deck machines. However, only two of the fourteen saloons materialised in 1948, numbered 107 and 108. These vehicles gained registration marks EBD234 and EBD235, and carried the Bristol L6B chassis.

The double-deck order fared a little better, when eight of the twelve vehicles were constructed and delivered during 1948. EBD216-223 were numbered 647 to 654 by United Counties. London Transport was suffering a severe shortage of buses in the capital and as a result, 651 to 654 were diverted on long term loan to London Transport, not returning to United Counties until the latter part of 1949. The intake of new vehicles allowed five elderly Leyland Lion saloons to leave the fleet.

It was the intention of the directors of United Counties to rebody some of the elderly Leyland Titan and Bristol J machines within the fleet, for which a number of ECW bodies were ordered for delivery over the course of 1948 and 1949. However, only one materialised in 1948, whilst the 1949 order never arrived with United Counties. The solitary bus that was completed in December 1948 was Bristol J05G 425 – VV6255. The outstanding bodies arrived in 1949.

1949

The outstanding four Bristol K machines from 1948 duly arrived with United Counties over the first couple of months of 1949, and were placed on loan to London Transport, joining the rest of this batch there. They remained on loan with London Transport until the end of 1949, early 1950. These vehicles were numbered 655 to 658, and registered EBD224-7.

A further twelve Bristol K machines were taken into stock by United Counties during 1949, these being from the order of nineteen such vehicles ordered for 1949 delivery. Registration marks EBD228 to EBD233 and ERP605 to ERP610 were allocated to these vehicles along with rolling stock numbers 659 to 670.

United Counties failed to receive any single-deck vehicles from the outstanding 1948 order, or the 1949 order during the year. However, two Beadle-Morris saloons were diverted from Brighton, Hove & District to the company during December. These vehicles took up fleet numbers 115 and 116, and were registered FBD915/6.

The intake of new vehicles during the year saw the demise of ten Leyland Lion saloons from the fleet. The outstanding bodies ordered by the company the previous year put in an appearance during 1949, when fifteen Bristol J saloons were rebodied, the work being undertaken at the former United Counties works at Irthlingborough, which had been occupied by ECW during the war.

Five Roe bodied Bristol K5G double-deck machines were taken into stock during May 1940, the difference in body styles between Roe and ECW was noticeable. This can be seen when compared with NV2272. Representing the batch is 567 – BBD811. *794 Preservation Group*

1948 saw the delivery of a small number of Beadle bodied Bedford OB saloons to the company. Representing the batch is DBD937, which became numbered 802. This vehicle was the only one not to pass to W. North, Leeds, in 1953, instead it was converted to a stores van in 1952, when it was renumbered to 25. *794 Preservation Group*

Bristol K6B 778 – EBD233 is seen loading passengers in Guildford Street, Luton, on a bleak, grey afternoon in January 1966. This vehicle was one of six new to the company in the summer of 1949. They transferred to Luton during 1956 when they displaced the former Eastern National Bristol K5Gs. The town's bus station can be seen on the right of the photograph. *Graham Smith*

1950–1959

1950

Compared to the previous decade, 1950 was a great year for United Counties when they received forty-one new vehicles.

EBD236 to EBD241 were six ECW bodied Bristol L6B coaches taken into stock during May and June 1950 numbered 809 to 814. Prior to the arrival of these vehicles, the coaching fleet of the company was becoming quite elderly, and these new vehicles were quite welcome.

The previous year, United Counties was successful in acquiring the order for a trio of Bristol L5G saloons from the Caledonian Omnibus Company, which at that time was absorbed into sister company Western Scottish. One each was delivered in March, May and June when they took up stock numbers 817 to 819, FNV117-9.

Other single-deck vehicles to enter the fleet comprised a Bristol L5G saloon and eight Bristol LL machines, all with ECW bodywork. The latter batch were longer and therefore could accommodate more passengers. 820 – FRP820 was the identity of the single Bristol L5G saloon, whilst the Bristol LL machines took up numbers 821 to 828, registered FRP821-828 respectively.

Twenty-three new double-deck machines were taken into stock by United Counties during 1950. This was split between thirteen Bristol K machines, and ten Bristol KSs, all with ECW bodies. The thirteen Bristol K machines were all delivered by June, and continued the fleet numbering sequence from 671 to 683, registered ERP611-23. The Bristol KS machines were numbered 684 to 693 by United Counties, these vehicles being registered FRP684-693.

A collision caused by fog took place between Leyland Titan machines VV6352 and NV1158 whilst in service in Burton Latimer. The former vehicle was repaired and placed into service, whilst NV1158 was converted into a recovery vehicle for the company, taking up fleet number 18 in the ancillary fleet.

1951

1951 was another busy year for the intake of new vehicles into the fleet. Thirty-two vehicles were taken into stock, with all but five being single-deck vehicles. The five double-deck machines were made up of four Bristol KS machines and a solitary Bristol KSW machine. The KS machines were registered FRP694 to FRP697, and carried fleet numbers corresponding to the numbers in their registration plates. The KSW model was numbered 698, and registered CNH698.

The coaching fleet received a further thirteen vehicles during February and March 1951. Numbered 832 to 844, FRP832-844, these vehicles had luxurious ECW bodies mounted on the Bristol LL6B chassis. By 1951, new vehicles were able to be built to the maximum width of 8 feet. This was the width that these vehicles were built to, with the chassis being smaller than the body. This led to problems with the distribution of heat created by the axles of the vehicles. 839 – FRP839, as a result of this problem, was burnt out whilst in service in London in June, a problem encountered not only by United Counties. Modifications later followed on this type to counteract this. 839 was later rebuilt by ECW and re-entered service with the company.

Yet another new chassis type was introduced to the United Counties fleet, this time being the Bristol LWL6B. Three of these new vehicles were taken into stock during March and April when they were numbered 829 to 831, FRP829-831. Eleven further LWL6Bs were taken into stock during the autumn and winter of 1951, when CNH845-855 (845-855) were delivered to the company.

Six Bristol J saloons were re-bodied by ECW during 1951 with bodies ordered by United Counties the previous year. 471 and 472 gained dual-purpose bodies, whilst 451, 461, 463 and 470 all received similar bus bodies.

The intake of thirty-two vehicles saw the disposal of twelve vehicles from the fleet.

1952

The intake of new vehicles between January and May 1952 saw twenty-six machines enter the fleet, split between six saloons and twenty double-decks. The six single-deck machines came in the form of the Bristol LWL6B model, which were numbered 856 to 861 by United Counties, carrying matching 'CNH' registration marks. The intake of double-deck machines were of the Bristol KSW6B model. These vehicles were numbered 699 to 718, registered CNH699 to CNH718 respectively.

A decision by the management of the British Transport Commission in 1952 saw the fleet of United Counties double in size. It was decided that the Midland area operations of the Eastern National Omnibus Company Limited be transferred to the control of United Counties. The operating area consisted of Bedfordshire, north Hertfordshire, the Aylesbury area of Buckinghamshire and Huntingdonshire. From 1 May 1952, 247 buses and coaches were added to the United Counties fleet garaged at Aylesbury, Bedford, Biggleswade, Hitchin, Huntingdon and Luton. On the same date, the Oxford to London express services operated by United Counties for a number of years were transferred to South Midland Motor Services Ltd of Oxford, along with eight Bristol coaches.

In preparation for this take-over, United Counties renumbered its fleet into a series that would also accommodate the acquired Eastern National vehicles. This took place on 1 March 1952. The company also introduced the use of metal fleet number plates on the vehicles to denote the garages. Northampton gained a green background; Stony Stratford green with black edges; Kettering became yellow; Wellingborough red; whilst Rushden gained red plates with black edges.

The acquired garages were allocated the following coloured plates. Bedford – light blue; Biggleswade – light blue with black edges; Huntingdon – light blue, yellow edges; Aylesbury – light blue with red edges; Luton – brown; and Hitchin – brown with black edges.

The vehicles taken into stock comprised a number of different types. Full details of these vehicles can be found below, but just to summarise, the fleet acquired was made up of eleven Dennis Lancets; eight Bedford machines; four Leyland saloons; twenty Bristol J05G saloons; fifteen pre-war and twenty post-war Bristol L5G saloons;

three Bristol L6B coaches; nine Bristol LL5Gs; four Bristol LWL5Gs; three Leyland Titan TD1 double-decks; four Titan TD2s; five Titan TD3s; ten Titan TD4s; eight Titan TD5s; twelve Titan PD1s; eighty-nine pre and post-war Bristol K5G machines; five KS5G machines and nine KSW5G double-decks.

Four additional vehicles were taken into stock by United Counties from Eastern National but were not numbered by the company. These vehicles were acquired in a withdrawn state and were not operated in service by the company.

101 – 107   Dennis Lance   ECOC

101	AEV785	103	AVW468	105	BTW487	107	AVW458
102	AEV791	104	BTW484	106	BTW494		

111	GPP497	Bedford OWB	Duple

112 – 118   Bedford OB   Duple

112	LPU620	114	LPU625	116	LPU627	118	ONO85
113	LPU622	115	LPU626	117	ONO84		

158	EKX691	Dennis Lancet	Perris Faulker
159	GPP473	Dennis Lancet	Willowbrook
160	MPP450	Dennis Lancet	Yeates
161	TM6312	Leyland Lion	Stratchen
162	TM6311	Leyland Lion	Stratchen
163	TM6904	Leyland Lion	Stratchen
170	KKX408	Leyland Tiger	Duple

182 – 226   Bristol JO5G   ECW (except 194 – Willowbrook)

182	DEV456	187	ENO944	192	ENO953	222	FNO792
183	DEV461	188	ENO947	193	ENO955	223	FNO793
184	DEV463	189	ENO948	194	ENO960	224	FNO796
185	DEV465	190	ENO949	220	FHK751	225	FNO798
186	DEV469	191	ENO951	221	FNO791	226	FNO800

250 – 342   Bristol L5G   ECW

250	GPU413	259	GPU433	305	KNO604	320	MPU28
251	GPU417	260	GPU435	306	KNO605	321	MPU29
252	GPU418	261	GPU436	307	KNO606	324	MPU35
253	GPU420	262	GPU437	308	KNO607	327	NNO109
254	GPU422	263	GPU438	311	KNO612	328	NNO110
255	GPU423	264	GPU416	312	KNO613	333	ONO45
256	GPU424	302	KNO599	315	KNO621	341	ONO990
257	GPU425	303	KNO602	316	KNO623	342	ONO994
258	GPU430	304	KNO603	317	KNO624		

352	PTW107	Bristol L6B	ECW
353	PTW108	Bristol L6B	ECW
354	PTW109	Bristol L6B	ECW

349 – 389   Bristol LL5G   ECW

349	ONO995	384	RHK122	386	RHK125	388	RHK130
350	ONO998	385	RHK124	387	RHK128	389	RHK132
351	ONO999						

390	RHK136	Bristol LWL5G	ECW
391	SHK514	Bristol LWL5G	ECW
399	TNO667	Bristol LWL5G	ECW
400	TNO668	Bristol LWL5G	ECW
513	TM3734	Leyland Titan TD1	ECW
514	TM6408	Leyland Titan TD1	Beadle
515	TR5295	Leyland Titan TD1	Short
521	DR9838	Leyland Titan TD2	Weymann
522	DR9864	Leyland Titan TD2	Weymann
528	AEV796	Leyland Titan TD2	ECOC
529	AEV797	Leyland Titan TD2	ECOC
543	BTW495	Leyland Titan TD3	ECOC
544	BTW496	Leyland Titan TD3	ECOC
545	BTW497	Leyland Titan TD3	ECOC
546	BTW498	Leyland Titan TD3	ECW
547	BTW500	Leyland Titan TD3	ECOC

556 – 565   Leyland Titan TD4   ECW/Brush

556	DEV483	559	DEV486	562	ENO934	565	ENO937
557	DEV484	560	DEV487	563	**ENO935**		
558	**DEV485**	561	DEV488	564	**ENO936**		

Note: 558, 563-565 carried ECW bodywork.

569 – 576   Leyland Titan TD5   ECW

569	FEV175	571	FEV177	573	FEV179	575	FEV181
570	FEV176	572	FEV178	574	FEV180	576	FEV182

583 – 594   Leyland Titan PD1   ECW

583	MPU36	586	MPU39	589	MPU42	592	MPU46
584	MPU37	587	MPU40	590	MPU43	593	MPU47
585	MPU38	588	MPU41	591	MPU45	594	MPU53

609 – 818   Bristol K5G   ECW

609	FPU508	618	FPU518	628	GNO693	641	GTW889
610	FPU509	619	FPU523	629	GNO694	642	GTW890
611	FPU510	620	FPU513	630	GNO696	643	GTW891
612	FPU511	624	GNO688	631	GNO697	644	GTW892
615	FPU515	625	GNO689	632	GNO698	645	GTW894
616	FPU516	626	GNO690	633	GNO699	646	GTW895
617	FPU517	627	GNO692	640	GTW888	672	JEV411

673	JEV412	689	JEV428	725	MPU9	770	TTW268
674	JEV413	690	JEV429	726	MPU10	771	NNO103
675	JEV414	691	JEV430	727	MPU11	788	ONO55
676	JEV415	692	JEV431	728	MPU12	789	ONO56
677	JEV416	693	JEV432	732	MPU13	790	ONO57
678	JEV417	694	JEV433	733	MPU16	791	ONO61
679	JEV418	695	JEV434	734	MPU18	792	ONO62
680	JEV419	696	JEV435	735	MPU19	793	ONO70
681	JEV420	702	JPU640	736	MPU23	814	ONO73
682	JEV421	711	KHK513	755	NNO96	815	ONO74
683	JEV422	712	KHK514	756	NNO97	816	ONO75
684	JEV423	713	KNO443	757	NNO98	817	ONO77
685	JEV424	715	KNO597	758	NNO99	818	ONO79
686	JEV425	716	KNO598	759	NNO100		
687	JEV426	723	MPU1	760	NNO101		
688	JEV427	724	MPU2	761	NNO102		

825 – 829   **Bristol KS5G**   **ECW**

825	RPU521	827	RPU525	829	RPU527
826	RPU522	828	RPU526		

875 – 883   **Bristol KSW5G**   **ECW**

875	SHK511	877	SHK520	879	SHK527	881	TNO674
876	SHK519	878	SHK524	880	TNO673	882	TNO677
883	TNO678						

3423	AEV793	Dennis Lancet	ECOC
3484	AVW462	Dennis Lancet	ECOC
L121	ABH358	Leyland Cub	Duple
L122	APP528	Leyland Cub	Duple
L123	CPP236	Bedford WTB	Duple
L125	FPP545	Bedford WTB	Duple

United Counties took a Bristol LS4G saloon on demonstration from Eastern Counties during 1952, registered MAH744. The vehicle proved popular with the company and a number of similar vehicles were purchased later in the year.

Further vehicle orders for 1952 consisted of six double-decks; nine underfloor saloons and four similar coaches. The order for five double-decks and three single-decks were also taken by United Counties from Eastern National, along with two double-deck and one single-deck bodies for the re-bodying programme introduced by Eastern National the previous year.

The two double-deck bodies mentioned above were already being built by ECW when Eastern National transferred. These were fitted to 624 – GNO688 and 702 – JPU460 and arrived during May with United Counties.

The combined double-deck order totalled eleven vehicles, split into two batches. The original United Counties order gained fleet numbers 908 to 913 – HBD642-7. The Eastern National order was allocated rolling stock numbers 917 to 921, with registrations HNV733 to HNV737 respectively. The only difference between these two batches were the engines mounted in them.

Delivery of the coaches took a while, the first arriving in October 1952, the last in February 1953. All carried the Bristol LS5G chassis. These were the first under-floored vehicles to be purchased by United Counties and gave a modern appearance to the company's coaching fleet.

The combined order for single-deckers in 1952 called for twelve, but sixteen saloons in total were delivered to United Counties. Three Bristol LS5G saloons arrived between October and November registered HNV729 and HBD630/1. These vehicles were numbered 436, 441 and 442, and carried dual-door ECW bodies. The specification for the remaining order was changed so that the vehicles carried dual-purpose bodies rather than the standard bus body. The vehicles affected by this change were numbered 452 to 462, registered HBD632-641 and HNV730-2, out of sequence. It is believed that the single-deck body ordered by Eastern National was delivered as HNV729 mentioned above.

United Counties found that Bristol saloon ENO960 (194) was not fit for purpose. To combat this problem, the Willowbrook body from withdrawn Leyland Lion RP6722 was fitted to the chassis of the former vehicle. Bedford OB 120 – DBD937 was converted to a covered stores van during April 1952 to allow the transportation of engineering supplies around the newly enlarged operating area. It was numbered 25 in the ancillary fleet.

1953

The order for new vehicles during 1953 originally comprised ten double-deck machines and seven saloons. These orders were combined with those placed by Eastern National in 1952, which called for a further ten double-decks; five single-decks and four luxury coaches.

Delivery of the four coaches was split between October 1953 and February 1954. The first pair to arrive were numbered 467/8 – JBD983/4; whilst the second duo were given fleet numbers 481/2 – JBD985/6. These were again ECW bodied Bristol LS machines.

The combined order of twelve single-deck vehicles arrived in the form of seven bus-bodied machines and five dual-purpose vehicles. Delivery of this batch was spread across a year, starting in October 1953 and was completed in October 1954. First to be delivered were 469-473, registered JBD987-991 which carried the dual-entrance, dual-purpose ECW body on the Bristol LS6B chassis. The remainder of the batch found their way to United Counties during 1954 in the bus-body form. They were numbered 474/5, 480 and 490-3, and carried registrations JBD992-8.

The original order for double-deck machines called for twenty, when in fact twenty-eight machines materialised. The 'Eastern National' order was completed during 1953 and came in the form of eighteen Bristol KSW6B machines. These vehicles were registered JBD965-982 and were allotted rolling stock numbers 928 to 945. The ten ordered by United Counties were of the new Bristol LD6B Lodekka model, an example of which United Counties trialled the previous year, leading to this order. The batch was allocated fleet numbers 950 to 959 along with registration marks JBD955-964. 950 was the only one of this batch to materialise in 1953, the remainder arriving with United Counties over the course of 1954. 950 was a pre-production model, this being the reason for it arriving early.

The rebodying of older Bristol K5G machines acquired from Eastern National continued in 1953 when twelve ECW bodies ordered in 1952 were fitted to some pre-war K5Gs. The vehicles chosen for this exercise were 673/6-8/80/3/7-8/92-3/5/6, all from the 'JEV' registration series.

The capacity of the acquired Bristol L5G saloons was lower than that of those that originated with United Counties. This was rectified when many of the former Eastern National fleet were up-seated from thirty-one-seaters to thirty-five-seaters.

1953 saw the acquisition of the operations and vehicles of Bedfordshire independent O.A. Bartle of Potton. With this came a number of services joining Potton with local villages, as well as services to St Neots, Royston and Bedford. The company also operated a town service in Biggleswade. The routing of the inherited services was left untouched by United Counties which adopted them into their network in the 190s series. Fourteen vehicles were acquired with the business, five Duple bodied Bedford OBs, 125-9 (EMJ999, FTM367, GBM302, GMJ267, HTM986); seven Thurgood bodied Guy Arab IIIs, 140-6 (EBM421/2, ETM649/50, FNM785, FMJ752) and a pair of Weymann bodied Guy Arabs, 516/7 (DMJ371, GMJ268). The expansion of the fleet led to withdrawn Leyland Lion RP8557 being used as a staff rest room at Biggleswade.

1954

1954 orders called for three single-decks; five dual-purpose vehicles and twenty double-decks. Fourteen of the total order of new vehicles arrived during the allotted year.

United Counties received the five dual-purpose vehicles over the course of the year. Registered KNV29-33, these vehicles were numbered 483 to 487 by United Counties. The batch carried the dual-door ECW body style on the Bristol LS6B chassis.

Nine of the double-deck machines came in the form of the Bristol KSW6B, and would turn out to be the last of this type to be purchased by United Counties. These vehicles became numbers 961 to 969 in the United Counties fleet, registered KNV334-342.

These two batches were not however the only new vehicles to be delivered to the company during the year. Thirty-two new vehicles entered the fleet, displacing thirty-six older vehicles. The details of the remaining new vehicles can be found under the 1953 heading.

Further Bristol K-type machines were rebodied during 1954; the vehicles selected this time were those delivered during the war. The vehicles concerned were Duple bodied 732/3 – BRP232/3 and Stratchen bodied 707-9 – CBD762-4, which had their original bodywork replaced by new ones constructed by ECW.

Several Bristol saloons were downgraded to normal bus work as a result of the delivery of the new dual-purpose vehicles. The vehicles selected for this were Bristol J05Gs 175 and 215, NV6639, VV6251; and Bristol L5Gs 320/4 – MPU28/35.

Another bus converted to an ancillary vehicle was Beadle bodied Bedford OB LPU622. This vehicle was converted to an open truck and replaced similar CEV394, inherited from Eastern National at Luton.

1955

The outstanding vehicles from the 1954 order duly arrived with United Counties between January and July 1955. The vehicles concerned were three Bristol LS5G saloons and eleven Bristol LD6B double-deck machines. The trio of Bristol saloons were delivered registered LBD258 to LBD260, and were given fleet numbers 494-6.

The eleven LDs materialised as 971 to 982 – LNV500-10. There were slight variations in the bodywork of different members of this batch, mainly concerning the seating capacity. Additionally, 971-8 were fitted with rear platform doors, whilst 979-82 were delivered as open-platform vehicles.

The original orders for 1955 delivery were made up of sixteen double-decks and eight single-deck machines, with four additional double-decks being added to the order. Ten of the twenty double-decks found their way to United Counties in 1955. Again they carried the Bristol LD6B chassis, with ECW bodies. They took up stock numbers 983 to 992 – MNV100-9, and were delivered between October and December 1955. Six of the eight saloons arrived during 1955, numbered 100 to 105 they carried registrations MNV759-764. These were again ECW bodied Bristol LS5G machines, with the body style varying from previous deliveries of the type, in that they only had an entrance at the front of the vehicle.

United Counties took a Bristol SC saloon on demonstration from Eastern National in January 1955. The loan of the vehicle, registered 724APU, led to the order of six similar machines for 1956 delivery. A second loan during the year saw a Bristol J05G registered BWT782 come to the company. The vehicle had been converted to a mobile office by West Yorkshire and was used by United Counties to assist in a recruitment drive.

1956

The outstanding vehicles from the 1955 order arrived within the first three months of 1956. The Bristol LD6B machines continued the fleet numbering system from 993 to 999, with additional numbers 500-502 being used. These vehicles were registered MNV110-119 and were of similar appearance to the previous year's batch. The remaining two saloons were numbered 106 and 107, registered MNV765/6 respectively.

The new vehicle programme for 1956 called for six lightweight saloons, two dual-purpose machines and twenty-two double-decks. First to arrive were the two dual-purpose vehicles which were numbered 110/1 – NBD900/1. These vehicles put in an appearance in May and carried the Bristol LS5G chassis.

Fourteen of the twenty-two double-decks ordered arrived during 1956. The batch was numbered 503 to 516 by United Counties, and were registered NBD902 to NBD915 respectively. Delivery commenced in June and continued for most of the year.

The training bus fleet gained three new members during 1956. Three withdrawn Bristol L5G machines were converted for such use over the course of the year. The first vehicles to be treated were VV7250/2 which were renumbered 1 and 2, and transferred to this use in February and March. The third member was converted for this use in December, registered GPU436 this vehicle was logically numbered 3. All remained in this guise for 5 or 6 years.

1957

January and February saw the delivery of the outstanding double-decks to the company. They took up stock numbers 517 to 524, and were registered NBD916-23. The outstanding Bristol lightweight saloons were also delivered during 1957. They were numbered 125 to 130 – ONV425-430 and were ECW bodied Bristol SC machines. The batch was split between Northampton and Stony Stratford. The Northampton allocation were used at the Welford outstation.

1957 orders called for eight single-decks and twenty double-decks. The term single-deck in this case can be lightly used, as the order in fact turned up as two luxury coaches, two other coaches and four dual-purpose vehicles.

First to arrive was the duo of luxury coaches which were employed on the extended tours run by United Counties. They were registered OBD901/2 and carried fleet numbers 114/5. These vehicles carried ECW bodies mounted on the Bristol LS6G chassis. A further two LS6Gs were delivered but were of slightly lower specification. They carried on the registration sequence as OBD903/4 and were numbered 116/7. The four dual-purpose vehicles arrived on the Bristol LS5G chassis. They were registered PNV218 to 221 and were allotted rolling stock numbers 118-121.

As with previous years, the intake of double-deck vehicles did not match the number ordered by United Counties. Of the twenty vehicles ordered, only seven were delivered in the designated year. Again these machines were ECW bodied Bristol LD6B machines. They were numbered 525 to 531 and carried registrations ORP25-31.

1958

The outstanding thirteen Bristol LD6B machines from 1957 were slow to materialise in 1958, being delivered between January and September. They were numbered 532 to 544 and were registered ORP32-44.

The order for new vehicles for 1958 called for thirty vehicles, twelve saloons and eighteen double-decks. This was altered to eight saloons and twelve double-decks. The full quota of new vehicles was again not fulfilled in the designated year.

Four of the eight saloons materialised in the designated year. These vehicles became known as 134 to 137 – TBD134-7. These vehicles bought in the new Bristol chassis, named the MW. Delivered between October and November, the first three were re-registered to SRP134 to SRP136, entering service in January 1959 instead of the predicted Easter period.

At the same time as the saloons, five of the twelve double-deck machines arrived with the company. These were numbered 545 to 549 by United Counties and gained registrations SBD545 to 549, and again carried the Bristol LD6B chassis.

1959

All of the outstanding 1958 orders arrived with United Counties between January and June 1959. The four Bristol MW saloons were numbered 138 to 141 – TBD138-141. The seven Bristol LD6B machines became 550 to 556, continuing the fleet numbering sequence, and were registered SBD550 to SBD556.

Orders for new vehicles in 1959 called for sixteen double-deck machines. The success in delivering these machines proved greater than the previous few years, with fourteen of these machines being delivered to United Counties. They became known as 557 to 570 and were registered TRP557-570, again being ECW bodied Bristol LD6B machines. Included in this batch was the 100th Lodekka machine purchased by the company. These vehicles were also the last LD6B machines to be purchased by the company.

December saw the arrival of a Bristol FLF6B double-deck machine from Bristol. The vehicle was loaned to the company for one day, after which orders for the type were soon placed. The vehicle in question was registered 995EHW.

Leighton Buzzard was in receipt of an office converted from Bristol J05G VV5697 which had been withdrawn by the company; it was put to use at the garage premises in that town.

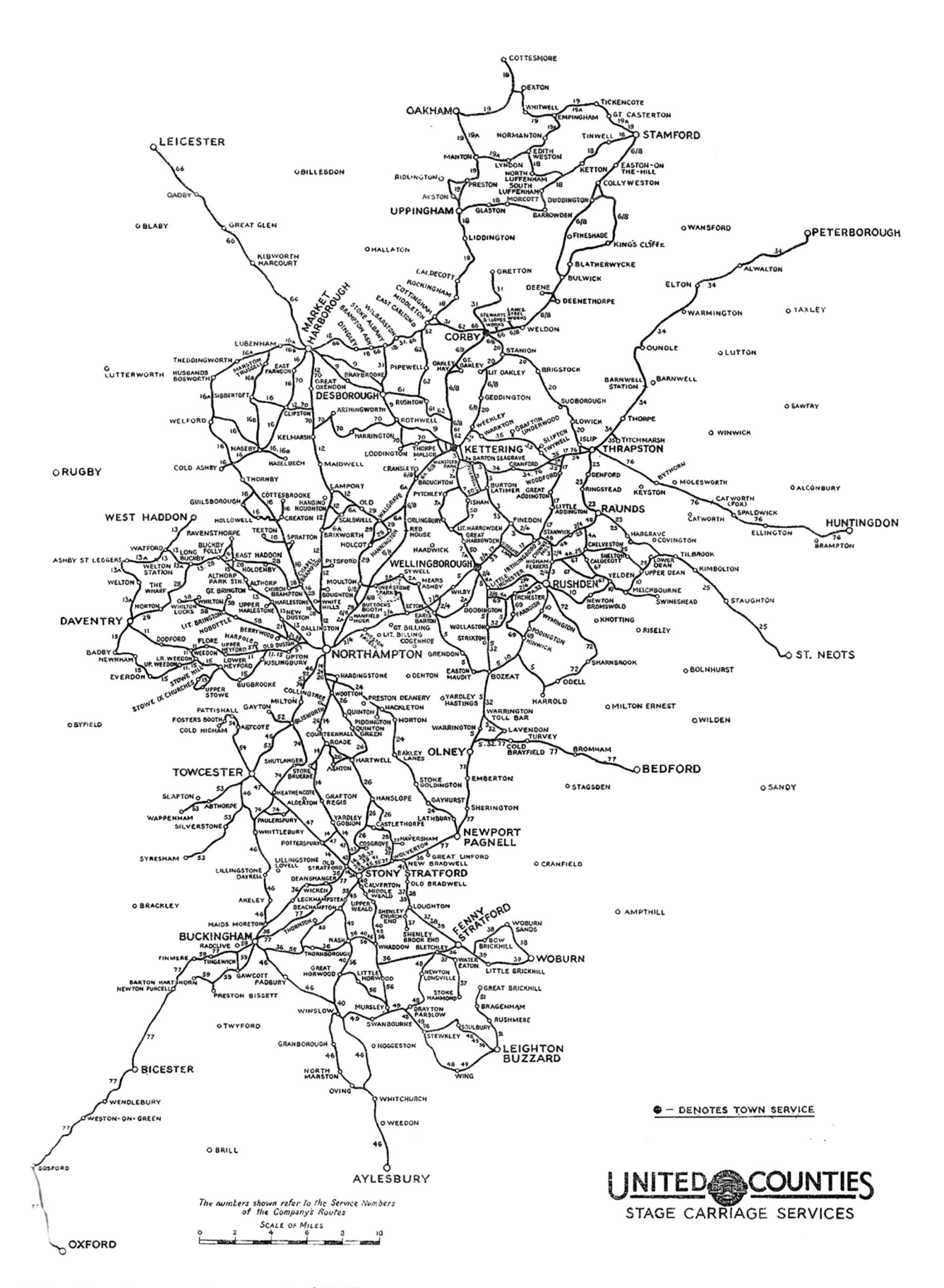

United Counties operating area – April 1949.

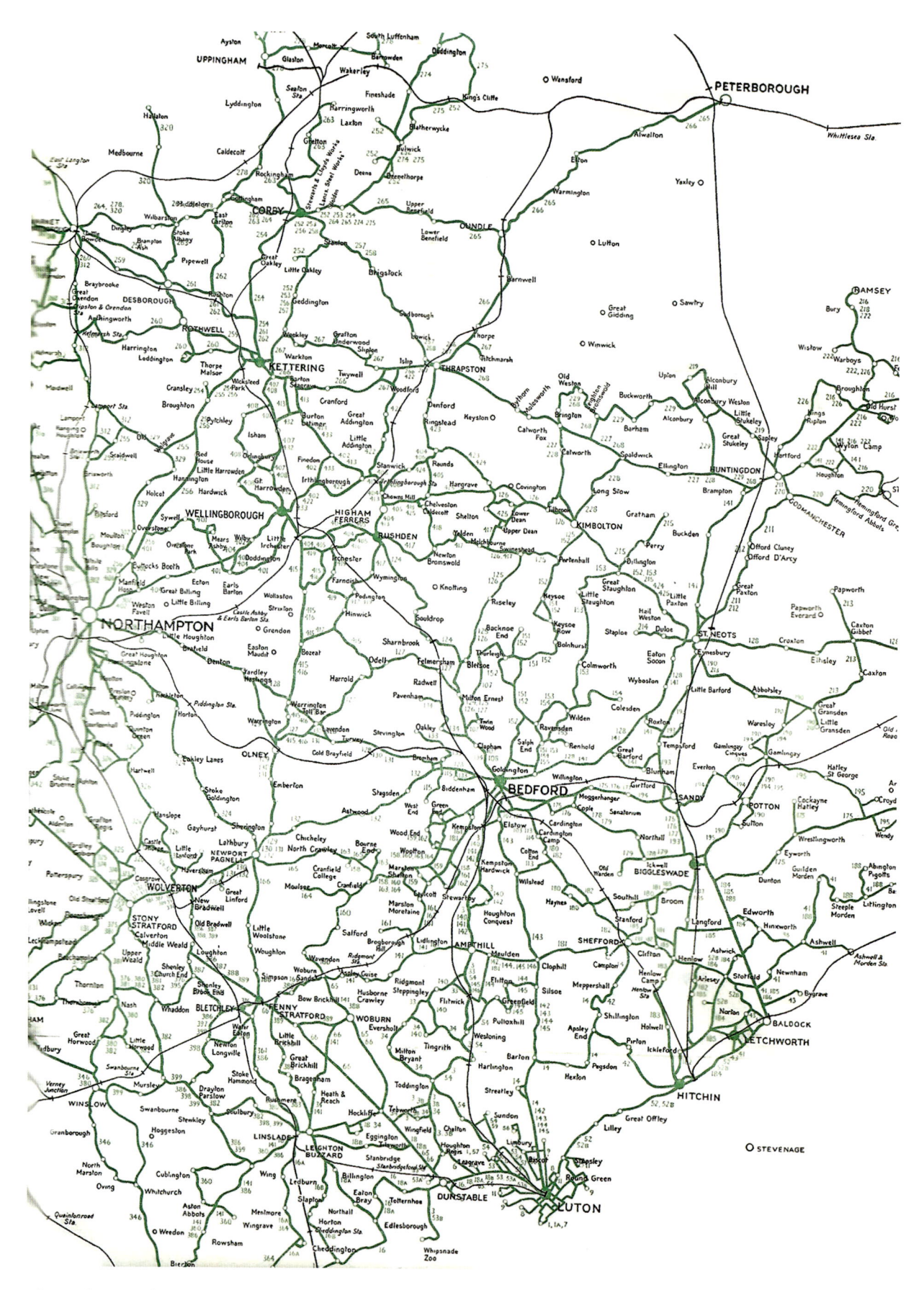

The main United Counties operating area after the addition of Eastern National - August 1959.

A number of Bristol L6B coaches were added to the United Counties fleet during 1950. 811 – EBD238 shows off the body style carried by these vehicles. EBD238 later transferred to Eastern National in November 1957, for which it is seen working in this photograph. *794 Preservation Group*

In amongst the double-deck deliveries, United Counties received three Bristol L5G saloons during 1950. March saw the arrival of 817 – FNV117 to the company. It is seen leaving Derngate, Northampton. *794 Preservation Group*

The slightly higher capacity Bristol LL5G saloon was also taken into stock by the company during 1950. FRP822 was one such vehicle, and gained rolling stock number 822. *794 Preservation Group*

851 – FRP694 was a unique vehicle in the United Counties fleet. In 1951 it was approved that 8ft wide buses could operate on British roads. At this time the company had four 7ft 6in wide Bristol KS chassis on order. To keep up with this new allowance, ECW were in a position to produce an 8ft wide body to fit these vehicles if the company required them to. United Counties soon took up this option. 851 was the only example to gain a Bristol engine, becoming a Bristol KS6B. Allocated to Northampton until 1966, 851 was reallocated to Luton where it was regularly found operating route 12 (Round Green – Town Centre – Roman Road). 851 is found at the Round Green terminus in this photograph taken in June 1969. *Graham Smith*

1950–1959 • **57**

GPU436 was amongst the numerous vehicles taken into stock with the acquisition of the Midland Area operations of the Eastern National Omnibus Company Ltd. in May 1952. This ECW bodied Bristol L5G was originally numbered 261 by United Counties and remained in passenger service until July 1956. After this time, it was put to further use by the company as a driver training vehicle and was given new rolling stock number 3. It is seen in use as the latter type of vehicle displaying its second fleet number. *S.J. Butler Collection*

436 – HNV729 was the first Bristol LS5G saloon to enter service with United Counties in October 1952. It spent most of its life operating from Hitchin garage, but was moved to Luton in 1968. The vehicle underperformed and was put to use on peak-time services. It is seen in April 1969 on service 13 between Vauxhall and Biscot Mill. *Graham Smith*

Eighty-nine ECW bodied Bristol K5G double-decks were taken into stock by United Counties with the acquisition of Eastern National in May 1952. 733 – MPU16 shows off this type whilst parked outside Bedford garage. *794 Preservation Group*

Another K5G taken into stock from Eastern National was 755 – NNO96. The vehicle was four years old when it was acquired by United Counties. This photograph shows the nearside of the vehicle well whilst parked at Stony Stratford garage. *794 Preservation Group*

For many years, Bedford garage would send members of its allocation to other garages as 'engineering spares' whilst other vehicles were sent to Bedford for repairs. Luton was often the recipient of these vehicles, which were placed on the Biscot Road local services 55 and 56. 877 – SHK520 was one of nine Bristol KSW5G double-deck machines acquired from Eastern National with the Midland area operations. 877 is seen at the Vicarage Street terminus in Luton in November 1966. The building site to the right was for an extension to Luton College of Technology – now the University of Bedfordshire – whilst the skyline is dominated by the towers and offices of Flower's Brewery – now long since gone! *Graham Smith*

A line up of three former Eastern National Bristol saloons is seen here, two JO5G models to either side and one of the Bristol L5G models in the middle. As can be seen, there was little difference in the body styling of the types. From left to right we see 256 (GPU424), 193 (ENO955) and 223 (FNO793). *794 Preservation Group*

60 • UNITED COUNTIES BUSES

Another of the nine Bristol KSW5Gs acquired from Eastern National May 1952 was 881 – TNO674. This vehicle remained at Luton for most of its operational life. It is seen in April 1966 at the Town Centre terminus of services 55 and 56 at Waller Street. *Graham Smith*

The Bristol KSW6B model was first purchased by United Counties during 1952 when a number of ECW bodied examples were taken into stock. 968 – KNV341 was delivered to United Counties in September 1954. The vehicle is seen loading at Corby Bus Station. *Thomas Knowles*

A smart looking single-deck to operate with United Counties was the ECW bodied Bristol LWL6B. Registered CNH865, this vehicle gained stock number 431 and was new to United Counties in May 1952. It is seen at Stamford Bus Station.
Thomas Knowles

From the same manufacturer comes 874 – CNH713, an ECW bodied Bristol KSW6B model. This vehicle was new to United Counties in May 1952.
Thomas Knowles

62 • UNITED COUNTIES BUSES

Over shadowed by the large intake of second-hand vehicles from Eastern National in May 1952 was a small batch of seven ECW bodied Bristol KSW6B double-deck machines. Representing this batch is CNH716, which was allocated rolling stock number 896. It is seen passing through Letchworth. *S.J. Butler Collection*

Five Bristol KSW5G/ECW vehicles were delivered to United Counties in October 1952. These were allocated rolling stock numbers that continued on from the similar vehicles acquired from Eastern National earlier that year. HNV733 was allotted rolling stock number 917. It is seen loading in Kettering. *794 Preservation Group*

New in November 1953 was this 55-seat ECW bodied Bristol KSW6B. Registered JBD981 it was numbered 944 by United Counties. It is seen parked in the rear yard of Bedford garage. *794 Preservation Group*

950 – JBD955 was one of the first Bristol Lodekkas to be operated by United Counties, and one of four pre-production models delivered to the Tilling Group. Unlike others in the fleet, 950 was built with an open-platform rather than having doors fitted. These at the time were revolutionary, with the new drop axle chassis which enabled a normal centre aisle upper deck without the offside sunken gangway. This LD6B model was new to the company in April 1953. Further examples of the type arrived during 1954. When compared with the photograph of 944 on the previous page, it can be seen how much more modern 950 would have appeared to the public. *794 Preservation Group*

The 1950s also saw the introduction of the Bristol LS6B saloon into the United Counties fleet. 482 – JBD986 was new to the company in February 1954 and was fitted with coach seating. It is seen operating an Associated Motorways service to Portsmouth. *794 Preservation Group*

March 1954 saw the arrival of four luxury Bristol LS6G coaches. The third of the batch, 116 (OBD903), is seen here on layover at Victoria Coach Station in the cream coaching livery. *S.J. Butler Collection*

October 1957 saw the delivery of four, less luxurious ECW bodied Bristol LS5G saloons for local work. 118 (PNV218) is seen demonstrating the local coaching livery. Kettering garage provides the backdrop to this photograph.
S.J. Butler Collection

Of the many Bristol saloons operated by United Counties, the SC4LK was not as popular as other models, with only six being taken into stock by the company. ONV 426 (126) represents this batch. It is seen parked at Derngate Coach Station, Northampton.
794 Preservation Group

66 • UNITED COUNTIES BUSES

Royston provides the backdrop for 134 (SRP134), an ECW bodied Bristol MW6G, which is seen passing through the town en-route to Buntingford on route 188. The Boars Pub is seen on the right of the vehicle, the road to the left is now the location of Royston's Bus Station.
S.J. Butler Collection

The company's Desborough garage provides the backdrop to this photograph. Here we find ECW bodied Bristol LD6B 541 – ORP41 which formed part of a batch of nineteen such vehicles delivered to United Counties over the course of 1958.
S.J. Butler Collection

1960–1969

1960

The first two of the Bristol FS6B double-deck machines arrived with United Counties in 1960. These two vehicles were outstanding from the 1959 order. Taking up rolling stock numbers 600 and 601, these vehicles were registered URP600/1.

The new vehicle orders for 1960 called for twenty vehicles, five single-decks and fifteen double-decks. The five saloons were ECW bodied Bristol MWs; whilst the double-decks were of the new Bristol FS Lodekka model. All five Bristol MW saloons arrived in June numbered 142 to 146. They carried matching WBD registration marks. Nine of the fifteen double-deck machines arrived over the months of June and September 1960. They were numbered 602 to 610, registered WBD602-10.

1960 saw a programme of changing the seating capacity on some of the single-decks in the fleet. In total, twenty-one saloons were re-seated to forty-five-seaters; the vehicles treated were 100-7, 436/41/2/74/5/80/90-6. The intake of new vehicles and the withdrawal of older vehicles were almost balanced during 1960, with sixteen vehicles being taken into stock, and fifteen older vehicles leaving the fleet.

1961

The outstanding vehicles from the 1960 order duly arrived during 1961. However, these vehicles took a while to put in an appearance with the company. The first three arrived during April, whilst the remaining trio didn't arrive until June and July. Following on from the previous year's deliveries, these vehicles were numbered 611-616 complete with matching WBD registration plates.

Sixteen vehicles in all were ordered for 1961 delivery, four coaches and the remainder being double-deck machines. The four coaches were delivered to United Counties over the months of May and June, numbered 200-203 – YBD200-3. These machines carried ECW bodies on a Bristol MW6G chassis and were put to use on the extended coach tours operated by United Counties.

It is no surprise that not all of the double-decks ordered by the company arrived in the designated year. Eight of the twelve materialised in the correct year. These eight vehicles continued the fleet numbering sequence from 617 to 624 and were registered YNV617-624 respectively. These were of the Bristol FLF6B variety. The intake of new vehicles in 1961 outweighed the number of vehicles taken out of the fleet, with eighteen arriving, and fifteen departing. At the close of 1961, the United Counties fleet totalled 439 vehicles, with an additional twenty-six vehicles awaiting disposal.

Four Bristol LS5G coaches were repainted during 1961. 437-440 lost their cream livery in favour of the standard green bus livery.

By 1961, the fleet of driver training vehicles were beginning to look their age. This led to their replacement by two Bristol L5G saloons registered KNO602/3 during November. These two machines gained new identities as numbers 4 and 5.

1962

The four outstanding Bristol FLF6B machines from 1961 found their way to United Counties in the first month of 1962. These followed on from their sister vehicles and gained stock numbers 625-628 – YNV625-8.

A modest twenty-six vehicles were ordered for 1962 delivery; broken down it called for fourteen saloons and twelve double-decks. The fourteen saloons were ECW bodied Bristol MW6G machines. They took up stock numbers 147 to 160, registered 147-160BRP. Delivery of the batch took place in three stages. The first five arrived during July; four more in September and the remaining five vehicles in October.

Again, the full quota of new double-deck machines was not reached during 1962, with only eight of the twelve vehicles being delivered. These machines took stock numbers 629 to 636 – 629-636BRP and were similar to the previous intake of Bristol FLF6B machines.

During 1953, United Counties had purchased a batch of Bristol LS5G saloons for use on long-distance coach work. By 1962, these vehicles were in a poor condition and therefore unsuitable for such use. Therefore, eleven were re-seated by United Counties and placed into service as normal stage-service buses.

Two Bristol coaches, 114/5 – OBD901/2, were sold to sister company Eastern National in March 1962. This was due to a policy adopted by United Counties to remove all but a small number of saloons that were of full coach specification from the fleet. This was aided by the repainting of Bristol LS6B saloons 467/8 in April, and the sale of Bristol SC saloons 125-27 to Red & White.

Twenty-six vehicles left the United Counties fleet during 1962, this greatly outnumbering the fourteen new vehicles that had entered service.

The United Counties ancillary fleet gained a new member during 1962. Withdrawn Bristol K5G 681 – JEV420 was converted to a tree-lopper. This machine was the first vehicle owned by United Counties that was specifically used for this work. An additional Bristol L5G saloon was also added to the ancillary fleet to be used as a driver tuition vehicle. 317 – KNO624 was the vehicle in question and was renumbered 6, replacing GPU436 from similar duties.

1963

Delivery of the four outstanding vehicles from 1962 was split between January and April 1963. 637 to 640 – 637-640BRP were the vehicles concerned.

Twenty-eight vehicles were ordered for delivery during 1963, but this was later reduced by two. As with previous years, few of the vehicles ordered were received during 1963. In fact, only ten of the double-deck machines saw service in the intended year. These were of the Bristol FS6B model rather than the specified FSF model ordered by the company, and were numbered 641 to 650, registered 641-650EBD. Delivery was spread between August and December, with the first six being allocated to Bedford, with the remaining vehicles finding their way to Northampton.

Two Bristol LS models were re-seated during January, the vehicles being numbered 461/2. United Counties had also introduced a programme to downgrade the coach fleet to dual-purpose vehicles. Four machines were converted under this programme; 481/2 – JBD985/6 and 116/7 OBD903/4.

United Counties discontinued operating extended coach tours after the 1962 season. This left four luxury coaches purchased in 1961 surplus to requirements. Three of the four were sold to sister company Eastern National, with 203 – YBD203 being retained. United Counties also sold the remaining Bristol SC buses to Cumberland Motor Services in February 1963. The tour licences were subsequently sold to Wallace Arnold of Leeds.

1964

The outstanding vehicles ordered the previous year arrived during 1964. First to arrive were four Bristol RE saloons, the first in January, numbered 250 – 250BRP. It was built to coach specification, but was painted into the green and cream standard livery. The remaining three were delivered between February and March, numbered 251-3 which were the first vehicles to gain the new 'B' prefix registration marks, taking registrations ABD251-3B.

Delivery of the outstanding Bristol FS double-deck machines was spread between January and August. The first arrived in January when five vehicles materialised. These took up rolling stock numbers 651 to 655, and were registered 651-5EBD. The remaining seven took up stock numbers 656 to 662 and were registered in the new system as ABD656-62B.

The 1964 orders called for six Bristol RELH6G saloons and twenty-eight Bristol FS double-decks. All of the saloons were delivered in the designated year; however, only eleven of the double-deck machines arrived during 1964. The saloons were registered BBD254-9B, and carried fleet numbers 254 to 259 respectively.

The eleven Bristol FS6B machines that were taken into stock were numbered 663 to 673, registered CNV663-73B.

During 1964, an additional five Bristol LS saloons were downgraded to buses. 469-471/3 had the forty-one dual purpose seats removed in favour of forty-five bus seats.

1965

1965 saw the balance of the twenty-eight Bristol FS machines arrive with United Counties. Delivery of these vehicles still took a while, taking place between January and September. Twelve were taken into stock during the opening three months of the year. These were numbered 674 to 679 and carried matching DNV-C registration marks. The next trio came between April and June, with one arriving each month. These carried on from the previous batch, numbered 680 to 682 – EBD680-2C. The remaining eight took stock numbers 683 to 690 – ENV683-90C, the last of these arriving by September.

Orders for new vehicles for 1965 delivery called for a modest seven Bristol FLF machines. Unlike previous years, all seven arrived in the latter quarter of the year numbered 691 to 697, registered GBD693/4C and GRP695-7D. The latter three carried D registrations as, although they were delivered in 1965, they did not enter service until January 1966.

For the first time in twelve years, United Counties took in a stock of a number of second-hand vehicles during 1965. The first vehicles to arrive were two Bristol LS5G coaches acquired from Eastern National. They took stock numbers 476/7 and were registered WVX441/2. The next four vehicles were also sourced from Eastern National. This time they were Bristol LS6G coaches registered VVX367-9 and XTW152. They were numbered 463 to 466 by United Counties.

The company treated Bristol LS saloon 472 – JBD990 to a re-seat during the year. The intake of thirty vehicles into the fleet led to the displacement of twenty-six older vehicles.

1966

The modest number of new vehicles ordered for 1965 was more than compensated for in the 1966 orders. No less than twenty-nine buses and coaches were ordered by United Counties for delivery during the year. Broken down, the order called for twenty Bristol FS Lodekka machines, six Bristol SUL saloons and a trio of Bristol MW coaches. An additional Lodekka was added to the order, being diverted from an order for Lincolnshire Road Car.

The first ten Bristol Lodekka double-decks arrived during the first four months of the year. They continued the numbering system from 698 to 707 – GRP698-707D. Next to arrive were the trio of Bristol MW coaches, all bodied by ECW. These took rolling stock numbers 260 to 262 and carried registration marks GRP260-2D. A further four Bristol FS machines arrived numbered 708 to 711, HBD708-11D.

Some of the more unusual vehicles to be delivered to United Counties during the year were the six Bristol SUL4A saloons complete with ECW bodies. The first three, 300-2 HRP300-2D, replaced elderly Bristol saloons at the Welford garage. The remaining three, 303 to 305 – HRP303D, JNV304/5D, were stored by United Counties for a reasonably long period of time before a route that was suitable for them to operate was found. They eventually entered service on the 383 which ran between Leighton Buzzard and Great Brickhill. The final seven vehicles to be taken into stock were ECW bodied Bristol FS6G Lodekka machines. These were registered KBD712-8D and naturally took rolling stock numbers 712 to 718.

1966 saw the 800th anniversary of the Bedford town charter, and to celebrate this, United Counties repainted Bristol FS6B 678 – DNV678C into all-over cream, and applied dark blue lettering reading '1166 Bedford Charter Year 1966', positioned between decks, and placed the Bedford Arms on the bottom panels. In addition, the wings and wheels were also repainted dark blue. 678 remained in this livery between March and October 1966.

Bristol RE saloons 254 to 259 were repainted from the green with cream relief livery into the cream with green relief coaching livery. Bristol coach 117 – OBD904 was also treated to this livery. Coach 203, which was made surplus from the loss of the coach tours operated by United Counties, saw this vehicle up-seated to thirty-nine seats, and the green relief added to its cream livery.

United Counties tested an AEC Swift demonstrator in the Northampton area in April 1966. Registered FGW498C, this vehicle carried a Willowbrook body. This was the first demonstration vehicle to be hired by United Counties for a number of years. No further orders for this type were placed by the company.

1966 saw thirty-six elderly buses taken out of the fleet, replaced by thirty-one new vehicles.

1967

Thirty-six new vehicles were ordered for 1967 delivery. Broken down, this order comprised twenty Bristol FLF machines; eight Bristol RELH dual-purpose vehicles and eight Bristol RELL saloons. For the third year in a row, United Counties received all of these vehicles in the correct year.

First to arrive were eight Bristol FLF6B machines which were delivered in January and February. These vehicles took up stock numbers 719 to 726, registered KNV719-26E. The eight dual-purpose Bristol RELH6G coaches were next to arrive. These were delivered in the cream with green relief livery. These followed on from the previous batch, numbered 263 to 270 and were registered KRP263-70E.

The remainder of the Bristol FLFs duly arrived between March and June 1967. The first four, numbered 727 to 730 by United Counties, were registered LBD727-30E. The remaining eight quickly followed, taking stock numbers 731 to 738, registered LRP731-8E. The final intake of new vehicles comprised eight Bristol RELL6G saloons which were delivered in October 1967. They took stock numbers 306 to 313, registered NBD306-13F. Again, all new vehicles delivered carried Eastern Coach Works bodies.

A further two second-hand vehicles were purchased by United Counties from Isle of Wight-based Southern Vectis. The two vehicles in question were Bedford SBO machines, complete with the Duple Super Vega body style. These vehicles took fleet numbers 112 and 113, and were registered ODL48 and ODL51.

The coach fleet had four vehicles added to it during the year. This was achieved by the repainting of Bristol RELHs 250 to 253 and Bristol LS6G 116 – OBD903 into the new cream and green relief livery. Two Bristol MW6G dual-purpose coaches were re-seated to forty-five seaters, these being 139 – TBD139 and 142 – WBD142.

The intake of new and second-hand vehicles almost balanced with those that were disposed of. Thirty-eight new vehicles entered the fleet, whilst thirty-six left, these mainly being older Bristol K double-deck machines.

1967 saw a further two demonstrators being used by United Counties. The first vehicle concerned was a rear-engined, front entrance Bristol VRL registered HHW933D, and was used for a day in the Northampton area in February. The second demonstrator was a Mercedes-Benz 0302 coach registered OLH302E, and was used on the Nottingham-Leicester-Northampton service, and was loaned during April.

1968

A large order was again placed for delivery in 1968. Four Bristol VRs, twenty Bristol RELL saloons and six Bristol RELH express saloons were ordered, the order being slightly altered, swapping two of the RELL chassis for two Bristol LH saloons, these being constructed during 1969. The majority of new vehicles arrived in 1968.

First to arrive were six Bristol RELH6G express coaches. They were all delivered wearing the cream and green relief coach livery, taking stock numbers 271 to 276, ORP271-6F. The eighteen Bristol RELL6G saloons arrived between August and September 1968, taking stock numbers 314 to 331, with matching RBD-G registrations. The four Bristol VRT machines did not materialise until 1969.

Four second-hand Bristol saloons of the LL6B and LWL6B models were taken into stock by United Counties during January 1968. Acquired from Hants & Dorset Company, Bournemouth, these vehicles were numbered 432 to 435, registered KEL731-3 and KRU996. These four vehicles lasted just over a year and a half with United Counties.

In addition, six second-hand saloons were taken into stock during October, in the form of Bristol LS5G saloons sourced from Red & White Services Ltd. These vehicles were allocated stock numbers 478/9, 488/9 and 497/8, registered LAX635/9 and MAX104/8/9/14.

Two Bristol LS saloons were re-seated during 1968, with 110/1 – NBD900/1 gaining 45 bus seats. The forty-four new and second-hand vehicles taken into stock displaced thirty-three elderly vehicles from the fleet.

1969

As a result of the Transport Holding Act of 1968, the infamous National Bus Company was formed, taking effect from 1 January 1969. As of this date, United Counties came under the ownership of the National Bus Company. United Counties lasted under the ownership of the National Bus Company until 1986.

The four Bristol VRTs outstanding from 1968 arrived during January 1969. Like the vast numbers of Bristol vehicles that had entered the fleet during the years, these buses carried bodies supplied by Eastern Coach Works. These vehicles took up stock numbers 750 to 753, registered RRP750-3G and introduced the first front entranced double-decks into the United Counties fleet. The two outstanding Bristol LH6L saloons took up stock numbers 400 and 401 – SRP400/1G.

A further four Bristol VRT machines were ordered as part of the 1969 order, along with sixteen Bristol RELL6Gs, eight Bristol RELH6Gs, and two further Bristol LH saloons. United Counties was successful in receiving all but two of these vehicles during 1969.

Five Bristol RELL6Gs were the first vehicles to arrive. They took stock numbers 332 to 336, SRP332-6G. Next to arrive were the pair of Bristol LH6L saloons, which followed on from the previous two, being numbered 402/3 – TBD402/3G. May and June saw the arrival of the eight Bristol RELH6G dual-purpose saloons with United Counties. They carried registrations TBD277-84G, and were numbered 277 to 284. Delivery of the Bristol VRT machines was spread over the course of 1969. The first two arrived during May, and the remaining two in September. The first two were numbered 754/5 – TBD754/5G, the last two took stock numbers 756/7, registered UBD756/7H.

The batch of Bristol RELL6Gs for 1969 arrived in August numbered 337 to 342 with registrations UBD337-42H. The final deliveries of 1969 saw three additional Bristol RELL6G saloons arrive between October and November, following on from the previous batch from as 343 to 345, registered URP343-5H.

September 1969 saw the remaining stage carriage services of Birch Bros. of Kentish Town, London, acquired by United Counties along with a number of vehicles. Included in the sale were twelve Leyland Leopard coaches, the first of this type for the company. 170 – 173 (DUC70-3C) carried Marshall bodies, 181/2 – 81/2CYV Willowbrook bodies and 190 to 195 (90-95FXD) were bodied by Park Royal. All were allocated to Rushden garage.

Dual-purpose 250/1/3/6 and Bristol MWs 148/50/5/8 were downgraded by being repainted into a green with cream waistband. In addition, eight vehicles, four Bristol MW6Gs and four Bristol LS5Gs, were downgraded by the removal of their dual-purpose seats with 45 bus seats. The vehicles concerned were Bristol MWs 134/5/6/8, and Bristol LSs 118-121.

The intake of forty-six vehicles saw twenty-six vehicles withdrawn from the fleet.

During 1969, the driver training fleet was replaced using withdrawn Bristol LS5G saloons 437 to 440, HBD626-9, which were converted between May and June 1969. They were renumbered 8 to 11 in the ancillary fleet series.

Numerous examples of the Bristol MW6G model were purchased by United Counties between 1958 and 1962. All carried bodywork by ECW as is shown here by 143 – WBD143. *794 Preservation Group*

602 – WBD602 is seen entering Bedford Bus Station having travelled from Cambridge on a 128 service. The vehicle would have continued on its journey to Northampton. The service would later be renumbered as X3 with the introduction of the Coachlinks network in the 1980s. 602 was one of the first Bristol FS6B Lodekka models to operate with United Counties. *Bruce Pyne*

The Bristol
FS6B model was introduced into the United Counties fleet in 1962. 642 – 642EBD was delivered to the company during 1963. The batch, 641-648, was different from other FS models in the fleet in that they had driver operated doors for use on Bedford town services 100 and 101. It is seen on layover at Bedford Bus Station.
Bruce Pyne

Bristol RELH6G express coach 252 – ABD252B waits in Luton's first Bus Station during April 1968 before running empty to Sundon Park Skefko to operate a journey on works service 23 to Dunstable. Unusual shift working hours at Sundon SKF meant these journeys often operated at abnormal times, and were usually one-man operated, this being at a time when very little mileage was worked without a conductor.
Graham Smith

Four ECW bodied Bristol LS6G coaches were acquired from sister company Eastern National in December 1965. They helped to give the company's coaching fleet a smart, modern appearance. 465 – VVX369 represents this batch, dating back to 1953. It is seen parked in the rear yard of Bedford garage. *S.J. Butler Collection*

United Counties acquired a pair of ECW bodied Bristol LS5G saloons in July 1965 from Eastern National. The pair were consecutively registered, the first being WVX441, which took up fleet number 476. It is seen parked outside Kettering garage. *794 Preservation Group*

United Counties took stock of just six Bristol SUL4A buses with 36-seat ECW bodies. Three of the original four were allocated to Northampton garage which allowed two to be available for out stationing at Welford, where two short, low-height single-deck machines were required. The fourth was allocated to Rushden garage. 304 – JNV304D was allocated to Luton garage from where it entered service in 1967. It was mainly allocated to the Leighton Buzzard outstation where it operated market day services on a Tuesday and Saturday and some summer Sunday workings. During the week, it was mainly used on the peak time Luton – Leighton Buzzard services, resting at Luton garage during the day where it was often put to use. It is seen here operating a Vauxhall Works service to the Stopsley area of Luton. *Graham Smith*

The shorter Bristol FS6G Lodekka machine was taken into stock during the mid-1960s. Representing the batch is 715 – KBD715D, which was delivered to the company during November 1966. This vehicle shows off the basic National Bus Company green livery well. *Bruce Pyne*

1960–1969 • 77

A pair of Bedford SBO coaches were acquired from Southern Vectis Omnibus Company in December 1967, initially for a rail replacement service after the closure of the line between Bletchley and Oxford. They both carried the stylish Duple Vega coach body making them stand out from other coaches in the fleet at that time. ODL48 was one of the pair and it gained rolling stock number 112. It is seen parked at Kettering garage. *794 Preservation Group*

A busy Victoria Coach Station finds 263 (KRP263E) on layover having operated a journey on the X6. The difference in livery styles worn by express coaches from around the country at the time can be seen by the other vehicles viewed in this photograph. *S.J. Butler Collection*

ECW bodied Bristol FLF6B 720 – KNV 720E was new to United Counties in January 1967 and is seen here at its home depot of Wellingborough. Wellingborough was at one time the disposal point for many United Counties life-expired buses and a couple of Bristol SUL4A saloons can be seen in this photograph. *794 Preservation Group*

Another of the numerous Bristol Lodekka machines to operate with United Counties. 731 – LRP731E was new to the company in June 1967. It is seen passing through the Bedfordshire village of Cople bound for Bedford on route 176. *S.J. Butler Collection*

314 – RBD314G shows off the ECW bus body fitted to the Bristol RELL6G saloon. The green livery with white relief band is seen clearly in this photograph as is the brown fleet number plate applied to vehicles allocated to Luton garage. This is the location where we find 314. *Bruce Pyne*

Another photograph taken at Victoria Coach Station. This time we find Bristol RELH6G 271 (ORP271F) which has completed a journey on the MX5 service, advertising itself as a 'Motorway Express' service to London Victoria. *S.J. Butler Collection*

Numerous Bristol LL6B saloons were taken into stock by United Counties in the 1950s along with three second-hand versions from Hants & Dorset. KEL731 was one such vehicle acquired from this operator and was numbered 432. It was acquired in January 1968. It is seen here after its career with United Counties. *794 Preservation Group*

Six ECW bodied Bristol LS6G saloons were taken into stock by United Counties during October 1968 from Red & White. LAX635 was one such vehicle which gained fleet number 479 for its time with United Counties. It is seen parked at the open-air garage area at Skinners Hill, Rushden. *S.J. Butler Collection*

1960–1969 • **81**

Six ECW bodied Bristol LS6G saloons arrived from Red & White in October 1968. 498 – MAX108 was numerically the last of the half dozen single-deck machines. It is seen operating route 89 to Pirton from Luton. *794 Preservation Group*

Marshall bodied Leyland Leopard DUC72C was new to Birch Bros. in July 1965. United Counties took over the Birch Bros. operations in September 1969. The company slotted the acquired vehicles into their fleet numbering sequence. Fleet number 233 was allocated to this vehicle which is seen loading at Bedford Bus Station. *Thomas Knowles*

In September 1969, United Counties acquired the operations of Birch Bros. of Rushden, bringing with it twelve Leyland Leopard coaches with various body styles. The majority of them carried Park Royal bodies as is seen in the photograph above. 240 – 93FXD is seen at Bedford Bus Station wearing the coaching livery. *794 Preservation Group*

326 – RBD326G was new to United Counties in October 1968. This ECW bodied Bristol RELL6G is seen loading in a semi-busy Leighton Buzzard town centre on a local service. *Gary Seamarks*

1960–1969 • 83

A number of shorter Bristol LH6L saloons were taken into stock by United Counties during 1969. Representing this batch is 401 – SRP401G which is seen entering Stamford Bus Station. *S.J. Butler Collection*

Delivery of the ECW bodied Bristol VRT machines commenced in January 1969 with the last new VRTs arriving in 1981. 753 – RRP753G was one of four delivered in January 1969 to the company with the flat front body style. It is seen loading in Aylesbury town centre. *S.J. Butler Collection*

1970–1979

1970

One of the more significant acquisitions in the history of United Counties took place in January 1970, when the operations of Luton Corporation were purchased. In total, seventy-five vehicles were acquired, thirty of these being single-decks, the remainder double-decks.

The single-decks acquired were all pretty modern vehicles in the form of the Bristol RELL6L model, the oldest of which dated back to 1967. These vehicles were registered in five different registration series. 361 to 370 were registered MXD101-5E and NXE106-10F. The second batch, 371 to 380, were registered PXE111/2F and PXE113-20G. The final ten vehicles were registered UXD121-30G, and were numbered 381 to 390. Although licensed in July 1969, 387-90 were never used by Luton, and all were built to dual door specification. In addition, five Bristol LHs were also acquired but were not operated by United Counties and passed unused to Eastern Counties as WNG101-5H.

The forty-five double-deck machines were not as uniform as their single-deck counterparts. Twenty-one Leyland Titan PD2s; sixteen Albion Lowlanders and eight Dennis Lolines were taken into stock. The first of the two Titans were allotted rolling stock numbers 800/3, registered RNM140/3. The pair carried MCCW bodywork, and lasted less than two months with United Counties. Sister vehicle RNM141 was also acquired in a state of cannibalisation. Four similar vehicles gained stock numbers 804 to 807, registered RMJ144-7. Both of these batches were not repainted into United Counties green, instead they remained in the red livery of Luton Corporation. They also failed physically to gain the allotted fleet numbers. These vehicles remained in the fleet until June 1970. The next five PD2s again carried the MCCW body style, registered UNM148-152. They took up fleet numbers 808 to 812, and were treated to the United Counties green livery unlike their counterparts. Further Leyland Titans to be acquired were numbered 813 to 817, and carried Weymann bodywork. These vehicles were registered WTM153 to WTM157. The final batch of Leyland Titans to be taken into stock were numbered 818 to 822, and were registered 158-162ANM, this batch introducing a third body style on this type to the fleet, this time being of East Lancs build.

The next two vehicles, numerically, were a pair of Dennis Loline machines. As with the last batch of Titans, these vehicles carried East Lancs bodies. They continued the fleet numbering system on and became 822 and 823, registered 163/4ANM. The remaining six Lolines were bodied by Neepsend. New in 1965, these vehicles took up stock numbers 841 to 846 and were registered FXD181-6C.

The sixteen Albion Lowlanders taken into stock comprised two batches. The first batch took stock numbers 825 to 830, registered 165-170EMJ. These again carried East Lancs bodywork. The final ten Lowlanders were allocated stock numbers 831 to

840, and were registered 171-180HTM. The first four were bodied by East Lancs, the remaining six being bodied by Neepsend Coachworks of Sheffield, under contract to East Lancs. The final vehicle to be acquired from Luton Corporation was a Leyland Titan PD2 machine registered RNM139. The vehicle was used as a driver training vehicle.

Moving onto the fleet replacement programme for 1970 now, and the year saw an order placed for fifteen Bristol VRTs, nine Bristol RELH saloons and nine Bristol LH saloons. The complete order was delivered over the course of the year. However, the first two new vehicles to enter the fleet were the outstanding RELL6G saloons from 1969. They arrived in January and were numbered 346/7, registered URP346/7H. They were allocated to Bedford and Kettering garages respectively. In addition to the above order, United Counties also took delivery of the vehicles ordered by Luton Corporation. Between February and March 1970, ten Bristol RELL6G saloons were delivered to United Counties registered VNV348-357H, and naturally took up stock numbers 348 to 357. Due to these vehicles being ordered by Luton Corporation, they were delivered in dual-door layout.

The fifteen Bristol VRT machines arrived at Northampton between April and November. The first five arrived in April, taking stock numbers 758 to 762; they were registered VNV758-62H. A further two followed in June 1970, numbered 763 and 764, VNV763H and WBD764H. The next arrived between July and September 1970, numbered 765 to 768, WRP765-8J. The final four arrived in October and November, with two being delivered each month. These vehicles were registered XBD769-72J, and numbered 769 to 772 respectively. Allocation of these vehicles were split between Bedford, Kettering, Northampton, Rushden, Aylesbury and Wellingborough.

The order for nine Bristol RELH6G dual-purpose saloons was fulfilled between May and July 1970. These vehicles took up stock numbers 285 to 293 and were registered WBD285-293H. These vehicles were all painted in United Counties cream and green coaching livery. Two of these vehicles were allocated to Rushden to operate the former Birch Bros. route to London, with the remainder being shared between Northampton, Bedford, Kettering, Luton and Wellingborough.

The final nine new vehicles taken into stock were Bristol LH saloons which arrived between September and October 1970. These vehicles were registered XBD404-12J, and took stock numbers 404 to 412. This batch was distributed between Corby, Kettering, Bedford, Biggleswade, Northampton, Stony Stratford and Hitchin depots. The intake of 115 new and second-hand vehicles saw sixty-four older vehicles leave the fleet.

In October 1970, Bristol RELL 325 – RBD325G was involved in a serious accident in Bletchley involving a car and a taxi. The petrol tank of the car ignited the bodywork of the bus, and as a result, it was gutted by fire, although the chassis did not gain serious damage.

Bristol RELH 252 was downgraded in March 1970, and was repainted into an alternative style of United Counties livery. It gained green up to the waist band, and cream from the waist upwards.

1971

1971 vehicle orders comprised fourteen Bristol VRTs, nine Bristol RELH coaches and eight Bristol LH saloons, which were later swapped for the RESL model instead.

First to arrive were the nine RELH coaches. The first four arrived during March, taking stock numbers 205 to 208, registered YNV205-8J. The remaining five followed in April and were numbered 209 to 213, carrying registrations YRP209-13J. These vehicles were split between Northampton, taking four, Luton two, and Bedford, Kettering and Rushden one each.

June saw the delivery of the eight Bristol RESL buses commence, with the first three arriving during the month. These took up stock numbers 420-2, ANV420-2J. The remaining five vehicles arrived over the course of the latter quarter of 1971, and followed on from the three delivered in June, taking fleet numbers 423 to 427, BRP423-7K. This batch was shared between Huntingdon, Stony Stratford and Kettering depots.

The first of the fourteen VRTs ordered duly arrived in June, numbered 773 to 776, registered ANV773-6J. The next four arrived at Northampton during December 1971, numbered 777 to 780 – CBD777-80K. The remaining six failed to materialise during 1971, arriving in 1972. Of the eight that were received, Northampton received three, Bedford a pair, and Kettering, Stony Stratford and Rushden one each. 778 was inspected by West Midlands PTE in February 1972 for a day but not used in service.

The intake of new vehicles saw further Bristol KSW6Bs and Bristol LS saloons leave the United Counties fleet.

The former Luton Corporation Leylands and Albions became more unreliable during the year. This led United Counties to source fifteen older Bristol/ECW machines that were being withdrawn from other National Bus Company operations. The first two arrived in January in the form of the Bristol LD6B model, numbered 948/9 – LFW320/3. These vehicles came from Lincolnshire Road Car Co. Ltd. Allocated to Bedford depot, they displaced two United Counties vehicles to Luton depot. The next three to arrive came in the form of the Bristol LD6G. Two were sourced from the Nottinghamshire & Derbyshire Traction Co. Ltd, and the other from Midland General. The first two buses to arrive were registered 21/22DRB. The vehicle acquired from the latter company was registered 259NHU. The trio became numbered 571 to 573, and were allocated to Luton.

A more sizeable batch were acquired from Red & White Services of Chepstow, from where United Counties sourced six Bristol LD6G models, all arriving in June. They took up stock numbers 920 to 925, registered LAX624-9. Again, all six were directly allocated to Luton depot, and entered service after a repaint from red to green. Cumberland Motor Services Ltd was the source of two LD6G machines registered UAO376/8, which became known as United Counties 946/7. These vehicles were both allocated to Northampton depot. The final two were sourced from Midland General and the Mansfield District Traction Co. Ltd, arriving in August and September. The first was registered 523JRA, which received United Counties stock number 574, and was allocated to Luton. The bus acquired from the latter company took stock number 599 – 565ERR, and was slightly different to the others, being a Bristol FS6G machine. Originally allocated to Kettering, this vehicle was soon reallocated to Luton depot. All fifteen received a repaint before entering service.

Midland General Omnibus Co. Ltd also provided a trio of Bristol MW saloons which were used to replace three of United Counties' Bristol LS saloons which were ageing considerably. The vehicles in question were allocated stock numbers 124 to 126 and were registered 24-6DRB. These vehicles arrived in December 1971, entering service during January 1972. They were allocated to Biggleswade and Hitchin depots.

The final second-hand vehicle to be taken into stock during 1971 was a Dennis Loline III, bodied by Alexander. 396COR became United Counties 847 and was purchased from Aldershot & District as a source of spare parts for the Luton Corporation Dennis vehicles.

Bristol saloon 325, destroyed by fire in 1970, was rebodied by ECW during 1971. When rebodied, this vehicle gained a curved windscreen style body which differed from its original body style.

A number of vehicles were repainted into the green up to the waistband, and cream above livery. Vehicles treated to this livery were Bristol MWs 149/51/3/4/6/7/60 and younger Bristol RELH coaches 254/5/7/8/9. May 1971 saw Bristol MW 148 re-seated to forty-five bus seats.

1972

1972 proved to be a difficult year for United Counties, which had to operate services with an ageing fleet which put a strain on the operation of some routes. The original order for new vehicles for 1972 delivery called for twenty-eight Bristol VRTs, five Bristol RELH express coaches and three Bristol RELLs. However, due to the poor performance of United Counties in 1970 and 1971, the order for the VRTs and RELH coaches was cancelled, and the RELL order replaced by an equal number of Leyland National saloons, which was later increased to six. This order again changed, when a deal was made with Trent Motor Traction to exchange three of the Nationals for three VRTs. During the year, United Counties struggled to provide a good level of service to its customers with its current fleet. This led to a further twelve Bristol VRT machines being diverted from other National Bus Company operators. Ten were diverted from Eastern Counties, the other two from Eastern National.

Although this deal had been made, United Counties only received five of the twelve in 1972. The first new vehicles to be delivered in 1972 were the outstanding six Bristol VRTs from 1971. The batch was numbered 781 to 786, registered CBD781-6K, the first three materialised during March, with the remainder arriving during July 1972. Five of this batch were put straight into service, the sixth member being retained until August. This resulted in this vehicle being registered FRP786L instead of the above registration. Bedford, Kettering and Northampton were allocated two each of this batch. These were also the last Bristol VRT machines to be delivered to United Counties featuring the flat windscreen.

Next to arrive were three of the Bristol VRT machines that were diverted from Eastern Counties. 787 to 789 were registered GRP787-9L and were delivered to United Counties in November 1972, all three being the first VRT machines to be allocated to Luton garage. The final two of the year arrived in December and were the two that were originally intended for Eastern National. They followed on from the three diverted from Eastern Counties and took stock numbers 790/1 – GRP790/1L. These two vehicles were allocated to Bedford depot.

The remaining seven VRTs and the additional three swapped with Trent for three Nationals did not materialise until 1973. The order for three Leyland Nationals arrived over the final month of 1972, and first month of 1973. The first two, 450/1 – GBD450/1L, put in an appearance in December and 452 – GBD452L arrived in January 1973, all three were allocated to Luton.

The acquired Albion Lowlanders were giving United Counties further problems in 1972, and their eventual demise came. As United Counties was not in a position to purchase new vehicles, they were again successful in acquiring a dozen second-hand Bristol machines that had been made surplus from other companies. The first arrived in February in the form of three Bristol LD6B machines which came from Lincolnshire Road Car. These originated from the same batch of similar vehicles which United Counties had acquired the previous year. The three vehicles in question took stock numbers 917-9, and were registered LFW325/7/8, being allocated to Bedford and Northampton depots. Next to be acquired was a quartet of similar vehicles from

Western National. Registered TUO489, RTT961, 998, 962, and allocated stock numbers 915/6, 926/7, these four vehicles were pressed into service from Wellingborough, Kettering and Northampton depots. A solitary LD6G model was sourced from West Riding Automobile Co. Ltd. Taking stock number 575, this vehicle was registered WAL437 and allocated to Luton depot. The final four vehicles arrived from Crosville Motor Services. They arrived at Northampton in November where they were allocated fleet numbers 576 to 579, registered 620-3LFM. Allocation of these four vehicles was split between Kettering, Bedford, Northampton and Rushden depots.

The Bristol LS saloons also gave United Counties their fair share of trouble. Rather than the company spend money on rectifying the problems, five MCCW bodied Leyland Tiger Cub saloons were acquired from East Yorkshire Motor Services Ltd. The first three arrived in May, registered 6682/4/5KH when they took up stock numbers 196 to 198. The remaining two made their way to United Counties in July; numbered 199 and 200, they were registered 6680/1KH and were allocated to Bedford, Luton, Kettering and Northampton.

The intake of thirty new vehicles saw off seventeen of the ex-Luton Corporation double-decks, as well as further Bristol KSW6Bs and Bristol LSs.

Driver training vehicle 9 was involved in an accident during the year which resulted in it being replaced by withdrawn Bristol LS6B 475 in June. This vehicle was quickly renumbered 12 in the ancillary numbering sequence.

The autumn of 1972 saw the National Bus Company adopt a corporate identity which resulted in the standardisation of liveries worn by buses in the fleet. It was specified that the local bus fleet had to be painted either leaf green or poppy red with a single relief band, with fleet names being applied next to a reflected 'N' symbol. United Counties appropriately chose the leaf green version of the livery. The dual-purpose coaches were re-classified as local coaches, which saw a livery of a vast expanse of white from the waist band up. Coaches in the fleet were to receive an all-white livery with the word NATIONAL in large red and blue lettering.

Prior to the introduction of this livery change, United Counties had repainted a further two Bristol MWs from the 'BRP' batch in March 1972 into the green up to the waist band and cream above, with 152/9BRP being the two vehicles concerned. The first to go into the new NBC green and white bus livery was 155/8BRP which were treated in October 1972. RELH6G 289 – WBD289H was the first United Counties coach to receive the all white coaching livery in September 1972, quickly followed by 275 – ORP275F and 263 – KRP263E.

The first all-over advertisement bus to operate with United Counties did so in 1972. Bristol FLF 733 – LRP733E was adorned with such an advert for Lillywhites of Luton, completed in July 1972. This idea soon caught on with a second vehicle being treated to an all-over advertisement in September, with VRT 771 receiving one for Brookside Garages, Wellingborough.

1973

Before looking at any new vehicle orders for 1973, we take a look at the outstanding vehicles from the 1972 order. This comprised a solitary Leyland National saloon which has already been mentioned above, and a trio of VRTs that were exchanged with Trent, plus seven that had been diverted from Eastern Counties. The Trent VRTs were first to be delivered in January 1973 to Northampton. They were allocated stock numbers 792 to 794, GRP792-4L. These three were allocated to Bedford, Kettering and

Northampton depots. May and June saw the seven diverted VRTs find their way to United Counties. These followed on from the previous batch delivered, taking stock numbers 795 to 801 along with registrations JRP795-801L, and all entered service from Luton depot.

Orders for 1973 delivery called for twenty-eight Bristol VRT machines, five Bristol RELH express vehicles and three Bristol RESL saloons, which, like the previous year, were substituted for three Leyland National saloons.

During the year, United Counties was presented with a number of problems with its ageing fleet, in particular the vehicles inherited from Luton Corporation. To compensate for this, the National Bus Company arranged for twenty Leyland National saloons to be diverted from other subsidiaries to United Counties. These came from Northern General (nine), Eastern National (four), East Midland (three), Lincolnshire (two) and Yorkshire Traction and West Yorkshire one each.

The arrival of new vehicles came in the form of five Bristol RELH6G express vehicles which took registrations KRP214-8L and were allocated stock numbers 214-8. These five arrived over the course of June and July in the National white coach livery, with the first three being allocated to Northampton, and the remaining two being allocated to Kettering and Luton garages respectively.

The trio of Leyland Nationals were next to arrive in July 1973. They were allocated fleet numbers 453 to 455, registered NBD453-5M. Northampton, Bletchley and Kettering depots received one each, and these were the first Leyland National saloons for these garages.

The twenty-eight Bristol VRTs that were due for 1973 delivery did not materialise in the designated year, being received instead between February 1974 and February 1975. However, twelve of the twenty Leyland Nationals that had been diverted from other National Bus Company subsidiaries did arrive during 1973, the balance arriving in January 1974. These twenty took up stock numbers 456 to 475, registered ORP456-75M.

United Counties had the opportunity during 1973 to purchase six Willowbrook bodied Bedford YRQ saloons through Kirkby Central Ltd, Anston. These six were allocated registration plates ONV430-5M, which were soon changed to PNV430-5M, and they naturally became numbered 430 to 435. Three found their way to Hitchin depot, and the remaining three were shared between Biggleswade, Huntingdon and Stamford depots.

1973 saw a further twenty-four second-hand Bristol machines acquired from various sources. The first arrived in February when three Bristol LD6G machines were acquired from Cumberland Motor Services. These vehicles took stock numbers 580 to 582 and were registered ORM136, ORM144 and RAO728. However, the trio were in a poor condition, with 581 being sent for body attention at ECW prior to it entering service; 582 was in a very poor condition and was used as a source of spare parts for sister 580. The latter vehicle was the first to enter service in December 1973, closely followed by 581 in January 1974. Both vehicles were allocated to Stony Stratford.

Mansfield District Traction Company provided three Bristol MW6G saloons, which took stock numbers 127 to 129, registered 266NHU, 27/32DRB. The former vehicle already wore a green and cream livery so did not need repainting before entering service. The other two wore the dual-purpose livery, and were quickly repainted into the green and white local coach livery. These three vehicles were allocated to Kettering, Northampton and Rushden garages respectively.

Next to arrive were two Bristol FSF6G machines, arriving in March from Southdown Motors Services Ltd. Numbered 597/8 they were registered VAP34/5 and were put into the care of the company's Luton depot.

The largest batch of vehicles to be acquired at this time was a batch of nine Bristol LD6G machines from Southern Vectis. These vehicles were allotted stock numbers 931 to 939, registered KDL402-410 and were allocated to Luton depot.

The final seven to be acquired came from Cumberland Motor Services Ltd, and were a mixture of Bristol LD6G, FS6G and FLF6G models. Three were of the LD6G model and took stock numbers 940 to 942, registered UAO379/81/2. Three of these seven were Bristol FS6G machines which were registered 110-2DRM, to which United Counties allocated stock numbers 594 to 596. The final vehicle was a solitary FLF6G which was registered 508BRM, and took stock number 739. Luton took stock of the LD6G; with the FS6Gs and FLF6G machines being shared between Kettering and Corby depots. In addition, a further LD6G model was acquired from S. Twell of Ingham, originating with Lincolnshire, but was not operated by United Counties, instead it was used as a source of spare parts. The remains returned to Twell in 1974.

The National Bus Company made a deal with the Scottish Bus Group to exchange a number of Bristol FLF machines for Bristol VRTs. As part of the deal, United Counties was due to send 735 to 738, LRP735-8E north to Scotland but in practice only 736 was transferred, being swapped for LFS288F. However, the deal was soon cancelled as 736 had a Bristol engine rather than the Gardner engine specified by the Scottish Bus Group. LFS288F stood unused at Northampton prior to moving on to Southdown for further service.

A number of vehicles were placed on loan to help United Counties overcome staff shortages and mechanical difficulties being experienced. First to come were eight Bristol FLF machines from Eastern National in February 1973. The vehicles concerned were registered 184/5XNO, RWC604/8, BVX668B and KNO949C and AVX874/5G. The first six were Bristol FLF6Bs and the remaining two were FLF6Gs. The vehicles' Eastern National fleet numbers, 2600, 2602, 2603/5/6/8/13/4, were used by United Counties. This batch were built to CH37/16F layout, featuring additional luggage space at the rear of the lower deck. They retained their Eastern National livery and fleet names.

Trent Motor Traction Co. Ltd also stepped in to help United Counties by providing a number of Leyland Tiger Cubs, totalling ten in all. The vehicles concerned were YRC182/3/5/8/9/90/2/3/4/6 and had matching stock numbers.

October 1973 saw three AEC Reliance saloons hired from Maidstone & District Motor Services Ltd over a six month period. The three were registered 266/9/79DKT which were numbered 3266/9/79. The last vehicles to be taken on loan were six LD6B and FS6B models from West Yorkshire Road Car Co. Ltd. These vehicles retained their West Yorkshire fleet numbers whilst with United Counties, these being 1667, 1697, 2675-7 and 2693, and were registered TWY609, 9755WU, XYG831-3 and 2227WW. These six vehicles were loaned to United Counties at various periods between October and November 1973.

A number of vehicles were repainted during 1973, the first being 116 – OBD903 which gained the green and white bus livery. Next was 156 – 156BRP which was repainted into the dual-purpose livery in October 1973. RELH6Gs 251-3 and 290/1/3 were repainted into the dual-purpose coach livery from the cream coach livery. An additional coach to be repainted into the green and white local coach livery was former Birch Bros. Leopard 192 – 92FXD. A number of vehicles also received the white National coach livery, vehicles being treated so were REs 264-274/6, 285-8, MWs 203 and 261, which completed all the main coaches into this livery. Finally, on the livery front, VRT 786 gained an all-over advert during January 1973 for Charles Wells Brewery.

Four vehicles were added to the driver training fleet in 1973 in the form of four withdrawn Bristol KSW machines. The vehicles concerned were 911 – HBD647; 933/4 – JBD970/1 and 964 – KNV337. The latter vehicle was first to be converted, completed in February, followed by the remaining three in June 1973. They took stock numbers 13 to 16, and replaced saloons 8, 10-12.

1974

The outstanding eight Leyland Nationals from the batch 456 to 475 duly arrived in the first part of 1974, and were the first new vehicles to be taken into stock that year. At the same time, the outstanding Bedford YRQ 434 – PNV434M also entered the fleet, all doing so in January.

The outstanding order for Bristol VRTs from 1973 also materialised during 1974, when, over the period of February and March, four arrived numbered 802 to 805, registered PRP802-5M. The order was split between twelve ultralow-height machines and sixteen standard low-height vehicles. The four that arrived were of the ultralow-height model. Four more followed in June when RRP812-5M arrived, taking rolling stock numbers 812-815 respectively. The final four low-height machines were taken into stock during November when vehicles registered GNV331 to 334N arrived with United Counties. They were numbered 822-825 by the company. However, the full complement of the normal height VRT machines was not received during 1974, with twelve of the sixteen materialising. The first six arrived over the course of March and April 1974. They took up stock numbers 806-11 with matching RRP-M registrations. Of this batch, 807 was delivered in readiness for an all-over advertisement for Tricentrol of Dunstable to be applied. These vehicles were shared between Biggleswade, Luton, Bedford, Kettering, Stony Stratford and Rushden depots. The next six arrived between August and September 1974 at which time they were allocated stock numbers 816 to 821, and registered SRP816-21N. These vehicles were a little less spread out, with Northampton, Bedford and Corby receiving two each.

Moving on now to the 1974 orders, United Counties required eleven Bristol VRTs, twenty-four Leyland National saloons and five coaches. As with the 1973 order, none of the Bristol VRT machines were manufactured and delivered during the year. The Leyland Nationals fared a little better with twenty being received, the four outstanding machines materialising during 1975. United Counties was however successful in receiving its full complement of coaches ordered.

The coaches featured the Bristol RELH chassis complete with Plaxton bodywork. These vehicles were registered SBD219-223M and took up stock numbers 219 to 223 respectively. They were delivered in National white coaching livery between May and June 1974, and were allocated to Northampton depot where they were initially put to use on the Nottingham to London express service.

The twenty Leyland National saloons were delivered in two batches of ten. The first ten were delivered between June and July 1974, and when received by United Counties, they took stock numbers 476 to 485, registered RNV476-85M. The next batch arrived over the course of November and December 1974, and followed on from the previous batch, numbered 486-495, but failed to gain matching registration plates due to industrial action taking place at the time at licensing offices. Instead they were registered GNV653-62N. Twelve were allocated to Luton depot, with the outstanding eight being distributed between the depots.

A large order for fifty Bedford saloons was placed during 1974 and was split into two batches. The first called for twenty-two Bedford YRT 53-seat machines, the second twenty-eight Bedford YRQ saloons, all bodied by Willowbrook. To make room for the order, the ex-Birch Bros. Leyland Leopards taken into stock as 170-3, 182/3 and 190-5, were renumbered to 231 to 242 in February 1974. At the same time, United Counties renumbered the six Bedford YRQ saloons purchased by them during 1973 from 430 – 435 to 161-6, allowing the Bedfords to be numbered in the 100 fleet number series. The final vehicles to be renumbered to make room for this batch were Bristol LS saloons 100-2/4-7/10/1/6-21, which became 428 to 442 respectively.

First to arrive were the twenty-two Bedford YRT machines. Taken into stock between March and August 1974, they took up rolling stock numbers 101 to 122 as anticipated, and carried registration marks RBD101-16M and TBD617-22N. All but three of the twenty-eight Bedford YRQ saloons also arrived during 1974. These vehicles slotted into the rolling stock sequence as 167 to 195. Bristol RESL 423 was involved in a serious accident in June 1974, resulting in a twisted chassis. This led to a further YRQ being ordered by United Counties as a replacement, one originally intended for Jolly of South Hylton, and was the only United Counties YRQ to feature a luggage boot. The vehicle in question was numbered 185, registered GNV983N and allocated to Rushden.

The YRQs were registered in five different registration series. 167 was the only example to gain an 'M' registration, registered RBD167M due to its arrival in June. The remaining saloons all gained 'N' registrations, with 168 to 173 being registered TBD168-73N, 174-9 being allocated registration marks GNH528-33N and the penultimate batch, 180-5, taking registrations GNV978-83N. The final batch took registrations GRP914-23N and rolling stock numbers 186-195.

During 1974, United Counties received two second-hand vehicles. The first was a Bristol FSF6G machine originating with Southdown Motor Services Ltd. The vehicle in question was registered VAP32 and became numbered 593 with United Counties. Arriving with the company in December 1974, the vehicle failed to enter service until June 1975, and was allocated to Stony Stratford. The second vehicle acquired was a Bristol LS6G saloon registered MFU107, and was sourced from Lincolnshire Road Car Co. Ltd. Although it was allocated stock number 443, this vehicle never saw service with the company, instead it was used as a source of spare parts.

United Counties acquired the operations of Court Line Coaches on 9 December 1974 after the company went bankrupt. The fleet comprised eight 'K', 'L' and 'M' registered Ford R192 and R1014 coaches with variants of the Plaxton Elite bodywork. The poor condition of the vehicles meant that these coaches initially had to be replaced by Bristol LS saloons. The eight coaches took up stock numbers 196 to 203 and were registered LXD424/33/4/535/6K, SXD557L and YXD458/9M.

For the second year in a row, United Counties took a number of vehicles on loan from other National Bus companies. First to arrive were five 'F' registered Bristol RELL6G saloons from West Yorkshire Road Car Co. Ltd, which remained on loan for two to three months. These vehicles were registered TWR453/4F, SYG847/53F and TWU241F. All retained their West Yorkshire rolling stock numbers whilst operating with United Counties. Next came a trio of vehicles from Cumberland Motor Services Ltd. United Counties allotted temporary fleet numbers 582-584 to these three Bristol LD models which carried registrations VAO383/5 and XAO606.

A more significant loan took place in August 1974 when an arrangement was made with Northampton Transport to hire six Roe bodied Daimler CVG6 machines. Daimlers 228-30/2/4/5 (ONH 228-30/2 RNH234/5) were briefly hired by United Counties, but due to trade union opposition to the operation of these vehicles at Kettering depot, they were soon returned to Northampton Transport.

Another saloon to arrive at Northampton was TXE755L, a Bedford YRQ coach complete with Willowbrook bodywork. It was loaned to United Counties by Vauxhall Motors over a number of occasions between January 1974 and January 1976. This vehicle was frequently used on the service between Northampton and London. Another Bedford YRQ was loaned to United Counties from Vauxhall Motors for similar reasons, this time carrying an Alexander body. The vehicle concerned was registered WXE264M, and was again used on the Northampton to London service.

The ageing fleet of Bristol MW dual-purpose vehicles was downgraded with their forty-one coach seats being replaced by forty-five bus seats, and a fresh repaint into green and white livery. Vehicles treated to this were 149, 151/2/4/7/9. Similar vehicle 147 was re-seated but not repainted. Prior to this, 155/6/8/60 were also re-seated, and had received a repaint prior to the refurbishment.

The re-seating and repainting continued, with two of the ex-Birch Bros. Leyland Leopards (DUC71/2C), being re-seated with forty-nine bus seats, and a fresh coat of green and white paint applied. These vehicles were completed in October and June 1974 respectively. August 1974 saw Bristol RELH6G 255 – BBD255B gain the refurbished seats from former Birch Bros. Leyland Leopard 237 – 90FXD.

A number of other repaints took place over the course of the year, when Bristol MW6Gs 124/5/7/8/9 were repainted into dual-purpose livery; Bristol REs 250/4/5/7/77-84/7/92 and 205-13 gained the National Bus Company local coach livery. The final vehicles to gain repaints in different livery variations were Bristol REs 258/9 and Bristol MWs 260/2 which gained the National white coaching livery.

All-over advertisements adorned two United Counties vehicles over the course of 1974. First to be treated was 726 – KNV726E which wore a base colour of orange for the Solid Fuel Advisory Service in March 1974. The second vehicle was VRT 810 – RNV810M which gained an all-over advert for the *Milton Keynes Express* newspaper in October 1974.

Bristol RE 282 – TBD282G was damaged by fire in February 1974 and was sent to Eastern Coach Works for repair, where it was also repainted into the local coach livery, being completed in July.

1975

The four outstanding Bristol VRT machines from the 1973 order arrived long overdue in January and February 1975. They were numbered 826 to 829 by the company, registered HBD163-6N. They found homes at Aylesbury, Northampton and Rushden depots.

The four outstanding orders from 1974 called for four Leyland Nationals, eleven Bristol VRTs and three Bedford YRQs. The three Bedfords were first to be delivered, arriving in January 1975. These three were registered GRP920/1/3N, and took stock numbers 192/3/5. The first two were allocated to Kettering depot, with Stony Stratford taking stock of the final YRQ. Next to arrive were the four Leyland Nationals which were given rolling stock numbers 496 to 499, and carried registrations GVV887 to 890N. Two of these vehicles found their way to Bedford, the remaining two were allocated to Bletchley and Kettering depots.

Six of the eleven outstanding VRTs, all Series 2s, were delivered to Northampton between March and May 1975. Upon arrival they took up stock numbers 830 to 835, and were registered HRP670-5N. Northampton, Bletchley, Wellingborough, Luton, Kettering and Bedford depots were allocated one each. The remaining five were of the Series 3 type, and were delivered to the company in October. They carried on from the earlier VRTs, numbered 836 to 840, registered LBD836-40P. These vehicles were shared between Biggleswade, Bedford, Northampton and Aylesbury depots respectively.

Orders placed for 1975 delivery called for sixteen Bristol VRTs, five Bristol RELHs and fifteen Leyland National saloons. None of the Bristol products were received during 1975, and the order for the RELH saloons was superseded by one for Leyland Leopards. United Counties successfully received ten of the Leyland Nationals during the year, with the remainder arriving in 1976. They arrived with the company between July and August 1975. The first five took stock numbers 500 to 504, KNH500-4P arriving in July. The remainder, 505-9 – KNV505-9P, arrived in August. To make way for the Leyland Nationals, the Bristol LD machines numbered in the 500 series were renumbered into the 900 series. In September, Bristol MWs 124/5 were also renumbered to 130/1 to make way for new vehicle deliveries.

A trio of Bristol LD6G machines were acquired from the Bristol Omnibus Co. Ltd for spare parts to keep others on the road. The vehicles concerned took stock numbers 943-945, registered WHY952, WHY933 and YHT952.

United Counties gained a contract for an experimental Dial-a-Bus service in the Woughton area of Milton Keynes. A small batch of minibuses were required for this operation, and United Counties ordered six Mercedes-Benz L406D parcel vans which were converted to minibuses by Williams Deansgate. These vehicles found their way to United Counties during January and February 1975. The vehicles concerned took stock numbers 1 to 6 and were registered HBD167-72N. These minibuses were painted yellow with red doors and wore branding reading 'Woughton Dial a Bus', with NBC Milton Keynes fleet names in place of United Counties ones. The service proved popular and to relieve the struggling Mercedes minibuses, two Bedford CFL minibuses, again bodied by Williams Deansgate, were hired from Dial-a-Ride Ltd, Manchester, between October and November. The vehicles concerned were registered CMA407N and CMA409N.

Two additional vehicles were also taken on loan for short periods of time during the year for demonstration purposes. First was Ford R1014 coach JWC525N which came from Ford Motors to operate on its services. This vehicle carried a Duple Dominant body and was loaned to the company during June and July. July saw the demonstration of another Ford bus. This time, an Alexander bodied Ford A minibus registered GSA60N, owned by Grampian Regional Council, was assessed for its suitability on the Milton Keynes Dial-a-Bus services and for service in Leighton Buzzard.

The seven remaining Bristol LD6G machines that had been acquired from Southern Vectis were placed on loan to United Automobile Services Ltd, Darlington, between June and October 1975. The vehicles concerned were numbered 931/3/4/5/7/8/9. These vehicles were officially taken into stock by United in January 1976 where they were used as driver training vehicles.

United Counties replaced the Bristol K5G tree lopper during 1975 with Bristol LD6G 620LFM, which the company had acquired from Crosville Motors. It was converted for such use during October 1975.

More repaints took place over the course of 1975, with MWs 126/50/3 and Leopards 231/3 being repainted into the National Bus Company green bus livery. The ex-Court Line coaches 196-203 and REs 214-8, 285/6/8/9 were repainted into the local coach livery. RE coaches 253-7 were repainted into the white National coach livery. Prior to the repainting of 150/3 and 231/3 mentioned above, these four vehicles were re-seated with bus seats with a capacity of either 41 or 49 seats. MWs 140/1 and 143/4/6 were also re-seated to forty-five bus seats.

Two vehicles gained all-over advertisements during 1975. VRT 798 – JRP798L was treated to an all-over advertisement to celebrate the centenary of the Borough of Luton in 1976. The colours chosen were beige, white and olive green, and this vehicle was operated around Luton until May 1977. At the same time, withdrawn Bristol LD6G 580 was repainted into similar colours and operated by Luton Borough Council for various special non-psv duties in the area.

1976

Vehicles outstanding from the 1975 orders comprised five Leyland Nationals, five Leyland Leopards and sixteen Bristol VRT machines. First to put in an appearance were the Leyland Nationals, which arrived during February 1976. They took up stock numbers KNV510 to 514P and were allotted rolling stock numbers 510 to 514. The first two were allocated to Milton Keynes, the next two were allocated to Hitchin, and Aylesbury received the final National.

The Leyland Leopard coaches began to arrive during April and May, and were equipped with Alexander 'T' bodywork. They took up stock numbers 224 to 228 in the United Counties series and were registered MRP224-8P. These vehicles were painted into the National white coach livery and were initially allocated to Northampton depot.

The sixteen outstanding Bristol VRT machines arrived over the course of June and July. Taking up rolling stock numbers 841 to 856, these vehicles were registered in three different batches. The first four, 841-4, were registered OBD841-4P. 845 and 846 gained registration marks ONH845/6P. The final batch gained registrations OVV847-856R. Luton depot gained five, Northampton, Bedford and Kettering being allocated three each, and Huntingdon and Rushden depots gaining one each. Unlike other Bristol VRT machines to be purchased, this batch were fitted with Leyland 501 engines rather than the traditional Gardner ones. However, in 1982 they were re-engined with reconditioned Gardner engines sourced from the National Bus Company disposal centre at Lincoln.

The 1976 orders originally required twenty-eight Bristol VRTs, ten Leyland Nationals, ten Bedford YRQs and five Bristol RELH coaches. However, this order was changed significantly in June 1975 when the order for VRT machines was reduced to three, which was later raised to seven. The Leyland Nationals and Bedford machines were swapped for thirteen Leyland Nationals and three Bristol LH saloons, only to be changed again for five Nationals, ten Fords and three Bristol LHs. United Counties was unwilling to take stock of the Bristol LH saloons, and the order was altered again, calling for three Bedford YRTs. The order for five Bristol RELH coaches had by 1976 fallen by the wayside.

The three Bedfords were bodied by Willowbrook, and took stock numbers 123 to 125, LVV123-5P, which the company purchased through Kirkby Central Ltd. This was a Sheffield-based dealer which had supplied the previous batch of Bedfords operated by United Counties. These vehicles arrived with the company during March 1976. This trio were allocated to Northampton, Kettering and Hitchin depots respectively.

The next new vehicles to be delivered were the ten Ford R1014 saloons which carried Duple Dominant bodies. These vehicles took up stock numbers 51 to 60, OVV51-60R.

These ten vehicles were delivered between July and August 1976. Three were each housed at Northampton, Kettering and Bedford depots, with the remaining one being allocated to Aylesbury.

The five Leyland Nationals arrived over the course of August and September 1976. They took stock numbers 515-519, registered OVV515-9R, and were allocated to Milton Keynes, Wellingborough, Corby and Luton depots.

A similar number of the seven Bristol VRT machines ordered for 1976 delivery arrived in the specified year, arriving in December, the remaining two arriving in February 1977. The 1976 arrivals were numbered 857 to 861, registered RRP857-61R, the first three being allocated to Bedford, and the remaining two being allocated to Northampton.

Growth of the Woughton Dial-a-Bus scheme in Milton Keynes led to the purchase of a further two minibuses. These two vehicles had a higher capacity than the previous minibuses employed on this service. Converted by Charter Way, they were based on the Mercedes-Benz 309D chassis. They continued on from the previous batch, taking stock numbers 7 and 8, registered MNV7-8P.

In July, Bedford YRQ 190 – GRP918N was involved in a fatal accident on the road between the villages of Isham and Great Harrowden. It was in collision with a cattle truck, resulting in the fatalities of both drivers, and three passengers on board the vehicle. The vehicle was subsequently written off.

United Counties also lost Bristol RELL6G 353 – VNV353H in January 1976 when it was destroyed by fire. The following evening, sister vehicle 354 was also involved in a fire, but was later repaired and placed back into service.

The ancillary fleet received an upgrade over the course of 1976 when four Bristol LD6G double-deck machines were converted to driver training vehicles. Those chosen for this conversion were 578, 575, 579 and 574 (622LFM; WAL437; 623LFM and 523JRA). To fit in with their new role, these four vehicles received new rolling stock numbers 1023 to 1026 and were subsequently allocated to Luton, Bedford, Kettering and Northampton.

Compared with previous years, only a handful of repaints took place over the course of 1976. Three Bristol RELH6G saloons, 250 to 252, lost the local coach livery they were wearing in favour of the full National coach livery.

Bristol RELH6G 217 – KRP217L received a dedicated blue and white livery for the Corby Rail Link service that was introduced to run between Corby and Kettering. Appropriate branding was also applied to this vehicle.

Two Leyland National saloons gained all-over advertising for the Luton SuperRider scheme during 1976. This was a fast service operating between Luton and Dunstable. First to be treated was 473 – ORP473M which gained a livery of yellow and orange. It was treated to this livery during September. Stablemate 508 – KNV508P gained the same livery in November, and gained 'SuperRider 2' branding. 473 was rebuilt after being involved in a serious road traffic accident in August 1975.

A pair of Ford A series midibuses complete with Tricentrol bodywork was hired from Tricentrol PSV Sales for a period of six months over the course of 1976. They gained temporary fleet numbers 071 and 072, registered PKX271/2R. They were repainted into United Counties local coach livery, and had Bedfordshire County Council names applied to them. They were placed into service in the Leighton Buzzard area. A third was hired from the same source, registered LNM318P. This vehicle joined the previous two.

1977

Unlike the previous years, only two vehicles were outstanding from the previous years' vehicle orders. The two vehicles concerned were two Bristol VRT machines which took up stock numbers 862 and 863 along with registrations RRP862/3R. Kettering received the first, the second being allocated to Northampton.

Orders for 1977 comprised ten Leyland National saloons, five Bristol RELH coaches, thirty-five Bristol VRTs and ten Bedford YRQs, bringing the number of expected vehicles to the grand total of sixty. However, as with previous years, the orders were changed to fourteen Leyland Nationals, three Leyland Leopards and twenty-eight Bristol VRTs, reducing the total number of new vehicles to forty-five.

The first seven Nationals arrived in February which took stock numbers 520 to 526, SBD520-6R. The second half of the order arrived in July which took stock numbers 527 to 533 and were registered VRP527-533S. The first seven were allocated to Northampton, Wellingborough, Kettering, Aylesbury, Hitchin and Bedford depots; the second batch being shared between Northampton, Kettering, Rushden, Bedford, Biggleswade, Hitchin and Aylesbury.

The trio of Leyland Leopard coaches arrived with United Counties during July 1977. The first two, 229/30 – VRP229/30S, carried Duple Dominant bodies. The third taking stock number 231, registered VRP231S. This vehicle varied from the previous two, carrying a Plaxton Panorama Supreme Express body.

Fourteen of the twenty-eight VRT orders for 1977 delivery made it to United Counties in the specified year. The first ten arrived between May and June, taking stock numbers 864 to 873, registered TNH864-73R. The next quartet arrived over the course of September and October 1977, and were allocated stock numbers 874 to 877, registered WBD874-7S. The first ten were distributed between Luton and Bedford depots, and the four 'S' plate machines being allocated to Milton Keynes, Corby, Huntingdon and Luton depots.

1977 presented United Automobile Services Ltd of Darlington with a number of mechanical difficulties with their vehicles. To assist them with this trouble, United Counties loaned Bristol VRT 808 – RNV808M between February and May 1977.

United Counties hired a Ford Transit minibus from Tricentrol PSV Sales of Markyate over the course of 1977. The vehicle was registered TVD851R and was allocated temporary stock number 70. It was placed into service on the Lilbourne Community Minibus Scheme in Northamptonshire, an initiative sponsored by Northamptonshire County Council. This vehicle was later permanently added to the United Counties fleet.

1978

The fourteen outstanding Bristol VRT machines from the 1977 order put in an appearance over the course of March 1978. They continued the fleet numbering system from 878 to 891, registered XNV878-91S. Four were allocated to Northampton, three each being allocated to Milton Keynes and Kettering, and Corby and Wellingborough received two each.

Vehicle orders for 1978 comprised twenty-one Bristol VRTs, fifteen Leyland Nationals, five Leyland Leopards and a solitary Bristol LH machine. As in previous years, the Leyland Nationals were the first new vehicles to be delivered. They were taken into stock between February and April 1978, and took up stock numbers 534 to 540, XVV534-40S. Bedford and Luton each had two added to their allocations, whilst Biggleswade, Hitchin and Aylesbury took one each. The remainder of the batch arrived in August, taking fleet numbers 541 to 548 with matching BVV-T registration marks. These vehicles were shared between Milton Keynes, Kettering, Corby, Aylesbury, Luton and Hitchin garages.

Again, the full complement of Bristol VRT machines were not received during the designated year. Thirteen of the twenty-one machines ordered put in an appearance. The first five were delivered in May, and were registered 892 to 896 – YVV892-6S. The remaining eight arrived during September and followed on from the previous batch, taking stock numbers 897 to 904 – CBD897-904T. 904 was displayed on the Leyland stand at the 1978 Commercial Motor Show at the NEC in Birmingham.

The five Leyland Leopard coaches also failed to materialise during 1978, putting a strain on the ageing coach fleet. To help compensate for this, United Counties took a number of coaches on loan from National Travel (East) Ltd in the form of AEC Reliance and Leyland Leopard coaches. Between January and March 1978, fourteen coaches were loaned, with four or five of these being used as full time coaches.

The Engineering Research Department of Borg-Warner made arrangements with United Counties to operate a Leyland National fitted with an SRM Torque Converter Transmission from Luton depot for a period of three days during August 1978. The vehicle concerned was OAE759R from the Bristol Omnibus Company.

Just one repaint of National coach livery was completed during 1978. October saw Bristol RELH6G 270 – KRP270E lose this livery in favour of the local green and white coach livery. Two years later, this vehicle regained the National coaching livery.

By 1978, the 'C' registered Bristol FS6B machines were becoming quite elderly. Two of these vehicles were converted into driver training vehicles, the vehicles chosen being 685 and 689. To distinguish these two vehicles for their new role, they were renumbered to 1033 and 1034 and replaced 1023/4, which were sold.

A shortage of engineers at the company's Luton depot during 1978 saw Bristol MW6G 160 – 160BRP and FS6B 664 – CNV664B put to use as staff shuttles, ferrying engineers from Bedford depot to Luton. The former vehicle was used between April and June, with the latter continuing from June through to September.

The small batch of Ford A minibuses operated by United Counties in the Leighton Buzzard area began to experience difficulties during 1978. This led to the hire of a similar vehicle from Eastern Counties to assist the company with these difficulties. Registered NAH142P, this vehicle carried an Alexander body, and was loaned to United Counties between October 1978 and January 1979.

United Counties was looking for a replacement for the vehicles used on both the Leighton Buzzard services and the Milton Keynes Dial-a-Bus services. For this, an unregistered Bedford JJL midibus was loaned as a possible replacement. Another vehicle placed on loan, although not for this purpose, was a Ford R192 registered YHA389J. It was loaned from neighbouring Midland Red but no interest was shown in the type.

The entire batch of Bristol LH6L saloons were transferred to Crosville during 1978.

1979

The first new vehicles received by United Counties in 1979 were the five outstanding Leyland Leopard coaches from the 1978 order. They took up stock numbers 232 to 236, and were registered EBD232-6T. Luton and Wellingborough received one each, with the remaining three being allocated to Northampton.

The eight outstanding Bristol VRT machines were not received until March and April 1979. These vehicles took stock numbers 905 to 912, and were registered FRP905-12T. Three of these vehicles were allocated to Milton Keynes, the remaining five were allocated to Corby, Bedford, Huntingdon, Northampton and Kettering depots.

Orders for 1979 delivery called for eighteen Leyland Nationals, seventeen Bristol VRTs and five Leyland Leopard coaches. Again, the Leyland Nationals put in an appearance first, with the first eleven vehicles arriving between January and March 1979. These eleven took up rolling stock numbers 549 to 559 – ERP549-59T. The remaining seven arrived between August and October 1979, following on from the previous batch, taking stock numbers 560 to 566, registered KRP560-6V. With the exception of Huntingdon depot, all other United Counties depots received some from this batch.

The order for five Leyland Leopards again failed to materialise during 1979. Also, the full complement of Bristol VRT machines was not received during the year, with only eleven of the seventeen arriving. The first seven put in an appearance during July when they acquired stock numbers 913 to 919, registered HBD913-9T. This batch was distributed between Milton Keynes, Northampton, Kettering, Bedford, Biggleswade and Luton. Four more arrived during December, taking up stock numbers 920 to 923 – LBD920-3V. Wellingborough and Bedford were allocated two apiece.

United Counties placed a successful bid with the National Bus Company for thirteen Leyland National saloons that had become surplus to the company's fleet replacement programme. The vehicles took up rolling stock numbers 567 to 579 and registrations MNH567-79V. Five were allocated to Milton Keynes, Luton received three, Wellingborough and Bedford taking two each, with the last being allocated to Aylesbury.

Arsonists struck twice at United Counties premises over the course of 1979. The first was in February at Luton depot, the blaze destroying four buses and damaging a further five. The fire started at the rear of 378 and spread to 494 and 377 which were completely destroyed, as was the fate of 378. The fire also spread to 292 which was severely damaged and was beyond economic repair. 364 was also damaged by the fire, and no attempt was made to repair this vehicle as it was shortly due for withdrawal. The three remaining vehicles, 330, 357 and 480, were all repaired and returned to service.

The second attack happened at Wellingborough depot in November. The fire started in ex-Court Line coach 199, which was completely gutted in the attack. Sister vehicles 197 and 196 were also destroyed. Other vehicles severely damaged by the fire were 363, 364, 365, 368 and 738. The vehicles destroyed and damaged in this attack were vehicles that had been withdrawn rather than vehicles that were in service at the time.

Bristol RELL6G 346 – URP346H was prematurely withdrawn from service as a result of a fire in August.

Two Bristol FLF machines were hired from Eastern National due to the vast number of buses that were being recertified by the company. Stock numbers 991 and 992 were allocated to these vehicles by United Counties, which were registered BVX677B and AVW397F. They came on loan in March 1979 and returned in April (992) and July (991).

A further two Bristol RELH7G coaches were repainted and downgraded during 1979, the vehicles concerned being 272 and 273 – ORP272/3F.

Four Bristol VRT machines gained all-over advertisements during 1979. The first was a pair based at Northampton, 881 – XNV881S and 863 – RRP863R, both of which gained an advert for the Tesco Superstore at the Weston Favell Centre in the town.

They were treated in October and November 1979 respectively. 800 – JRP800L was repainted to advertise the new ticket types, the 'CityRider' which was available in Milton Keynes, in July of that year. Sister vehicle 801 gained an all-over advertisement for the 'Shopabout' ticket, being completed in October.

Withdrawn Bristol FS7B 705 – GRP705D was converted into a mobile office during August 1979. This was done for the National Bus Company M.A.P. (Market Analysis Project) scheme.

Numerous double-deck machines were taken into stock with the Luton Corporation take over in January 1970. UNM148 shows off the MCCW bodied Leyland Titan PD2 combination, dating back to October 1957. It was numbered 808 by United Counties and is seen here parked in Luton garage.
S.J. Butler Collection

Another Leyland Titan PD2 model is seen here, this time carrying a Weymann body. 816 – WTM156 is seen here parked in between some vehicles new to United Counties themselves. WTM156 was new to Luton Corporation in May 1959.
S.J. Butler Collection

1970–1979 • 101

Visually there was little difference between the above vehicle and the previous one. 818 – 158ANM carried an East Lancs body. The former Luton Corporation fleet was quickly repainted into the green United Counties colours.
794 Preservation Group

Another non-standard type inherited from Luton Corporation was the East Lancs bodied Dennis Loline II. Representing this type is 823 – 163ANM. This was the first front-entrance double-decker for Luton. The Loline featured the same drop axle chassis as the Bristol LD and was built by Dennis under licence from Bristol as the Bristol chassis was only available to Tilling and Scottish Bus Group companies.
794 Preservation Group

1963 saw a batch of East Lancs bodied Albion Lowlanders arrive with Luton Corporation Transport. Representing this batch is 176HTM which became known as United Counties 836. It is seen leaving the Northamptonshire village of East Haddon. *S.J. Butler Collection*

The newest double-decks acquired from Luton Corporation dated back to 1965. These were again another non-standard type for United Counties, this time in the form of East Lancs bodied Dennis Loline III machines. 842 – FXD182C shows off this type whilst resting inside Luton garage. *S.J. Butler Collection*

A sizeable batch of thirty ECW bodied Bristol RELL6G saloons were taken into stock in January 1970 when United Counties acquired the operations of Luton Corporation. The first of the thirty was registered MXD101E and gained rolling stock number 361 with United Counties. It is seen here at rest in Luton garage. *S.J. Butler Collection*

Another Bristol RELL6G saloon acquired from Luton Corporation was NXE109F which became known as 369 in the United Counties fleet. It is also seen at rest parked at Luton garage. The fleet was quickly repainted from red to green by United Counties. *S.J. Butler Collection*

104 • UNITED COUNTIES BUSES

The Bristol RELL6G saloons acquired from Luton Corporation were registered in three different registration sequences. The previous two photos have shown two of them, and the one above shows the third. 372 – PXE112F is seen here loading in Luton town centre before setting off to Luton Airport on service 30.
S.J. Butler Collection

The slightly less stylish-looking ECW bus body fitted to the Bristol RELH6G chassis is shown in this photograph of 290 – WBD290H seen in the green and white dual-purpose livery. The vehicle is seen on layover at Bedford Bus Station having completed a journey on the 152 service.
Bruce Pyne

1970–1979 • **105**

Over the course of 1969 and 1970, United Counties took stock of a small batch of forty-five-seat Bristol LH6L saloons. They were put to use on various local bus routes. 404 – XBD404J is seen on layover at Bedford Bus Station having last seen service on route 165. A difference in the depth of the window screen between this and 401 can be seen when comparing the two photographs. *794 Preservation Group*

The Bristol VRT/ECW combination became a firm favourite of United Counties during the 1970s. A large number of vehicles were taken into stock between 1969 and 1981. 758 – VNV758H was delivered to United Counties during April 1970 with the flat front style body. *794 Preservation Group*

United Counties' network reached Central London on the express network. Marble Arch was one location where the company's vehicles could be found passing through. Bristol RELH6G 207 (YNV207J) is found at this location heading towards Nottingham. *S.J. Butler Collection*

1971 saw the arrival of eight ECW bodied Bristol RESL6G saloons with United Counties. Several were allocated to Luton garage and subsequently moved on to Luton & District in 1986. 425 (BRP425K) is seen loading in Manchester Street, Luton. It shows the brown Luton garage fleet number plate well. *Roger Warwick Collection*

1970–1979 • 107

A trio of MCCW bodied Leyland Tiger Cubs were taken into stock by United Counties from East Yorkshire Motor Services in May 1972, followed by two further vehicles in July. 6684KH was one which became numbered 197 by the company.
S.J. Butler Collection

Four Bristol LD6 machines were taken into stock from Crosville Motors in 1972. 623LFM was originally numbered 579 by United Counties. In 1976, this vehicle was added to the driver training fleet and renumbered 1025. The company painted the front of their driver training vehicles yellow to make them stand out from the normal buses in the fleet.
Bruce Pyne

After the break-up of the United Counties operation in 1986, a new livery of green with orange and white stripes was introduced. 786 – CBD784K shows off this livery whilst exiting Huntingdon Bus Station whilst heading for Brampton. *794 Preservation Group*

In December 1974, United Counties acquired the business of Court Line Coaches, Luton. Included in the sale were numerous Ford coaches, mostly of the R192 model. A pair of Ford R1014 coaches complete with Plaxton body work were also taken into stock. YXD458M (202) is seen here wearing the dual-purpose livery at Luton garage. *Bruce Pyne*

794 - GRP 794L is pictured here at Biggleswade garage on its way to the North Weald bus rally in 1989. 794 is a Bristol VRTSL2/6G and is now in preservation. It has been owned by the 794 Group since 1999. *794 Preservation Group*

The Willowbrook bodied Bedford YRT was not the most attractive of vehicle designs. 109 – RBD109M is seen showing off the design and the green and white band livery applied to United Counties vehicles. The batch operated with United Counties for a relatively short period of time. It is seen parked at Stamford Garage. *794 Preservation Group*

As well as the YRT model, United Counties also took stock of the Bedford YRQ saloon, again these were bodied by Willowbrook. As can be seen there was no real difference in appearance between the two models apart from the length. 188 – GRP916N shows off the model in this view. *794 Preservation Group*

December 1974 saw the operations of Luton-based Court Line Coaches acquired by United Counties. With this came nine Plaxton bodied Ford coaches, predominantly the R192 model, the other being the R1014 model. 200 – LXD536K is an example of the Ford R192 model. *794 Preservation Group*

Five Plaxton Elite Express bodied Bristol RELH6L coaches were taken into stock by United Counties, all arriving in 1974. 223 (SBD223M) represents the batch and is seen loading in Great Central Street in London. This vehicle in particular was used on the National Express network of services operated by United Counties. *Roger Warwick Collection*

Seen parked at the rear of Bedford garage is 465 – ORP465M, representing the numerous Leyland Nationals that entered the United Counties fleet during the 1970s. The vehicle is seen blinded for Bedford town service 103 which ran to Kempston, just south of Bedford. *Bruce Pyne*

One of the smaller and less popular vehicles to enter the United Counties fleet during the 1970s were a small batch of Duple Dominant bodied Ford R1014 saloons. 54 – OVV54R is parked at Bedford garage in this view of the vehicle. *Bruce Pyne*

Kettering Bus Station finds ECW bodied Bristol VRT 856 – OVV856R. It is seen about to operate a journey on route 19 to the nearby small town of Desborough. *Gary Seamarks*

Six Deansgate bodied Mercedes-Benz L406D minibuses were taken into stock in 1975 to operate the Woughton Dial-a-Bus scheme in Milton Keynes. They wore a predominantly yellow livery for this service as depicted above. 1 – HBD167N is seen in Marlborough Street, Milton Keynes. *Roger Warwick Collection*

1976 saw the expansion of the Woughton Dial-a-Bus scheme which required an additional two vehicles. For this a pair of Mercedes-Benz 309D minibuses with Charter Way bodywork were taken into stock. The first of the pair, 7 – MNV7P, is seen at Wavendon Tower. These two vehicles were slightly larger than the previous six vehicles. *Roger Warwick Collection*

124 (LVV124P) is another of the numerous Willowbrook bodied Bedford YRT saloons allocated to the United Counties fleet in 1976. It is seen exiting Kettering Bus Station having just completed a journey on the 260.
S.J. Butler Collection

A small batch of Alexander T bodied Leyland Leopards were purchased by United Counties in 1976 for use on the company's National Express network. For this they were painted into a white based livery with National Express fleet names. Red United Counties names were also applied to the vehicles. 228 – MRP228P is seen sporting this livery at Aylesbury garage.
Bruce Pyne

The Leyland
Leopard became a popular choice for the coaching fleet. In particular, the Plaxton body style proved to be a favourite with United Counties too. 232 – EBD232T is a Plaxton Supreme bodied Leyland Leopard coach that was purchased for use on the National Express network. It is seen on layover at Bedford Bus Station.
Gary Seamarks

Leyland National
561 – KRP561V is seen about to enter Greyfriars Bus Station, Northampton. 561 was new to the company in September 1979.
Gary Seamarks

1980–1989

1980

The eleven outstanding vehicles from 1979 reached United Counties during 1980. The five Leyland Leopard coaches had been completed over the summer of 1979 but delays in fitting their bodywork held up their delivery. These five vehicles put in an appearance in January 1980 and were allocated rolling stock numbers 237 to 241, registered KVV237-41V. These vehicles were bodied by Willowbrook and were received in National white livery. Entering service in February, they were allocated to Kettering (237), Northampton (238-240) and Luton (241). The outstanding half-dozen Bristol VRT machines took a little longer to put in an appearance, arriving during May. They took up stock numbers 924 to 929 and were registered ONH924-9V. Allocation was again split, with the first going to Stony Stratford, the next to Aylesbury, 926 to Bedford and the final trio were allocated to Luton.

New vehicle orders for 1980 called for ten Leyland Nationals, twenty-seven Bristol VRT machines, fifteen dual-purpose Leyland Leopards and nine Leyland Leopard coaches. The Leyland Leopards failed to appear, whilst the Leyland Nationals and nine of the Bristol VRTs were received by United Counties.

The first half of the Leyland National saloons had been due to be delivered in January. However, delivery of the batch was delayed and spread across a number of months. The first arrived in February, followed by a further two in April, another in May and the final one in June. By this time, production of the MK I National had ceased, so these were the first of the MK IIs. The batch took registrations NRP580-4V and were allocated stock numbers 580 to 584. These five vehicles took up residence in Bedford, Hitchin, Luton and Bletchley, all of which received one each, except the latter depot which was allocated two. The second half of the batch arrived between August and October, and were numbered 585 to 589, SVV585-9W. The first two were garaged at Biggleswade, the next two at Hitchin and the final vehicle was allocated to Luton.

The Bristol VRTs arrived with the company during July but did not enter service until August. They took up rolling stock numbers 930 to 938, registered SNV930-8W.

A pair of Leyland Leopard coaches were delivered to Northampton during January 1980 for use on the Peterborough to Kettering Rail Link. The vehicles concerned took stock numbers 242 and 243, MRP242/3V. They were painted into the dedicated Rail Link livery, complete with appropriate branding. They were fitted with additional luggage racks on the offside of the saloon. The two Leopard chassis were diverted from an order placed by the Western National Omnibus Company Ltd.

A solitary Ford Transit machine was taken into stock in August 1980 registered OKV531W. The vehicle took up fleet number 72 and was used on a community transport scheme in the Rushton area of Northamptonshire. This vehicle was funded by Northamptonshire County Council and was initially garaged at Wicksteed Park in Kettering.

Delays in the receipt of the new rolling stock had a knock-on effect on the ageing coach fleet. A short-term solution was reached when an agreement was reached with National Travel (West) Ltd which transferred five Leyland Leopards equipped with Plaxton Elite bodies. The coaches concerned were numbered 244 to 248, registered SJA368-372J. The five coaches arrived with United Counties during November 1980 and were allocated to Northampton. This batch was ill-fated, with many of them being involved in accidents, the majority lasting only just over a year with United Counties.

United Counties had the expectation of receiving more Leyland National saloons, so made the effort to clear some fleet numbers to make way for their arrival. This meant that Bristol RESLs 420-2/4-6 were renumbered to 391-6 in August. However, no more Leyland National single-deckers were purchased new by United Counties.

The driver training fleet received four Bristol FS6G machines during 1980. The vehicles chosen were 715-8, registered KBD715-8D. They were converted between August and December 1980. These vehicles replaced tuition vehicles ENV685/9C and tree lopper 620LFM. Luton, Northampton, Kettering and Wellingborough were the recipients of these four vehicles.

Few vehicles received changes to their liveries during 1980. Bristol RELH coaches 270/2/3 were repainted out of local coach livery, gaining the white National coach livery, 273 in July and the other two in November. Leyland National 561 – KRP561V received an all-over advertisement for the Army Recruitment Centre during September 1980.

During 1980, United Counties were still looking for suitable replacements for the minibuses at Leighton Buzzard. Over the course of the year, two demonstrators were loaned to United Counties for this purpose. First to arrive was a Leyland Cub registered YBK129V. The other vehicle was a Ford R1014 midibus registered NWC66V.

1981

1981 was a bumper year for the intake of new vehicles, with no less than seventy being received by United Counties. Thirty-eight of these machines were outstanding orders from the previous year. The orders for 1981 called for twenty-one Bristol VRT machines, nine Leyland Olympians, eight Leyland Leopard coaches and three Bedford YRQ midibuses. This order was later modified and saw the order for nine Olympians being replaced by one for twenty Olympians, and the disposal of ten VRT machines to sister company Eastern Counties. The entire order for Bristol VRTs arrived in the assigned year.

The first were sixteen of the outstanding Bristol VRT machines from the 1980 order. The first nine arrived in January 1981, registered URP939-947W they took up stock numbers 939 to 947. These vehicles were allocated to Wellingborough, Northampton, Stony Stratford, Bletchley, Bedford and Luton. The next arrived over the course of March and April 1981. Numbered 948 to 956 they were registered VVV948-956W. Corby, Kettering, Northampton and Aylesbury received one each whilst Bedford gained three machines, whilst two found their way to Luton.

Five Leyland Leopard coaches arrived in May 1981, at which time they were allotted rolling stock numbers 150 to 154 – UVV150-4W. All five were received in the

National white coach livery, three were allocated to Northampton, whilst Luton and Kettering received one each. The coaching fleet received a boost with the delivery of the aforementioned Leopards, as well as a batch of Duple Dominant IV bodied Leyland Leopard coaches which continued the fleet numbering sequence from 155 to 169, registered VNH155-169W. The first eight were allocated to Northampton, one each to Kettering, Wellingborough and Bletchley, and two each to Bedford and Luton.

The first of the 1981 Bristol VRT machines were taken into stock by the company during April. They were numbered 957 to 967 and carried matching VVV-W registration plates. Entering service over the course of April and May, they were allocated to Luton and Northampton which gained three each, while Bedford and Kettering took two each. The final one of the batch joined the Corby allocation.

The remaining ten were delivered to United Counties in June when they were allotted stock numbers 968 to 977, and were registered VVV968-77W. However, these ten were placed into storage with United Counties and were never operated by the company prior to their sale to sister company Eastern Counties. These were the last new Bristol VRT machines, and the last Bristol/ECW vehicle combination purchased by United Counties who took 218 VRTs between 1969 and 1981. However, these were not the last to be taken into stock by United Counties, as a number of others were acquired over the course of the 1980s and 1990s.

The next vehicles to arrive were three Bedford YMQ midibuses which were the vehicles chosen to replace the Leighton Buzzard midibus network. They arrived with United Counties in April and May, registered WNH50-2W, and took up stock numbers 50 to 52. These three midibuses carried Lex bodywork and wore Bedfordshire County Council logos on the side, as they provided funding for these vehicles.

The first Leyland Olympians arrived with United Counties between August and December 1981, with the outstanding three being delivered in January 1982. These twenty Olympians took stock numbers 601 to 620 and were registered ARP601-20X, all carrying ECW body work. The first three were allocated to Northampton, Bedford took stock numbers 604 to 611, and the remainder (612-620), were allocated to Luton depot. The first eleven were diverted from Alder Valley and Southdown to United Counties.

United Counties received a further Ford Transit minibus for operation on a community minibus scheme. The vehicle received was registered TDU828W, it was allotted rolling stock number 71 and dated back to 1977. It was put to use on the Lilbourne Community minibus scheme.

A programme commenced in 1981 to convert thirty-seven of the company's Bristol VRT machines to Series 3 status. The vehicles concerned were 750 to 786, and 760 VNV760H was the first to be converted, shortly followed by 755 and 752. However, not all of this batch received this treatment due to early withdrawal. Two Bristol VRT machines were re-seated with dual-purpose seating from withdrawn Bristol RELH saloons, and these two VRTs were also treated to an all-over advertisement for National Holidays, a nationwide campaign by the National Bus Company for holiday tours. The two vehicles chosen were 918 and 919, HBD918/9T from Luton's allocation. After undergoing this treatment, 919 was reallocated to Bedford depot, whilst 918 remained at Luton. Both vehicles were fitted with tachograph equipment so that they were able to be used on private hire and excursion work.

September 1981 marked the 60th anniversary of the United Counties Omnibus Company Limited. To celebrate this, four Bristol VRT machines gained a special anniversary livery which featured similar colours to those worn by predecessor, the Wellingborough Motor Omnibus Company Limited. The vehicles treated were 800 – JRP800L, 828/9 – HBD165/6N and 834 – HRP674N, which were repainted into ultramarine blue, red and white livery in August. They entered service from Stony Stratford, Northampton, Wellingborough and Kettering depots. Other vehicles to gain repaints in 1981 were Bristol RE saloons 279, 281 and 283 which lost the local green and white coach livery in favour of the green bus livery.

Two Bristol FS6Gs were converted to driver training vehicles in January, these being former buses 713/4 – KBD713/4D which were renumbered 1004/5 in the ancillary fleet.

1982

1982 saw the arrival of the outstanding trio of Olympians from 1981 mentioned above. Also, the eight outstanding Leyland Leopards with ECW coach bodies were delivered to United Counties during the first quarter of the year. CNH170-7X, 170 to 177, found their way to the company in March. These vehicles were delivered in a revised version of the National white livery which comprised red and blue stripes with a black skirt. To make room for this batch, the withdrawn Bedford YRQ saloons still in United Counties ownership had their fleet numbers reduced by 100, for example 176 became 76. The first five were placed in service from Northampton in March, the remaining three were allocated to Bletchley, Luton and Kettering depots.

1982 orders originally called for twenty-seven Leyland Olympians and eight Leyland Leopards, and five Leyland Leopard coaches. This was changed to seventeen Olympians and eight Leyland Leopards in January, being reduced further to just eight Leyland Leopards in July.

Of the eight Leyland Leopards ordered, only six materialised in the designated year. These were similar to the previous batch, carrying the ECW B51 coach body. The batch took stock numbers 178 to 183, and were registered EBD178-81X and JNH182/3Y. The latter two entered service after August 1982, this explaining the 'Y' registration plates.

Former National Travel (West) Leyland Leopard 245 – SJA369J was severely damaged whilst on loan to Trent Motor Traction and was not worth repairing. In January 1982, this vehicle was replaced by similar Trent vehicle VCH14G. Trent also had two similar vehicles up for disposal and a month after the arrival of VCH14G, its two sister vehicles were taken into stock by United Counties. These two additional vehicles were registered VCH15/6G, and took up stock numbers 250 and 251, with VCH14G taking stock number 249. The latter two acquired vehicles replaced SJA368/71J. In July, SJA372J was overturned which only left SJA370J of this batch in service with United Counties.

A further five flat-fronted Bristol VRT machines were converted to Series 3 specification during 1982. The vehicles chosen were 750, 753, 754, 751 and 769. Another vehicle conversion undertaken over the summer of 1982 saw Leyland National 564 – KRP564V converted to allow it to carry passengers in wheelchairs.

Two more RELH6G saloons lost their local coach livery in favour of the bus livery in 1982, the vehicles concerned were 277 and 290, TBD277G and WBD290H respectively. One bus gained an all-over advertisement during December 1982. The vehicle in question was Luton-based Leyland National saloon 560 – KRP560V which gained a blue livery for the Arndale Centre at Luton which this vehicle retained until it was withdrawn by United Counties.

Three coaches gained special liveries and branding for a pair of express services operated by United Counties. The first two vehicles were Leyland Leopards 150 – UVV150W and 241 – KVV241V, repainted into a white livery relieved by malachite green and gold lettering for the 760 service between Northampton, Milton Keynes and Heathrow, a service jointly operated with London Country Bus Services under the Green Line name. The third vehicle was Aylesbury-based Leyland Leopard 238 – KVV238V which was painted into the same livery as the former two vehicles, but gained branding for service X15 between Milton Keynes and Reading, via Aylesbury and High Wycombe, a service operated jointly with Alder Valley.

1983

The remaining two Leyland Leopard coaches from the 1982 order duly arrived one apiece in January and February 1983. These two vehicles followed on from the Leopards delivered the previous year by taking stock numbers 184 and 185, registered in the same series as the latter two, as JNH184/5Y respectively.

During the 1980s, United Counties took on a lot of coaching work, but they soon found that the ageing Bristol coaches were not up to the task. As a result of this, United Counties took advantage and acquired a number of second-hand coaches. First to be acquired were a trio of 'L' registered Leyland Leopard coaches from Ribble and National Travel (West) Ltd. The vehicles acquired were registered XTF803/8/15L and gained rolling stock numbers 252/3/4 in the United Counties fleet. These coaches carried Duple Dominant coach bodies and entered service at Luton depot in February 1983. A fourth vehicle was inspected but rejected by the company. The next batch of second-hand coaches came in the form of six Duple Dominant bodied Leyland Leopards which the company sourced from Stanley Hughes Group of Gomersal. The vehicles were numbered 186 to 191 by United Counties and were registered locally as NNH186-91Y. 186 to 191 were built for use as dealer stock but remained unsold by Hughes. Therefore, they were new to United Counties and were unique coaches in the fleet for two reasons. Firstly, they were the only coaches to feature a one-piece door and were also the first 12-metre long vehicles operated by United Counties.

New vehicle orders for 1983 delivery comprised just seven Plaxton Paramount 3200 bodied Leyland Tiger coaches. All seven were delivered to United Counties in May 1983 registered NBD101 to 107Y, and took stock numbers 101 to 107. All seven were added to Northampton's allocation. An additional batch of seven Leyland Tiger coaches were taken into stock in November 1983 which continued the fleet numbering system on from 108 to 114. Registered A108-14TRP, these coaches also carried the Plaxton Paramount 3200 body style on a Leyland Tiger chassis, being fitted with a toilet at the rear.

United Counties was graced with three additional Leyland Tiger coaches in November 1983 when three of the coaches ordered for 1984 delivery arrived. These three took up stock numbers 81 to 83 and carried private registration plates 81CBK, 82LUP and 83CBD respectively. As a result of the new deliveries over the course of the year, the United Counties coaching fleet was given a modern appearance. United Counties ordered these vehicles to set up a high class private hire fleet. They were painted in a metallic silver/grey/white livery to make them stand out from other coaches in the fleet. Built with the Plaxton Paramount 3500 body style, these vehicles were fitted with toilets, video players and a small servery.

The final new vehicle to enter service during 1983 was another Ford Transit minibus, this time used on the Grendon Community Minibus scheme. Like the other Community Minibus schemes, this vehicle was funded by Northamptonshire County Council. The Ford Transit took up stock number 73 and was registered A511URP.

The rolling conversion of the Series 1 VRT machines to Series 3 specification continued over the course of 1983 when 772, 773, 775 and 776 were all converted as such over the course of the year. Similar vehicle 771 – XBD771J was destroyed by fire whilst in service in Arlesey. Fortunately, the passengers on board were evacuated from the bus.

A number of buses and coaches had their liveries altered during 1983. Bristol REs 280/2 lost their local coach livery in favour of the green bus livery. A new livery of green with orange relief was introduced to some of the coaching fleet during the year. The vehicles repainted into this livery were Leyland Leopards 150, 154, 161, 169, 189, 229, 233, 237 and 239. 229 and 233 were the first to wear it, although incorrectly, the stripes at the front of the vehicle being in the wrong order.

The National Bus Company introduced a new version of the National Express livery, with the first United Counties coach to gain this livery being Leyland Leopard 159 – VNH159W which was repainted in January 1983. Prior to this date a number of experimental liveries were trialled, with coach 157 being painted into a red and blue skirt stripe livery. An alternative coach livery was applied to Leopard 234 – EBD234T when it gained a red and yellow livery for operation on service 200 between Corby and Birmingham. The 'Midland Express' fleet name was applied to the vehicle, similar to that worn by Midland Red vehicles.

The pair of Bristol VRT machines that gained an all-over advertisement for National Holidays the previous year, 918/9 – HBD918/9T, gained a revised version during 1983. Huntingdon based Bristol VRT 961 – VVV961W gained a simplified version of the red, white and blue anniversary livery and was put to use on excursion work operated from the Huntingdon area. It was also refurbished with dual-purpose seating. Towards the end of the year, Luton based 955 – VVV955W was also treated to a similar livery for excursion work in the Luton area.

In May 1983, United Counties repainted Bristol VRT 859 – RRP859R into a two-tone green livery with Citybus logos applied to it following a recommendation that buses in the Milton Keynes area should have a different livery to others in the United Counties fleet. This livery, however, was not continued by the company, but the application of Citybus logos was made to all Milton Keynes-based vehicles. United Counties compromised with the Milton Keynes Development Corporation with regard to the livery of the vehicles, with a white band being painted onto the vehicles between the upper and lower decks, thus distinguishing Milton Keynes vehicles from other United Counties vehicles.

Coach 242 – MRP242V lost its Corby to Kettering rail link livery in 1983 in favour of an all-white livery, when it was branded with green 'Corby Leisure Bus' and 'Corby Civic' logos.

1984

United Counties received a solitary new vehicle during 1984. This was due to the batch of ten Leyland Tiger coaches ordered for 1984 delivery arriving early in 1983. The new vehicle was yet another Ford Transit minibus numbered 74 – A513EJB. It was put to use by United Counties on the Gayton and Tiffield Community Minibus Scheme in Northamptonshire, again being funded by Northamptonshire County Council.

Two second-hand Bristol VRT machines were taken into stock by United Counties in December. These two vehicles were sourced from West Riding Automobile Co. Ltd and were placed into service from Huntingdon depot after being repainted into green livery. The vehicles concerned were numbered 968 and 969, registered GHL194L and JHL775L.

The conversion of Series 1 Bristol VRT machines to Series 3 specification slowed during 1984, with only two being completed. The vehicles converted were 774 and 779. A third, 778, was started but it took two years to complete this vehicle and it stood in a semi-finished state for a number of months.

A second United Counties Leyland National was earmarked to be converted to a wheelchair bus during 1984. This time, Hitchin based 548 – BVV548T was the vehicle chosen and was converted in July 1984.

United Counties lost another vehicle as a result of fire in August 1984. This time, Hitchin based Leyland National 450 – GBD450L was engulfed by fire whilst in service at Stopsley, despite the efforts of the driver.

1984 saw eight United Counties vehicles gain all-over advertisements. Seven of these were Bristol VRT machines. 957 – VVV957W was the first to be treated to a red, white and blue livery for Interlink Express Carrier Service. This was shortly followed by 929 – ONH929V which gained a black and white livery for Jockey Shorts. 931, SNV931W gained a red and white livery for Y-Fronts. A white based livery was applied to 933 – SNV933W to advertise Chiltern Radio, whilst 949 – VVV949W gained a multicoloured livery for Berger Paints. The penultimate VRT, 940 – URP940W, gained a brown, orange and white livery for Hereward Radio. The final VRT, 894 – YVV894S, gained a white livery for Graham Home Improvements. The eighth vehicle to gain an all-over advertisement was Leyland National 2 587 – SVV587W; Ekins Estate Agents. Luton-based RELL saloon 344 – URP344H gained an all-over yellow advert complete with green writing to promote the Bedfordshire Road Safety Committee's work in Bedfordshire.

The orange, green and white coach livery was applied to a number of different coaches over the course of the year. Bristol RELHs 219 and 220 and Leyland Leopards 224-8, 238/40/1/2/3, 152 and 191 were all recipients.

The ancillary fleet gained a new member during April 1984 when Bristol RELH6G 277 – TBD277G was renumbered 1012. It was used as a staff ferry between the Central Works in Northampton and Milton Keynes depot. It was repainted blue and had 'United Counties Engineering' logos applied to it.

1985

An order was placed by United Counties in late 1984 for seven Ford Transit minibuses for use in the Luton area. This order was granted and the seven minibuses duly arrived with United Counties during April 1985. These vehicles carried Dormobile bodies and took up rolling stock numbers 21 to 27. Registrations B21-27HRP were booked for these vehicles, although in practice only one, 27, gained this registration. The remaining six were not licensed by United Counties until December when they took up registrations C21-6NVV. As a result, these vehicles operated for a very short period of time with United Counties before passing to the newly formed Luton & District.

Advertising on United Counties buses proved popular again during 1985. The first two vehicles were treated in January, Bristol VRTs 835 – HRP675N and 880 – XNV880S, both gaining a blue-based livery to promote National Travelworld travel shops. 835 was allocated to Bedford, whilst 880 went to Northampton. Bristol RELH 212 was repainted into all-over yellow and joined similar 344 in promoting the work of the Bedfordshire Road Safety Committee, being treated to this livery in January 1985. Milton Keynes based 843 – OBD843P was the last vehicle to be painted into an all-over advertisement in January with an unusual black based livery for Milton Keynes Television. March saw the repaint of the next vehicle, again a Bristol VRT, 943 – URP943W which gained a blue and yellow livery to advertise Barclays' one-stop banking in Milton Keynes. April saw 933 receive an updated version of the Chiltern Radio livery. The next all-over advertisement rolled out of the paint shop during August when VRT 845 gained an advert for Timms Electrical of Kettering. 923 and 939 also received all-over advertisements during August. Vindis Garage of Bedford used a white-based livery to advertise themselves on 923, and the *Kettering Evening Telegraph* used a blue based livery on 939. September saw VRT 868 painted white in order for it to gain T-shape and superside advertisements for Key West Ticketing of the West Country. December saw VRT 839 gain a blue and white livery to advertise Gibbs & Dandy of Bedford. At the same time, Leyland National 457 was repainted into a white livery for Quant Garages of Luton. The final all-over advertisement was applied to Leyland Leopard coach 169 – VNH169W. It gained an advertisement to promote Luton International Airport.

Further repaints into the orange, green and white coach livery were Leyland Leopards 153 and 230. Four similarly painted coaches lost this livery in favour of the National white coaching livery, the vehicles concerned being 150, 161, 189 and 191. Leyland Leopards 172 and 176 gained a special white and blue-grey livery, based on the Executive Coach livery for the Nene Valley Express X94 service between Northampton and Raunds.

Over the course of 1985, the National Bus Company made the decision to divide United Counties up into four smaller operating units at the closure of the year. The United Counties name was retained for one of the companies; the three new companies were named the Luton & District Bus Company, Milton Keynes Citybus and United Counties Engineering. This was in preparation for the selloff of the National Bus Company. The creation of the smaller operators would make it easier for them to be sold.

Luton & District took control of Hitchin, Luton, Leighton Buzzard and Aylesbury depots. Milton Keynes Citybus was responsible solely for the Milton Keynes depot. United Counties Engineering became a direct subsidiary of the National Bus Company. The new United Counties took control of Northampton, Kettering, Corby, Wellingborough, Bedford, Biggleswade and Huntingdon depots. The livery was changed to a darker green, different to the green used by the National Bus Company, relieved by orange, yellow and cream stripes. The United Counties name was applied in bold yellow lettering. The first vehicle into this livery was Bristol VRT 828 – HBD828N which lost the anniversary livery in favour of this new livery. In addition, United Counties repainted one bus into the Luton & District livery and one into the Milton Keynes Citybus livery. 615 – ARP615X which gained a livery of red and ivory for Luton & District. The Milton Keynes Citybus vehicle was former VRT 907 – FRP907T which MK Citybus had renumbered 3907. This vehicle gained a livery of mainly white with a predominantly yellow logo. In addition, United Counties also painted up Leyland National 518 and VRT 947 for Luton & District, and Nationals 505 and 540 for Milton Keynes Citybus.

1986

The original vehicle orders for 1986 called for thirty-seven vehicles, seven Leyland Tiger coaches and the remainder being Mercedes-Benz minibuses. However, as in previous years, the order was altered to just the Leyland Tiger coaches, the minibuses being deferred. United Counties was successful in receiving four Iveco minibuses as a result of competition in the St Neots area of Cambridgeshire.

The Leyland Tigers arrived with United Counties between March and May 1986. The first four carried the high-floor Plaxton Paramount 3500 coach body. They took up stock numbers 81/2/4/5 and were registered C81/2/4/5PRP and all were painted in the National Express Rapide livery. Similar vehicle 83 was painted out of the Executive Coach Livery and joined these four coaches in the National Express Rapide livery. 81-83 were allocated to Northampton and the last two were allocated to Kettering depot. The remaining three arrived during May and had the slightly lower Paramount 3200 bodies and were painted in the company's new white and blue-grey Coachlinks livery. This trio took stock numbers 120 to 122 and were registered C120-2PNV, and were added to Kettering's allocation for use on the newly introduced Coachlinks network.

The four Iveco minibuses found their way to United Counties during October 1986 when they took up stock numbers 21 to 24, registered D21-4WNH. These vehicles were branded as 'Street Shuttle', a brand used by the company until the early 2000s. They were put to use on the St Neots town network.

Towards the end of 1986, three former Leyland Leopard coaches were reacquired by the company from Milton Keynes Citybus. The vehicles were 150 – UVV150W and 155/6 – VNH155/6W, these vehicles regaining their original United Counties rolling stock numbers. These vehicles were also recipients of the new white and blue-grey Coachlinks livery. Leyland Olympian 601 – ARP601X was refurbished with coach seats and repainted into the Coachlinks livery to help to deal with the capacity problems United Counties was facing on the X3 service between Cambridge, Bedford and Northampton.

A former Yorkshire Woollen District Transport Co. Ltd. Daimler Fleetline, bodied by Alexander, was acquired by United Counties during 1986 and placed into their ancillary fleet. Registered JHD334J the vehicle concerned took up fleet number 1034 and was put into use as a mobile travel shop. The vehicle was branded as the 'Roadshop' by the company and was used to tour around the smaller villages and towns in the United Counties operating territory that didn't have a travel shop.

From April 1986, United Counties ceased to operate the community transport schemes in Northamptonshire which resulted in the company giving up its interest in the Ford Transit minibuses used on these schemes from this date.

Two serious incidents took place over the year involving two of the company's coaches. Firstly, whilst travelling up the motorway in service, Leyland Tiger coach 113 – A113TRP was badly damaged by fire. The coach was subsequently rebuilt by Plaxton and re-entered service in December. The second victim was Leyland Leopard 180. This vehicle was severely damaged in an accident whilst in the care of a Lincolnshire Road Car Co. Ltd driver in July 1986. This led to Lincolnshire lending United Counties a similar coach registered AVL746X which gained stock number 146. This vehicle was later acquired by United Counties.

All-over advertisements returned during 1986 with a number of Bristol VRTs being treated to such liveries. First was 962 (VVV962W) which received one for the

S.T. Piercy Ltd., and was completed in May. August saw 944 (URP944W) receive one to promote the Harpur Centre in Bedford using a blue and yellow livery. The *Bedfordshire Times and Express* placed a contract with United Counties to advertise on a bus for three years. The vehicle chosen was 773 (ANV773J). 754 (TBD754G) was used to promote the new Asda Store in Corby. 835, HBD675N, lost its advertisement for National Travelworld in favour of a new livery for Chiltern Radio. It was joined by similar 902 (CBD902T) and Leyland Olympian 604 (ARP604X). The final vehicle to gain an advertisement livery during the year was VRT 939 (URP939W) which gained one for the *Evening Telegraph*.

The programme started in the early 1980s to convert the Series 1 Bristol VRT machines to Series 3 condition. 778 – CBD778K was one such vehicle that underwent this treatment. Conversion had started in 1984 but was not completed until May 1986, taking a mere three years.

1987

The business of United Counties was acquired by Stagecoach Holdings Ltd of Perth in November 1987.

Prior to this, United Counties purchased two batches of minibuses for the newly introduced 'Street Shuttle' network. The first ten were taken into stock during April 1987 and pressed into service on the Kettering network. These vehicles were allocated stock numbers 25 to 34, registered D25-34BVV. These vehicles were Robin Hood bodied Iveco A49.10 Turbo Daily minibuses. Next to arrive were a similar batch of Iveco A49.10s, this time for the Bedford 'Street Shuttle' network. These vehicles followed on from the previous batch by taking stock numbers 35 through to 44, and were registered D35-44DNH. October 1987 saw the launch of the Corby 'Street Shuttle' network. Rather than purchasing a new vehicle, United Counties hired an Iveco minibus from Luton & District. The vehicle in question gained United Counties stock number 20 and was registered D771MUR, and was loaned for a period of six months. This vehicle was eventually acquired by United Counties in October 1988.

One other vehicle was acquired by United Counties during 1987. This was ECW bodied Leyland Leopard 146 (AVL746X) from Lincolnshire Road Car Co. Ltd. This vehicle had previously been on loan to United Counties after a native Leyland Leopard, 180, was involved in a serious accident whilst being driven by a Lincolnshire Road Car driver.

The successful conversion of Olympian 601 – ARP601X to Coachlinks specification saw three more of this batch converted to the same specification but with four less seats on the upper deck. The vehicles treated were 605, 602 and 606 – ARP605/2/6X. They were completed in May, July and September respectively. Bristol RE coaches also underwent this refurbishment and gained the white and blue-grey livery and gained Coachlinks branding. In addition to this, these coaches lost their original registration marks SBD222/3M in favour of private registration marks. It was intended that they were to become EIJ222 and 223FWW. 223 gained its intended new registration in April 1987. However, 222's new registration fell through and a new one had to be sourced. It took until July for a new one to be purchased by the company, at which point 222 became registered 222WFM respectively.

In contrast to the previous couple of years, only three buses were painted into all-over advertisements during 1987. Bristol VRTs 935 and 940 – SNV935W and URP940W gained advertisements for Northants 96 FM local radio. The third vehicle was also a Bristol VRT, the vehicle concerned being 930 – SNV930W which gained an all-over advertisement for the Computer Centre in Bedford.

Repaints into Coachlinks livery continued through 1987 with Leopards 151/3/4/74/7/84/5, 229/33/4/42/3 were treated to this livery.

1988

1988 was a busy year for United Counties. A number of new and second-hand vehicles were taken into stock, as well as a number of vehicles coming on loan. Also, a number of vehicles gained all-over advertisements during the course of the year.

The highlight of 1988 was when United Counties introduced the AEC Routemaster bus into the fleet. It was United Counties' intention to operate these buses on service 101 in Bedford which linked the estates in the northern part of the town to Kempston in the south. These vehicles were also introduced to the Corby town network, especially to use them on service 1. The first eight to arrive were numbered 701 to 708 by United Counties. They retained their London registrations WLT512/528/682/903, 68CLT, 647DYE and CUV122/192C. These eight gained coloured allocation plates and were repainted into the company's green with orange, yellow and white stripes livery which looked very smart on these vehicles. These eight vehicles were allocated to Bedford depot where they were branded as 'ROUTEMASTER' and gained route branding for cross town service 101. A further eight Routemasters were sourced from London Buses Ltd for use on the Corby town service 1. These vehicles took stock numbers 709 to 716 and were registered VLT51/255, WLT980/985, 224CLT, 685/820DYE and ALM60B. An additional Routemaster was sourced from Stagecoach Scotland and took up stock number 717, but had lost its London registration plate in favour of EDS48A. This vehicle was used as a spare for the Bedford and Corby networks. To keep the fleet of seventeen in working order, four additional Routemasters were acquired as a source of spare parts. The vehicles concerned were registered VLT167, WLT410, ALM40B and CUV195C, all acquired directly from London Buses Ltd, none of which gained United Counties rolling stock numbers.

The first acquisitions from a fellow Stagecoach company came from Hampshire Bus. Bristol VRTs KRU843/5-7/52W were taken into stock by United Counties in January 1988. Taking up rolling stock numbers 970 to 974, these vehicles were placed into service from Biggleswade garage in the company's green and striped livery.

A Dodge midibus came on demonstration to United Counties from Stagecoach as a possible vehicle to be used on the 'Street Shuttle' network. The vehicle in question was a Dodge G saloon registered D365OSU. It was deemed to be unsuitable for use on the network.

The first new vehicles to be delivered to the company under Stagecoach ownership were six Iveco A49.10 minibuses. The vehicles were allotted rolling stock numbers 45 to 50, registered E45-50MRP and were all allocated to Kettering depot where they were placed into service on the expanded 'Street Shuttle' network. All six were taken into stock in April 1988.

The coach fleet was further improved during 1988 with the introduction of new and acquired coaches into the fleet. First to arrive were a trio of second-hand Volvo B10M machines with Plaxton Paramount 3200 bodywork in May 1988. They took up stock numbers 125 to 127 and carried cherished registrations 4009SC, 7878SC and 9492SC, all being acquired from Stagecoach Scotland.

Six new coaches were delivered to the company over the course of the year. They were similar to the three coaches acquired, being Plaxton Paramount 3200 bodied Volvo B10M machines. The six vehicles in question were allotted stock numbers 130 to 135 and were registered E130-4ORP and F135URP. The latter vehicle was not taken into stock until August 1988, hence the 'F' registration plate.

More minibuses were taken into stock by United Counties between April and May 1988 when six Ford Transits were acquired from Stagecoach Hampshire Bus. The first, registered C33BPR, was acquired in April and originally numbered 71. This was shortly followed by C27-32BPR in May, taking up stock numbers 2 to 6. To fit in with these vehicles, 71 was renumbered to stock number 1. Allocated to Kettering, these vehicles were predominantly used in service in the Wellingborough area.

The first Mercedes-Benz minibuses were delivered to United Counties in June 1988 when three L709D models complete with Alexander bodywork were taken into stock. These vehicles took up stock numbers 10 to 12 and were registered E510-2PVV. All three were allocated to Bedford depot where they entered service on the 'Street Shuttle' network.

The arrival of these minibuses meant that three of the ex-Hampshire minibuses were no longer required by United Counties, and were subsequently disposed of. The remaining three Ford Transits were replaced by a similar number of Iveco minibuses diverted from Hampshire Bus. These vehicles were numbered 51 to 53 and were registered F494-6NTR. These three vehicles were placed into service during August 1988 at Kettering (51) and Bedford depots (52/3). Like previous batches of Ivecos, they were bodied by Robin Hood. Like the Mercedes minibuses, these vehicles were delivered to United Counties in Stagecoach stripes.

During 1988, Stagecoach decided to introduce a single livery to replace the numerous versions worn by the different operators they had acquired, giving the company a corporate image. The colour scheme chosen was a white based livery, relieved by orange, red and blue stripes.

The first new double-deck machines in seven years were received by United Counties during 1988. The vehicles concerned were numbered 620 to 627, registered F620 to 627MSL. These Alexander RL bodied Leyland Olympians were received in the Stagecoach striped livery. All were allocated to Northampton, where they were branded for service 51 which had been branded as 'The Great Eastern Line', on which route these vehicles entered service in September 1988.

A second batch of seven Alexander bodied Leyland Olympians were delivered to Biggleswade depot where they entered service on the company's services between the town and nearby Bedford and Hitchin. The vehicles followed on from the Northampton batch and were registered F628-33MSL and F634MSP, taking stock numbers 628 to 634. 634 was diverted from Cumberland Motor Services as a replacement for accident damaged Bristol VRT 835 – HRP675N, this being the reason for the different registration.

Three additional Iveco minibuses were transferred to United Counties in September in exchange for the three Mercedes-Benz L709D minibuses. The vehicles took up stock numbers 54 to 56, and were registered F491-3NTR.

A deal between Devon General and Stagecoach saw the acquisition of fifty Bristol VRT machines for the Stagecoach Group, with many being allocated to United Counties. The first arrived during October when FDV809/33V and

LFJ868W were allocated to United Counties as 731 to 733. They were repainted into Stagecoach livery at Bedford. Six more arrived in November when they took stock numbers 734 to 739, registered FDV812V, LFJ864/5W, FDV811/35V and LFJ869W. The final six to enter service with United Counties were numbered 740 to 745. The vehicle to have originally been 740 was registered FDV840V, but after a repaint, it was transferred to Cumberland Motor Services Ltd. The registrations for this batch were FDV832V, a replacement for FDV840V, LFJ882/3W, LFJ858/878/885W respectively.

August 1988 saw the acquisition of the local service between Northampton and Irthlingborough operated by Yorks Coaches of Cogenhoe. Included in the deal was a pair of non-conventional coaches, Plaxton bodied Ford R1014 machines registered LRP66V and RNH783V. These two vehicles were allocated rolling stock numbers 245 and 246 respectively.

Two vehicles were added to the ancillary fleet during 1988. These came in the form of a pair of Leyland Titan double-deck machines originating with Southdown Motor Services. These vehicles were registered PRX191B and PRX200B respectively and were acquired from Stagecoach Ltd, Perth. Taking up stock numbers 1010 and 1011, they were soon renumbered 1001/2. 1011 was received in February, and 1010 in November. Both were repainted yellow with a blue waist band, and displaced 1008 and 1005 as driver training vehicles. 1001 was allocated to Kettering whilst Bedford took stock of 1002.

Five buses were treated to all-over advertisements during 1988. First to be done was VRT 966 – VVV966W which was used to advertise the *Kettering Evening Telegraph* group of newspapers, in a base colour of orange and white. Bedford based Leyland National 552 – ERP552T received an all-over advertisement for Park Road Garage, Kempston. August saw the repaint of VRT 941 – URP941W into a red and yellow livery for the *Northampton Citizen*. Newly acquired VRT 732 – FDV838V received an advert for the Asda Superstore in Corby, replacing similar 754 which had previously carried an advert for the store. The last vehicle to be treated was another Leyland National from Bedford's allocation. 553 – ERP553T was used to promote Carlow's Television and Audio Shop.

A number of the company's vehicles were repainted into Stagecoach's corporate livery through the Bedford paint shop during 1988. This included a number of the National Express and white and blue-grey liveried coaches. The Ford Transit minibuses were repainted all white but never gained their stripes, these being completed during June 1988.

United Counties found it needed additional minibuses during 1988. To fulfil this need, Luton & District provided five Ford Transit minibuses registered C21/3-6NVV. These vehicles had originally been owned by United Counties, arriving just before the company was divided. They were allocated stock numbers 21A, 24A-26A as United Counties already had vehicles numbered 21, etc. 23A was returned to Luton & District two days after its arrival with United Counties. Luton & District also loaned United Counties an Optare minibus registered E169EJO, which was put to use as a driver training vehicle.

Cumberland Motor Services loaned a pair of minibuses to United Counties in the form of an Iveco and a Ford Transit. The Iveco was registered E66BVS, numbered 18 by United Counties it was placed into service at Bedford. The second vehicle, a Ford Transit with Mellor body work, was numbered 19 by the company, and carried registration D552URM. Kettering made use of this second vehicle.

1989

The opening two months of 1989 saw eleven Bristol VRT machines enter the fleet from Devon General. These vehicles took stock numbers 746 to 749 (LFJ859/861/884/886W) and 720 to 726 (LFJ857/862/85/863/852/854/855W). In May, an additional VRT was received by United Counties from the same source. This vehicle became numbered 727 – LFJ879W. A handful of these twelve vehicles received all-over advertisements once they had arrived with United Counties. 721 and 722 gained an all-over advertisement for the Royal British Legion; 723/4 for Northants 96 Radio. 749 was decorated to celebrate Northampton's 800th Charter Year in March 1989. The final vehicle to gain an all-over advertisement was 744 which was decorated for the new Texas DIY store in Wellingborough.

A further three were purchased by United Counties from Devon General in January 1989, registered FDV810/6, 784V. These vehicles were not operated by United Counties, instead being transferred to Magicbus, Glasgow.

Six Iveco minibuses were ordered for United Counties and were taken into stock between March and April 1989. Four took up rolling stock numbers 57 to 60, registered F57-60AVV, all being allocated to Bedford. The remaining two were registered F61/2AVV and were sold directly to Hampshire Bus upon arrival with United Counties.

A further fifteen new Leyland Olympian double-deck machines were received by United Counties during 1989. The first ten were fitted with bus seats, taking rolling stock numbers 635 to 638, F635-8YRP, and 639 to 644 – G639-44EVV. The 'F' plate machines entered service in July, the 'G' registered vehicles in August. Allocation was split between Bedford, Northampton and Biggleswade. The remaining five were delivered with dual-purpose seating and were allocated stock numbers 645 to 649 with matching G-EVV registration plates. Kettering took stock of 645, Northampton 646/7 and 648/9 were stabled at Bedford. These five were taken into stock during October and were branded for the Coachlinks network.

An unusual coach entered the fleet in September in the form of a Yugoslavian built Famos coach. The vehicle took stock number 100 (G100JNV) and was painted in National Express livery. Northampton was the recipient of this vehicle.

A further six Iveco minibuses complete with Robin Hood bodies were taken into stock by United Counties during October 1989. They were given fleet numbers 61 to 66, registered G61-66JVV. The first two were allocated to Bedford, the next pair to Northampton and the final two at Kettering. An additional Iveco minibus, this time with Pheonix bodywork, was taken into stock to replace similar Robin Hood bodied Iveco, 21 – D21WNH, which was destroyed by fire in December. The vehicle followed on from the previous six mentioned, becoming number 67 in the United Counties fleet, registered G67LVV.

A pair of Leyland Leopard coaches were acquired from Southdown Motor Services Ltd in December 1989. Both carried the Plaxton Supreme coach body and were registered OUF56, 66W and were numbered 144 and 145 respectively. Acquired wearing National Express livery, these vehicles were repainted into Coachlinks livery in January 1990.

The ancillary fleet gained a solitary vehicle during 1989. This came in the form of an Alexander bodied Ford A minibus which arrived in June from Cumberland Motor Services. The vehicle took up stock number 1003 and was registered LSO84P. The vehicle was allocated to Bedford and was used on a Park and Ride service in the town.

Four coaches gained new registrations over the course of the year. First to be done was Leyland Tiger 105 – NBD105Y which became 83CBD. The vehicle was also treated to London Express fleet names on a National Express style livery. Coaches 125 to 127 lost their cherished registrations in favour of registrations A332ANH, A320ANH and A333ANH in June and July. The private plates were sent back to Stagecoach Scotland for further use.

Three Bristol VRT machines gained all-over advertisements during 1989. Firstly, 939 – URP939W regained its all-over advertisement for the *Kettering Evening Telegraph*. It was joined by 940 – URP940W which gained a similar livery, replacing the advertisement for Northants 96 previously worn. 966 – VVV966W lost its advert for the *Kettering Leader* in favour of Stagecoach stripes. The third vehicle treated was 952 – VVV952W which was given an advert for Chiltern Radio, being treated in September 1989.

A number of vehicles were loaned to United Counties during 1989. United Counties also loaned four Leyland National saloons to Frontrunner Southeast Ltd in April 1989. The vehicles concerned were 494, 534, 546 and 555.

A number of minibuses were acquired by United Counties during 1989. First was Luton & District Iveco D766MUR which came on loan for a three-week period. This was replaced by a Freight Rover Sherpa registered D956WJH from Hampshire Bus. This vehicle was given temporary fleet number 17 by United Counties. Two Iveco minibuses were also loaned to the company from Stagecoach in July. The two vehicles concerned were temporarily numbered 15 and 16, registered F25/6PSL. Both were used at Bedford, operating for just over a month. They returned to their rightful owner in August when a further two minibuses were taken on loan from Cumberland Motor Services. First was former United Counties Mercedes-Benz minibus E512PVV which gained its original fleet number 12, being joined by D29SAO which became temporarily known as number 13. The latter vehicle was a Reeve Burgess bodied Renault machine. Both operated from Bedford depot until November. Hampshire Bus loaned three Freight Rover Sherpa minibuses from August 1989. Registered D958-960WJH, these vehicles were numbered 8 to 10. Bedford was again the recipient of these vehicles, from where they were used on a Park and Ride service. Number 8 returned to Hampshire Bus in December 1989, whilst the other two stayed until April 1991.

Two demonstrators were also loaned to the company during 1989. The first was a Mark II Leyland National from South Wales Transport. Registered KEP829X, this vehicle took temporary stock number 999. It was loaned to United Counties over the course of February and March and was put to use in Bedford on town service 102. The second vehicle was a Bristol VRT owned by The Bee Line Bus Company. The vehicle was registered HJB461W and was numbered 14 by United Counties. It was allocated to Northampton for its stay during March where it was used in service.

New in January 1980 were seven Willowbrook bodied Leyland Leopard coaches. Two years later, United Counties applied dedicated branding to 238 – KVV238V which is seen above. The vehicle was chosen to work the X15 between Milton Keynes, Aylesbury and Reading for which appropriate branding was applied to the vehicle. This service was jointly operated with Alder Valley. It is seen wearing this branding above whilst posing for the camera on the Brackmills Industrial Estate in Northampton. *Roger Warwick Collection*

242 - MRP 242V, a Plaxton bodied Leyland Leopard, is seen here at Kettering Railway Station. This vehicle and sister 243 were diverted from Western National to United Counties to operate a limited stop service linking Kettering and Peterborough railway stations via Corby and Oundle. They wore British Rail blue and grey InterCity livery and carried route branding for the service. *794 Preservation Group*

132 • UNITED COUNTIES BUSES

United Counties only received a small number of Mark 2 Leyland National saloons. Showing off the type is 587 – SVV587W which is seen having just reversed off bay at Bedford Bus Station. The blue Bedford fleet number plate can be seen clearly on this vehicle. *Gary Seamarks*

A trio of Lex bodied Bedford YMQ midibuses were taken into stock by United Counties to operate town services in the Leighton Buzzard area. Upon privatisation in 1986, these three vehicles transferred to Luton & District. 52 – WNH52W is seen loading in Leighton Buzzard town centre. *Bruce Pyne*

United Counties operated several community minibus schemes during the 1980s in Northamptonshire. One such scheme was focused on the Lilbourne area where it is photographed. The vehicle selected for the different schemes was the Ford Transit. Dating back to 1977, TDU828W was allocated rolling stock number 71 by United Counties. This vehicle differed slightly from the other three similar vehicles taken into stock in that it carried bodywork by Deansgate. *Roger Warwick Collection*

November 1983 saw the arrival of a third Ford Transit minibus with United Counties, this time for Grendon community minibus scheme. This vehicle was numbered 73 by the company, registered A511URP. It is similar in appearance to the previous vehicle illustrated, but it carries a Ford body. The small village of Castle Ashby provides the location for this photograph. *Roger Warwick Collection*

Further Leyland Leopards were taken into stock by United Counties, this time with Duple Dominant body work. A handful of these vehicles survived privatisation with the company and saw operation with Stagecoach. 163 – VNH163W is seen parked on the forecourt of Kettering garage in full Stagecoach stripe livery, complete with Coachlinks logos. *Gary Seamarks*

Twenty Leyland Olympians complete with ECW bodywork were taken into stock by United Counties in 1981. 601 – ARP601X was one of many refurbished and is seen in Coachlinks livery travelling through Cambridge on an X3 service from Northampton. *Gary Seamarks*

965 - VVV 965W was part of the last batch of Bristol VRTs delivered to United Counties before the Leyland Olympian came along. It is pictured in glorious sunshine at Wollaston School on a contract to the nearby village of Bozeat. *794 Preservation Group*

Fifteen ECW bodied Leyland Leopard coaches were allocated to United Counties in 1982, with another arriving the year after. 172 – CNH172X shows off the type and is seen loading at Heathrow Central Bus Station in full National Express livery. A similar vehicle operated by London Country can be seen behind 172. *Gary Seamarks.*

New to United Counties in November 1983 was Plaxton Paramount bodied Leyland Tiger 83 (83CBD). It is seen here wearing the Stagecoach livery complete with Coachlinks names. This vehicle was exported to Malawi operations during May 1989, only to return to United Counties in January 1994. It is seen heading to the Showbus 1994 rally at Woburn.
794 Preservation Group

The Plaxton Paramount bodied Leyland Tiger coach became the popular choice of coach during the 1980s. Two models were taken into stock, the 3200 and 3500. 109 – A109TRP is seen wearing a revised National Express livery whilst sitting on the forecourt of Kettering garage.
D.J. Hancock

United Counties acquired a pair of Duple Dominant bodied Leyland Leopard coaches from Ribble Motor Services in January 1983. Representing this batch is XTF808L which took up rolling stock number 254. They were put to use on National Express contracts operated by United Counties. It is seen passing Luton Airport operating service 750 (Hemel Hempstead-Waltham Cross), one the company jointly operated with London Country. *S.J. Butler Collection*

Shortly before United Counties was divided into three operating companies, they received a batch of seven Carlyle bodied Ford Transit minibuses for operation in the Luton area. Representing the batch is 25 (C25NVV) which is seen loading in George Street, Luton. All seven minibuses passed to the newly formed Luton & District company in January 1986. 25 is seen here operating in March 1986 with its new owners. *Roger Warwick Collection*

A third National Express livery is shown here on Paramount 3500 bodied Tiger 81 – C81PRP. It is seen having just dropped passengers off at Victoria Coach Station. The red United Counties fleet names can be seen here next to the larger 'Rapide' logo. *Gary Seamarks*

United Counties acquired a Daimler Fleetline during September 1986 for use as a mobile travel office. It visited locations around the operational area that did not have a travel office. One such place was the small Cambridgeshire town of St Neots where we see 1034 (JHD334J) parked in use. Two Iveco minibuses on the Street Shuttle network can also be viewed. *794 Preservation Group*

Minibus operation came into its own with the introduction of the Street Shuttle network in Bedford, St Neots and Kettering over the 1986-1988 period. The original Street Shuttle network was operated by a number of Robin Hood bodied Iveco A49.10 minibuses. 35 – D35DNH represents this type of vehicle, with the largest number of these vehicles arriving in 1987. It seen loading in Midland Road, Bedford, bound for the suburb of Fenlake. *Gary Seamarks*

Biggleswade Market Square finds Robin Hood bodied Iveco 49-10 F60AVV, numbered 60. It is seen sporting the Street Shuttle brand, one that was applied to the company's minibus fleet from the late 1980s. *794 Preservation Group*

In 1988, the coaching fleet changed from the Leyland Tiger to the more modern Volvo B10M. The bodywork remained with Plaxton, again on the Paramount model. Five were taken into stock during the year. A more modern appearance was given to these vehicles, displayed here by 134 – E134ORP. It is seen in full Coachlinks livery operating an X64 service to Birmingham. *Gary Seamarks*

Two non-standard Plaxton Supreme bodied Ford R1114 coaches were acquired from York Bros. of Northampton in August 1988 along with services between Northampton, Wellingborough and Irthlingborough and Northampton to Nether Heyford. 245 (LRP66V) is seen here at the Irthlingborough end of the Northampton to Irthlingborough service. *Roger Warwick Collection*

1988 saw the first intake of new double-deck machines by United Counties since 1981. Over the coming three years, a number of Alexander RL bodied Leyland Olympians were taken into stock by United Counties for various duties. The initial batch were allocated to Northampton where they were placed onto town service 51 between the town centre and Blackthorn, via the Weston Favell shopping complex. The Weston Favell Centre is where we find 621 – F621MSL, the first of the new order of Olympians taken into stock by United Counties. *Gary Seamarks*

Five of these Olympians were taken into stock with dual purpose seating. They were put to use on the Coachlinks network. 649 – G649EVV is seen departing Huntingdon Bus Station heading for Peterborough on the X1. The X1 was the longest of the Coachlinks routes, originally travelling between Peterborough, Huntingdon, Bedford, Luton and Heathrow Airport. *Gary Seamarks*

The Stagecoach Group saw the potential of the Routemaster and acquired a large number during the late 1980s from London Buses Ltd. United Counties was successful in gaining seventeen operational Routemasters, plus several spares. 702 – WLT528 was allocated to Bedford garage, where they were used on cross town service 101, for which route branding was applied to the smart green livery. It is seen parked at Bedford Bus Station.
D.J. Hancock

Corby was the other garage to gain a small allocation of Routemasters. 710 – VLT255 represents the Corby allocation, parked at Corby Bus Station. These vehicles gained route branding for town service 1. United Counties appropriately branded the vehicles 'Routemaster'.
Gary Seamarks

October 1988 saw the arrival of a pair of Northern Counties 'Queen Mary' bodied Leyland Titan PD3s from Southdown Motor Services. Originally numbered 1010, PRX191B was later renumbered 1002. Both were repainted yellow and put to use as driver training vehicles. It is seen here at the former United Counties Head Office and Garage in Rothersthorpe Avenue, Northampton. *794 Preservation Group*

Another non-standard bus entered the United Counties fleet in June 1989 in the form of an Alexander bodied Ford A minibus registered LSO84P. It was originally purchased for use as a driver training vehicle, but was later used on Park and Ride duties in Bedford. It is seen loading outside the Woolworths store on Midland Road, Bedford, in plain white livery, relieved only by small blue United Counties fleet names. The vehicle was numbered 1003 in the ancillary fleet numbering system. *Roger Warwick Collection*

144 • UNITED COUNTIES BUSES

December 1989 saw the arrival of a pair of Plaxton Supreme bodied Leyland Leopard coaches from Southdown Motor Services. Delivered to the company in National Express livery, these vehicles were repainted into Stagecoach stripes and branded for the Coachlinks network prior to entering service. 145 (OUF66W) was one of the two vehicles and was allocated to Huntingdon garage. It is seen travelling along Emmanuel Street, Cambridge, heading for Huntingdon on route 74. *Roger Warwick Collection*

G100JNV was a unique vehicle in the United Counties fleet. The coach was a Yugoslavian built FAP Famos. Northampton garage took stock of the vehicle which took up stock number 100. As can be seen, it initially wore the National Express livery for use on the company's National Express contracts. It is seen at journey's end at Northampton Bus Station. *Gary Seamarks*

1990–1999

1990

The first vehicles to enter the United Counties fleet during April and May were eight second-hand Iveco A49.10 minibuses that originated with Magicbus, Scotland. Registered G27-9/31-3PSR and G40/1SSR, these vehicles took up rolling stock numbers 68 to 75. In June, the first three were renumbered out of numerical order, with fleet G27-9PSR becoming 70, 68 and 69. They all received the 'Street Shuttle' livery and three were allocated to Corby depot for the introduction of the brand to this town. Another was added to Kettering's allocation, whilst the remaining four found their way to Bedford depot.

June and July saw the arrival of six Volvo B10M coaches with Plaxton Paramount bodywork for use on National Express work. Registrations G386-391PNV were allocated to these vehicles along with rolling stock numbers 86 to 91. Four were allocated to Northampton, the remaining two joining Kettering's allocation.

Five Alexander RL bodied Leyland Olympian machines were taken into stock during 1990. They carried on from the existing Olympian fleet, numbered 650 to 654. Registered H650 to 654VVV, the first four were allocated to Huntingdon, with 654 being allocated to Northampton, but was quickly reallocated to Kettering where it remained for a large part of its working life. The first four arrived in September, whilst 654 arrived a month later in October.

A second batch of eight Iveco minibuses were sourced from Ribble Motor Services, arriving in September. These vehicles were acquired to operate a new network of services in Corby which the company branded as the 'Corby Magic Mini'. This was a scheme introduced to entice people away from the taxis operating in the town and onto United Counties buses. Allocated rolling stock numbers 301 to 308, these vehicles carried registrations D406FRV, D724/6/8/9/31/5YBV and D859FOT. They were decorated in a distinctive black and gold livery in the style of the Stagecoach stripes.

Six of the company's vehicles gained all-over advertisements during 1990, many of which were allocated to Bedford. Again, numerous Bristol VRTs were chosen for this use. First was 920 (LBD920V) which was used to advertise the *Bedfordshire Times & Chronicle*, this being completed in May. The next two were similar vehicles 916 (HBD916T) and 949 (VVV949W) in July. The first vehicle gained one for The Computer Centre, Bedford, whilst 949 was used to promote the Newlands Shopping Centre in Kettering. It was the turn of 926 (ONH926V) in August receiving an advertisement for Kwik Printing of Bedford. Auto Trader used Leyland National 552 to promote themselves from October, based on a grey and white livery. The final vehicle of the year was VRT 952 which was used to promote the Aspects Leisure Park in Bedford, being completed in December.

The career of Leyland National 544 – BVV544T came to an end in January 1990 when it was hit by a tree during gale-force winds.

Three double-deck machines were loaned to United Counties during 1990. The first was Cumberland Motor Services tri-axle Alexander RL bodied Leyland Olympian 1201 – F201FHH. The second was Southdown's Bristol VRT 621 – UWV621S, both of which were used in the Huntingdon area to counteract new services implemented by Whippet Coaches. The VRT put in a second appearance with United Counties during November for the Children in Need appeal. Finally, Stagecoach Megadekka F110NES was loaned from East Midlands to United Counties during November to promote Stagecoach's slogan 'Buses mean business'.

1991

United Counties was not fortunate enough to receive any new rolling stock during 1991, however a handful of second-hand vehicles did enter the fleet.

February 1991 saw the arrival of three Iveco minibuses from Ribble Motor Services, all carrying Robin Hood bodywork. The first two were registered D610 and 613BCK and gained rolling stock numbers 310 and 309 respectively. They were placed in service from Corby depot where they were used to enhance the town's 'Magic Mini' network, and were subsequently repainted into the black and gold livery. The third was registered D612BCK and gained stock number 76, and was painted into the company's 'Street Shuttle' livery, being allocated to Bedford. The intake of these additional vehicles allowed the Freight Rover Sherpa minibuses that were on loan from Hampshire Bus to return to their rightful owner.

Next to be taken into stock were seven Alexander bodied Leyland Olympians from Northern Scottish Omnibuses Ltd, arriving in July 1991. The vehicles had been built to dual-door layout, but the centre door was removed and four additional seats fitted prior to them entering service with United Counties over the course of August and September, many of them in as-acquired condition. These vehicles took stock numbers 612 to 618 and were registered D382/3/4/79XRS and GSO6/7/8V respectively.

Four Iveco minibuses were taken into stock during August from Cumberland Motor Services. The first was a vehicle that had previously been on loan to United Counties during 1988 and 1989. Registered E66BVS, this vehicle gained rolling stock number 77 and was allocated to Bedford depot where it replaced accident damaged 22 – D22WNH. The remaining three were numbered 311 to 313. Registered D618/9BCK and D725YBV, these vehicles were added to Corby's allocation. Like those acquired earlier in the year, these vehicles were painted into a black and gold livery for the 'Corby Magic Mini' network. The introduction of these minibuses saw the reduction in the Routemaster operation on the Corby network.

The final vehicle to be taken into stock during 1991 was a Duple 340 bodied Leyland Tiger coach. The vehicle was acquired from Fife Scottish Omnibuses Ltd. Registered MSU465, this vehicle gained rolling stock number 115. This vehicle was repainted into National Express livery and was acquired to replace the FAP Famos coach 100 – G100LNV.

Two vehicles were taken on loan to United Counties over the course of 1991. The first was sourced from Cumberland Motor Services Ltd. It went on loan between February and March 1991. The vehicle in question was a Duple Laser bodied Leyland Tiger coach registered B106HAO. This vehicle was swapped for United Counties

Leyland Tiger 81 – C81PRP which was required by Cumberland for National Express contracts. The second vehicle was taken into stock from Centrewest London Buses Ltd. The vehicle was registered JDZ2372 and was loaned for one day for evaluation purposes.

Two vehicles were treated to all-over advertisements during 1991. Both vehicles were Bristol VRTs and were both treated in April 1991. 950 (VVV950W) received an advertisement for Harcros Timber & Building Supplies of Northampton and 965 (VVV965W) was painted into an advertisement for the Harborne Groups' Wellingborough branch.

Three vehicles were re-registered by United Counties during 1991. First was AEC Routemaster 705 which lost its cherished registration 68CLT in favour of ABD892A in April. Sister vehicle 704, which had been withdrawn after suffering accident damage, donated its registration WLT908 to Volvo B10M coach 125, which in turn had lost its registration A332ANH. Two additional Routemasters were due to be re-registered during 1991 but this did not take place. The vehicles concerned were 712 – WLT985 and 715 – 820DYE.

United Counties withdrew its Daimler Fleetline Roadshop vehicle during October 1991.

1992

Thirty-nine new and second-hand vehicles were taken into stock over the course of 1992.

The first few months of the year saw an additional minibus requirement which led United Counties to source six minibuses, three Ivecos and three Dodge machines from Stagecoach Scotland, Cumberland Motor Services, East Midland Motor Services and Fife Scottish Omnibus Ltd. First to arrive was a Robin Hood bodied Iveco minibus registered D938ECR which took up stock number 314. The vehicle was taken into stock from Stagecoach Scotland and entered service at Corby in May 1992 in the black and gold 'Corby Magic Mini' livery. Next to be acquired was a similar vehicle from Cumberland Motor Services. Registered D217NUR, this minibus took up stock number 18. Again, the third vehicle was of the same specification and came from East Midlands. It was registered D936EBP and gained rolling stock number 19. Both 18 and 19 gained 'Street Shuttle' livery and were pressed into service from Kettering depot during April 1992.

The trio of Dodge minibuses were all sourced from Fife Scottish during May. These vehicles were registered E638/9/45DCK and were originally allotted rolling stock numbers 2, 3 and 1 but were renumbered during July 1992 to 5, 6 and 4 respectively. A further two Dodge minibuses were acquired in August which were registered D634/41DCK which took stock numbers 15 and 16. These two additional vehicles were also sourced from Fife Scottish. The first four Dodges were allocated to Bedford depot, with the fifth joining Northampton's allocation. A further Iveco minibus was also sourced during August from Ribble Motor Services. The vehicle in question was registered D411FRV which became number 17, and was allocated to Northampton depot.

Competition between United Counties and Whippet Coaches for school contracts in the Cambridgeshire and Bedfordshire areas increased during 1992. United Counties was successful in winning a number of contracts in this area and required a number of vehicles to operate them. It was hoped that the order for new Leyland

Olympians would arrive in time to allow the cascade of older Bristol VRT machines for these contracts, but this did not happen. Instead, a number of Bristol VRT machines were acquired from other Stagecoach operations, either permanently or on loan. Only three were acquired by United Counties from Cumberland Motor Services Ltd. The vehicles in question were registered FAO417-9V and took up stock numbers 750 to 752. The first two were acquired in Cumberland livery, whilst the third had been repainted into Stagecoach stripes by Cumberland. The latter two were quick to receive the Stagecoach stripe livery. All three were stabled at Huntingdon depot from where they operated the aforementioned contracts as well as being used on normal service work.

The remainder of the vehicle requirement was fulfilled by hired vehicles from Ribble, Sussex Coastline and East Midlands, with fourteen in total being sourced from these three operators. Ribble Motor Services loaned four Bristol VRT machines registered LHG445T, DBV26/8W and FDV784V. The first three of which took up stock numbers 718, 754 and 755. Sussex Coastline provided the majority of the fourteen, with eight being taken on loan from this operator. The first four were allotted temporary stock numbers 756/7/8/61 and carried registrations AAP662/70-2T. The remaining four took stock numbers 719, 760 and 759/62 respectively. These vehicles carried registrations LHG437T, UWV617S and EAP977/8V. The final two were hired from East Midlands Motor Services. The first was numbered 753, registered KWA219W, the second became 764 – DWE191V. United Counties required to hire an additional Bristol VRT machine but none were available, so instead a Leyland National MK II saloon was hired from Cumberland Motor Services. Registered LFR860X, this vehicle took up temporary stock number 542.

October 1992 saw the arrival of fifteen Leyland Olympians with Northern Counties bodywork enter the United Counties fleet. These vehicles were the first Northern Counties bodied vehicles to be purchased by United Counties. They were also the last Leyland Olympians to be taken into stock by the company. The batch were registered K655-65/7-70UNH and gained rolling stock numbers 655-65/7-70. Eleven were allocated to Northampton, and the remaining four to Bedford.

United Counties was successful in acquiring the Stagecoach Megadekka which had a 110 seating capacity. The vehicle was acquired to combat a capacity issue on the morning service between Biggleswade and Bedford. The vehicle was registered F110NES and took stock number 600. This vehicle was acquired from sister company East Midland which took United Counties 618 – GSO8V in exchange.

The last vehicles to be taken into stock during 1992 were ten Alexander bodied Mercedes-Benz 709D minibuses, arriving in December. These vehicles took stock numbers 350 to 359 and were registered K350-9ANV. All ten joined Bedford's allocation where they replaced older Iveco minibuses on the 'Street Shuttle' network.

Between April and August 1992, a number of the company's Routemasters were re-registered to allow United Counties to retain the cherished registrations. 701-3/6/9/10/4 were re-re-registered between this time, the registrations being allocated to three staff cars, Volvo B10M coach 126 and Leyland Olympians 612/4/5. Four Routemasters were disposed of to Ribble and Stagecoach Scotland. 702, 707 and 716 went to Ribble, whilst Stagecoach Scotland took 713.

A Plaxton Paramount bodied Volvo B10M coach was taken on loan by United Counties to allow modification work to be carried out on native coach 87. The vehicle concerned took registration F411DUG.

Four additional minibuses were required for the 'Corby Magic Mini' network, one of which is mentioned at the start of the 1992 section. The additional three vehicles were existing United Counties Iveco machines 22 – D22WNH, 20 – D771MUR and 26 – D26BVV. The trio were repainted into the gold and black livery and renumbered 315 to 317.

Leyland Olympian 601 – ARP601X lost its blue and white Coachlinks livery in favour of the Stagecoach stripes livery and gained blue Coachlinks fleet names.

Just one vehicle received an all-over advertisement during 1992. Bristol VRT 722 – LFJ863W lost its Chiltern Radio advert in favour of one for Beazer Homes in December.

1993

1993 saw no less than ninety new vehicles enter the United Counties fleet along with four second-hand vehicles.

United Counties received two second-hand coaches from Stagecoach Malawi in 1992 which were placed into store. The vehicles arrived in a poor state and after standing unused for a number of months, work commenced on putting these vehicles back into service. The first was completed by February 1993 when it gained rolling stock number 116 and UK registration B357KNH, later being re-registered VLT255, a former plate carried by a Routemaster. This vehicle was a Duple Laser 2 bodied Leyland Tiger and was allocated to Northampton from where it worked the Coachlinks network.

The first batch of new vehicles to be delivered to United Counties came in the form of five Plaxton Premiere 320 bodied Volvo B10M coaches for use on the company's Coachlinks network. These five coaches took up stock numbers 150 to 154, K150-4DNV, two of which were allocated to Huntingdon depot, the remainder being allocated to Bedford.

The four acquired vehicles were next to be taken into stock. The first were a pair of MK II Leyland National saloons from Cumberland Motor Services. These two vehicles were registered LFR862/4X and took up rolling stock numbers 500 and 501. These two vehicles were allocated to Bedford depot. The other pair of acquired vehicles were ECW bodied Bristol VRT machines which came from East Midlands Motor Services. The pair carried registration plates BAU178/9T and took stock numbers 900/1. Northampton received this pair of vehicles. In exchange, Leyland Nationals 580 and 586 moved to East Midlands Motor Services.

Volvo B10M coaches 86 to 91 dating back to 1990 proved themselves to be unreliable. This led to the number of National Express contracts worked by United Counties being reduced when the new summer timetable was introduced. As a result, all existing National Express work was transferred to Kettering depot. To replace coaches 86 to 91, five coaches were acquired by United Counties. Three coaches were acquired from Parks of Hamilton (92/3/6) and Rainworth Travel, a subsidiary of East Midlands (94/5). The five coaches took up rolling stock numbers 92 to 96 and were registered J430/9/45/6/50HDS. All were repainted into National Express livery and were fitted with destination equipment.

July 1993 saw the arrival of seven Alexander Dash bodied Dennis Dart saloons for use in the Northampton area. These seven Darts had originally been intended for Ribble Motor Services but were diverted. These vehicles did not gain local registrations, instead carried the booked registrations K104-10XHG, and were allotted rolling stock numbers 450 to 456. These vehicles were taken into stock to operate services 80/85, services introduced to compete with Northampton Transport.

A further eight Plaxton Premiere bodied Volvo B10M coaches were taken into stock during July 1993. These vehicles took up stock numbers 155 to 162, L155-62JNH. All eight were allocated to Kettering depot where they were used on the Coachlinks network to Birmingham and London.

Fifteen new double-decks were taken into stock between August and September 1993. By this time, the Leyland Olympian had been renamed the Volvo Olympian, and this batch again carried Northern Counties bodywork. Following on from the previous Leyland Olympians, these vehicles were numbered 671 to 685, and were registered L671-84HNV and L685JBD, all being allocated to Northampton.

A sizeable batch of twenty-one Alexander Dash bodied Volvo B6 saloons were taken into stock by United Counties between August and October 1993. These vehicles took stock numbers 401 to 421 with matching L-JBD registration plates. All twenty-one were allocated to Bedford depot, where they entered service on the town network, displacing Routemasters and conventional double-decks and Leyland National saloons. 420 was exhibited by Volvo at the Coach & Bus 93 show at Birmingham's NEC. 420 was also the 1000th new vehicle purchased by Stagecoach Holdings Limited.

Twenty-one Mercedes-Benz 709D minibuses complete with Alexander bodywork were taken into stock over the course of September and October. Fleet numbers 360 to 380 were allotted to these vehicles which were registered L360-80JBD. Thirteen were allocated to Bedford and the remainder to Northampton. The introduction of these vehicles replaced further Iveco and Dodge minibuses on the 'Street Shuttle' network. Three more were taken into stock in October numbered 381 to 383, L381-3NBD. 381 was another one of the company's vehicles displayed at the Coach & Bus Show 93 in Birmingham.

The final batch of new vehicles to enter the fleet were a further ten Alexander Dash bodied Volvo B6 saloons. 422 to 431 were registered L422-31MVV and were purchased by United Counties to replace the seven 'K' registered Dennis Dart saloons which found their way to Bluebird Buses Ltd. However, 429 and 430 did not operate with the company, whilst 431 never made it to United Counties. The competition between United Counties and Northampton Transport ceased in December 1993, at which point 423 to 428 transferred to Ribble Motor Services Ltd, with 422 – L422MVV being the only one of the batch being retained by United Counties.

Two vehicles received all-over advertisements during 1993. The first was Leyland Olympian 610 – ARP610X which gained an advertisement for Northamptonshire Training and Enterprise Council. It gained this livery during May 1993. The second vehicle was Iveco minibus 73 which was used to promote Kettering's new leisure village.

Alexander bodied Ford Minibus 1003 was renumbered 3 and gained a fresh livery of Stagecoach stripes, placed into service on the 'Street Shuttle' network in Northampton. Leyland Tigers 81/2/5 were painted out of National Express livery and gained the Stagecoach stripes Coachlinks livery.

United Counties sold eight withdrawn former Devon General Bristol VRTs (741-3, 745-749) to Ribble Motor Services during 1993.

United Counties wished to show the Bedford councillors the investment that they were making in the Bedford fleet, showing that they were modernising the fleet. For this purpose, United Counties hired Hampshire Bus Alexander Dash bodied Dennis Dart 529 - J529GCD, as the Volvo B6 was a new model and had not yet been completed. The vehicle was loaned for three days, at which time Mercedes-Benz 709D minibus 354 – K354ANV was loaned the other way.

Hampshire Bus also loaned Leyland Titan PD3/4 FCD292D to United Counties over the summer of 1993. This vehicle was used by United Counties on driver training duties.

1994

It has already been mentioned above that United Counties received two coaches from Stagecoach Malawi in 1992. These two vehicles underwent extensive refurbishment before entering service. The first was numbered 116 by the company. The second vehicle entered service during January 1994. This vehicle was originally owned by United Counties, numbered 83 it was exported to Malawi in 1989. The vehicle gained registration A294ANH before it regained its original registration once Leyland Tiger 105 gained new registration RBD397Y. This vehicle also gained Stagecoach stripes complete with Coachlinks logos.

The first of the two batches of new rolling stock comprised eight more of the Alexander Dash bodied Volvo B6 saloon. The first six were registered L423-428XVV, with the remaining two becoming M429/30BNV. This batch gained stock numbers 423 to 430 and were allocated to Huntingdon depot where they were used on the St Neots 'Street Shuttle' network, replacing six minibuses and two coaches.

Whilst no new double-deck machines were taken into stock by United Counties, ten Alexander bodied Leyland Olympians from Stagecoach's Scottish operations were acquired. The first six were sourced from Fife Scottish and were allocated stock numbers 708 to 713, registered J808WFS and K709-13ASC. Four of these vehicles were allocated to Kettering depot and the remaining two to Huntingdon. These machines arrived during July 1994. The remaining four were sourced from Bluebird Buses Ltd and arrived in September. First was 618 – GSO2V; this vehicle was from the same batch that United Counties had acquired some examples of during 1991; and replaced the original 618 which was transferred to East Midlands during 1992. The remaining three were registered J620-2GCR, which gained stock numbers 714 to 716. The former vehicle was allocated to Bedford depot, whilst the three latter vehicles were added to Northampton's allocation.

The second batch of new vehicles to enter the fleet during 1994 came in the form of seventeen Alexander bodied Mercedes-Benz 709D minibuses. These vehicles were allocated stock numbers 332/4-49 and were registered M332/4-49DRP. All were delivered during October 1994 and replaced Iveco minibuses on the Kettering 'Street Shuttle' network.

The replacement of the Ivecos by these Mercedes-Benz minibuses allowed some of them to be cascaded to the 'Corby Magic Mini' fleet, replacing the ageing 'D' registered minibuses. Ivecos 63 and 67 were the first to be converted and were completed during September 1994. Similar 50, 66, 70/4/5 were treated the same over November and December 1994.

A number of Ivecos were placed on loan to various Stagecoach companies. 58 to 61 were loaned to newly acquired Stagecoach Selkent in the Bromley area. These vehicles were repainted red and went on loan over the course of September and October, returning to United Counties in January 1995. Similar 51 to 53 were loaned to Stagecoach Darlington to help out in that town. Other vehicles to go on loan were Leyland Leopards 174, 184 and 185 which went on loan to Sussex Coastline which had suffered severe flooding at their Chichester garage. Routemaster 703 also went on loan to the same company for a short period of time. Midland Red South hired coaches 174/8/9, Leyland Nationals 500/1 and Leyland Olympian 611 for short periods over the course of 1994.

United Counties repainted their remaining Routemaster fleet into Stagecoach stripes, forming a reserve fleet. The vehicles concerned were 701, 703, 706, 708, 709 and 710, and all were completed between January and February.

Six of the Volvo B6 saloons at Bedford gained all-over advertisements over the course of 1994. First to be treated was 421 (L421JBD) which received a black based livery for Michael Peters in February, and was the first of four vehicles to gain an advertisement for this company. Next to be done was 420 (L420JBD) painted into a grey based livery for the same company, being completed in March. The third vehicle was 419 (L419JBD) which became purple for Michael Peters, also being completed during March. The fourth and final vehicle to advertise this company was 418 (L418JBD) in a black and blue livery, being completed in October. 406 (L406JBD) gained an all-over advertisement for Oakley Garage and was completed in October. The final Volvo B6 to gain an all-over advertisement was 417 (L417JBD). It was repainted in a red and cream livery for Woodfine Solicitors of Bedford and Sandy. Corby based Bristol VRT 948 (VVV948W) had Safeway logos applied, as did Kettering based 724 (LFJ852W), and were used on a free shuttle to the Safeway stores at Corby and Rushden.

United Counties re-registered a number of vehicles during November 1994. Coaches 125/6 were re-registered from WLT908 and 647DYE to A729/8ANH. The cherished registrations along with the cherished registration from a staff car was adorned by coaches 81/2/5, which gained registrations WLT683, WLT908 and 647DYE respectively.

Work had to be carried out on the fleet of Volvo B6 saloons during 1994. This resulted in the loan of similar saloon L163AVC which was placed on loan from Volvo Bus Ltd, Warwick, between October and November 1994. This allowed the work to be carried out on the native Volvo B6 machines.

1995

1995 was a slow year for the intake of vehicles into the United Counties fleet. No new vehicles were purchased; however, twenty-five second-hand vehicles were taken into stock.

The first half of the year was a quiet period, but over the summer, thirteen Leyland Fleetline double-deck machines of varying bodywork were sourced from Cleveland Transit, Busways Travel and G & G Travel Ltd. These vehicles were 'high' vehicles and as a result, all thirteen were allocated to Corby depot, and the Bristol VRT machines from the Corby allocation being reallocated to depots that were in need of vehicles for school contracts.

Numerically, the first seven were bodied by Northern Counties which came from Cleveland Transit. These vehicles were registered GAJ125-8V and YVN5202/4T, and they were allocated rolling stock numbers 980 to 986. The next four were sourced from Busways Travel and carried Alexander bodywork. These continued the fleet numbering sequence from 987 to 990 and were registered OCU801/2/4/8R. To complete the batch, SDA651S and SDA715S were acquired from G & G Travel of Leamington Spa, and took up rolling stock numbers 991 and 992 respectively.

The Fleetlines did not last long in service with United Counties, with most being withdrawn by the end of 1996.

United Counties were successful in sourcing a solitary Bristol VRT during 1995. The vehicle came from Circle Line registered LEU261P and was dual-doored, allotted fleet number 840 by the company. It was added to the Bedford allocation.

The majority of the remainder of acquired vehicles came in the form of two batches of coaches. The first were four 1983 Leyland Tiger coaches which were acquired from East Kent Road Co. Ltd. These vehicles carried Plaxton Paramount 3200 bodywork and came with cherished registration plates TSU639-642. Taking stock numbers 86 to 89, these vehicles were put to use from Bedford depot.

The second batch of coaches were of the more modern Plaxton Premiere bodied Volvo B10M model. They were acquired to operate the newly introduced Stagecoach Express X5 service which ran between Oxford and Cambridge, via Bicester, Buckingham, Milton Keynes, Bedford and St Neots. The vehicles were initially taken on hire by United Counties before being purchased from Roadlease Ltd. These vehicles took stock numbers 144 to 149 and were registered J752/3CWT and K758-61FYG. Allocation was split, with the first two being allocated to Bedford, the next pair at Northampton and the final two were added to Huntingdon's allocation. The X5 became a great success for United Counties and a number of coaches were acquired and purchased over the coming years for the service.

To complete the acquisitions for 1995, a 'new' driver training vehicle was taken into stock. Two years before, United Counties hired a Leyland Titan PD3 registered FCD292D from Hampshire bus. This vehicle was taken into stock by the company in July 1995 when it took up ancillary rolling stock number 1003.

The final Iveco minibuses operating the 'Corby Magic Mini' network were withdrawn over the course of 1995. Members of the original batch, 301 to 314, were replaced by newer Ivecos 59-62/4/5/8-71 which in turn had been displaced by the intake of Mercedes minibuses.

1995 saw another crop of buses gain all-over advertisements. Two additional Volvo B6 machines were added to the small number already wearing advertising wraps. January saw 408 (L408JBD) used to promote the company's Goldsaver Bedford freedom ticket. June saw similar 414 (L414JBD) gain an advertisement for Richard Tebbutt's Toyota dealership in Bromham. Northampton based Volvo Olympian 677 (L677HNV) received an all-over advertisement for Airflow Garage in Northampton to promote the multi-carwash facility. United Counties won the contract for transport to and from Cambridge Regional College. For this, two Bristol VRT machines were repainted into a silver livery advertising the college. The vehicles used were 871 (TNH871R) and 903 (CBD903T). A trio of Bedford based vehicles gained adverts for the Travelwise scheme introduced by Bedfordshire County Council. Between September and October 1995, Mercedes minibus 350 (K350ANV), Volvo B6 409 (L409JBD) and Leyland Olympian 639 (G639EVV) gained varying versions of this livery. At the same time, Leyland Olympian 636 (F636YRP) was painted black to advertise the *Bedfordshire Times and Citizen* newspaper. A fifth vehicle, 610 (ARP610X), was also treated to an all-over advertisement during October. This vehicle was decorated to promote the Northants Chamber of Commerce, Training and Enterprise. The final vehicle to be treated to an all-over advertisement was Bristol VRT 940 (URP940W) which was used to promote *Northants Evening Telegraph*.

A couple of other livery changes to note for 1995 were of coach 115 losing National livery in favour of the Stagecoach stripe Coachlinks livery, this being done during May 1995. Not so much a livery change, but the application of branding was applied to a pair of Iveco minibuses at Northampton depot. The company did this as a response to competition from Trinity Bus & Coach of Northampton on the service between Northampton Town Centre and Weston Favell. Two new routes were introduced, the 80 and 81, operated predominantly by Ivecos 51 and 53 which were adorned with 'Weston Favell Stagecoach' and 'Eastern District's Own Friendly Service'.

Volvo B6 422 – L422MVV had to be returned to Volvo Bus UK in June and did not return until July. During this period of time, Volvo loaned similar vehicle M262KWK to United Counties to allow the work to be carried out. The vehicle was placed into service wearing an all-white livery relieved by United Counties names.

During 1995, London United placed an order for 10.3m long Alexander bodied Volvo Olympian double-deck machines to replace older MCW Metrobus machines on the King's Cross to Heathrow Airport Airbus service. There were concerns that the length of these vehicles would create traffic problems at the King's Cross terminus. To help demonstrate that this would not be a problem, United Counties Leyland Olympian 714 – J620GCR was placed on loan for a day in June to London United.

Three double-deck vehicles were taken on loan by United Counties during 1995. The first were two Bristol VRT machines from Cumberland Motor Services which were allocated to Huntingdon and Kettering for the duration of their stay with United Counties. The vehicles were registered KRM432/3W; these two vehicles were given temporary stock numbers 968 and 969. A solitary Leyland Fleetline open topper, registered MBE613R, was hired by United Counties from Grimsby-Cleethorpes Transport during December 1995, returning to its rightful owner in March 1996. This vehicle was put to use as a tree lopper by United Counties.

1996

The lack of new rolling stock for 1995 was compensated for during 1996 when new vehicle orders consisted of twenty-nine Mercedes-Benz 709D minibuses, six Volvo B10M coaches, seven Volvo Olympian double-decks and three Dennis Dart midibuses.

The order for the Mercedes minibuses was reduced by three vehicles to twenty-six. These were all taken into stock during May and June 1996 when they took rolling stock numbers 301 to 326, registered N301-326XRP. Three were allocated to Northampton, eleven to Kettering and the remaining twelve to Bedford. The introduction of these minibuses allowed the withdrawal of the remaining Iveco minibuses, as well as some of the earlier Mercedes-Benz minibuses to be cascaded onto the 'Corby Magic Mini' network. 355 – K355ANV was down seated from twenty-five to twenty-one seats as an experiment prior to others of the batch being done. This proved successful, resulting in 350-365 being converted in October. The three that were not taken into stock were reallocated around the Stagecoach group.

Before looking at any more new deliveries, it should be noted that on 2 January 1996, two vehicles were involved in a fire at Northampton depot. The vehicles concerned were Leyland Tiger 109 – A109TRP and AEC Routemaster 709 – HVS936. The Routemaster was severely damaged in the fire, whilst the Leyland Tiger was written off. A replacement for the Leyland Tiger was sourced, in the form of a Plaxton Paramount 3500 bodied Volvo B10M coach from Premier Travel Services. The vehicle in question was registered F107NRT and gained matching fleet number 107. The vehicle was painted into Stagecoach stripes complete with blue Coachlinks logos.

To give the Coachlinks fleet a more modern appearance, six Plaxton Premiere bodied Volvo B10M machines arrived with United Counties during October 1996. These vehicles took up stock numbers 168 to 173 – P168-73KBD and all were put to use from Kettering.

The seven Volvo Olympians put in an appearance during October and November 1996. Bodywork had reverted from Northern Counties to the Alexander RL model which had been updated since the last had been taken into stock by United Counties. These vehicles took stock numbers 686 to 692 – P686-692JBD and were allocated to Northampton where they displaced older Olympians to Corby, Kettering and Bedford. The registrations of three of these vehicles did not correspond with the chassis numbers held by the DVLC, the problem being rectified by January 1997.

The last vehicles to enter the fleet arrived during December in the form of three Alexander Dash bodied Dennis Dart saloons. Northampton garage again benefited from these new vehicles which became numbered 450 to 452 (P450-2KRP). By this time, the Alexander Dash body had been remodelled to give it a more modern appearance, giving these vehicles a different look from the numerous Alexander Dash bodied Volvo B6 saloons in stock with the company.

Bristol VRT 939 (URP939W) was the first vehicle to gain an all-over advertisement during 1996, joining sister vehicle 940 in a similar livery for the *Northamptonshire Evening Telegraph*. A fifth vehicle was added to the fleet of vehicles advertising Bedford based Michael Peters. Again, the vehicle used was a Volvo B6, this time 402 (L402JBD) was treated. Volvo Olympian 681 (L681HNV) was painted into an all-over advertisement for Northampton Market. A similar advert was applied to Northampton based Volvo B6 saloon 422 (L422MVV) promoting Bedford Market. This advert was applied to 422 by mistake, being intended for 401 (L401JBD). To rectify the mistake, 422 was reallocated to Bedford in exchange for 401. June saw the application of an advertisement for the Vindis Audi garage in Bedford applied to Volvo B6 405 (L405JBD). Two Mercedes-Benz 709D minibuses gained all-over advertisements during 1996. The first was 370 (L370JBD) which was used to promote De Montfort University, Bedford. The second was sister vehicle 371 (L371JBD) which gained one for Gareth Woodfine Solicitors of Bedford and Sandy, joining Volvo B6 417 which was already in this livery.

Work had to be undertaken on some of the company's fleet of Volvo B10M coaches during the year. To cover for their absence two similar vehicles were loaned to United Counties. The first coach was registered G33TCU and was loaned to the company between February and March 1996, arriving from Kirkby Bus & Coach Sales. The second vehicle was registered G150XFT and was loaned between April and November, and like the other vehicle hired, they both carried the Plaxton Paramount 3500 body.

1997

Thirty-one vehicles entered the United Counties fleet during 1997, with all but one being new.

Before considering the new rolling stock, we look at the solitary acquired vehicle. January 1997 saw a Ford R1114 coach taken on loan from Stagecoach Midland Red. The vehicle was registered MKV86V and was loaned for driver training duties. This vehicle proved popular with United Counties which purchased it in May 1997. Upon entry into the fleet, it took up rolling stock number 1004, replacing driver trainer 1002 as a driver training vehicle, the latter vehicle becoming open-top for use as a tree lopper.

The first new vehicles came in the form of thirteen Plaxton Premiere Interurban bodied Volvo B10M coaches. These were delivered in place of the desired Alexander PS bodied Volvo B10M saloons required by United Counties. The coaches arrived between October and December 1997, taking stock numbers 174 to 186, registered R174-186DNH. All thirteen were garaged at Kettering where they replaced older Volvo B10M coaches to Bedford depot where they in turn replaced Leyland Tiger coaches.

Twenty Alexander RL bodied Volvo Olympians were also allotted to United Counties. The order was split between ten dual-purpose and ten bus-seated models. The order was slightly reduced to nineteen when one of the dual-purpose machines was diverted to another Stagecoach operator. Further to this, only nine bus-seated buses were received, as one of these was delivered as a dual-purpose vehicle in error. These vehicles took stock numbers 693-9, 701/2 and were registered R693-9, 701/2DNH. To distinguish them, the dual-purpose vehicles took up stock numbers 560 to 568 and were registered R560-8DRP. The additional dual-purpose vehicle was to have been numbered 703 – R703DNH, and this vehicle originally carried this stock number. It was soon renumbered to 559 in line with the other dual-purpose seated vehicles in the fleet. In January 1998 this vehicle was re-registered WLT528. 567 and 568 were not received by the company until January 1998. The dual-purpose vehicles were allocated to Bedford where they were branded for the Coachlinks network; the bus-seated Olympians finding a home at Northampton.

The withdrawal of the Leyland Tiger coaches from service led to a number of re-registrations during November. Coaches 83/6/7/8/9 lost registrations 83CBD and TSU639-642, gaining registrations A294ANH and FKK839-42Y. The cherished registrations were reallocated to the Volvo B10M coaches operating the X5 service. 144/5 – J752/3CWT gained registrations TSU639/40, 146 - K758FYG gained registration 83CBD and 148/9 – K760/1FYG became TSU641/2.

More all-over advertisements were applied to United Counties vehicles over the course of the year. To stand out, Leyland Olympian 661 (K661UNH) gained a semi-advertisement where it retained Stagecoach corporate livery but the slogan 'Follow Bedford Bear and shop in Bedford' was applied to it. The first full all-over advertisement was applied to Volvo B6 419 (L419JBD) which joined 422 promoting Bedford Market, being completed during May. Around the same time a trio of Olympians gained an advertisement for the Airflow Garage of Northampton. The chosen vehicles were Leyland Olympians 658/9 and Volvo Olympian 673, and were completed in April, May and June respectively. Leyland Olympian 636 (F636YRP) received a revised white-based version of an advertisement for *Bedfordshire Times and Citizen* newspaper group. Next, Volvo Olympian 678 (L678HNV) was treated to an all-over advertisement for Comtel. The final vehicle to gain an advertising wrap was Leyland Olympian 660 (K660UNH) which gained a pink based livery for British Petroleum.

Following a requirement laid out by the Office of Fair Trading, Stagecoach Holdings PLC was forced to sell their operations in Milton Keynes and Huntingdon. Milton Keynes had fallen into the hands of sister company Stagecoach Cambus. In due course, Huntingdon, along with Milton Keynes, was sold off to Julian Peddle who was operating as MK Metro Ltd. The Office of Fair Trading originally wanted Bedford and Biggleswade to be sold off by Stagecoach instead of Milton Keynes and Huntingdon. This deal took effect from 15 April 1997, although Huntingdon vehicles began to operate with MK Metro discs prior to this date. In total, thirty-four vehicles were transferred to MK Metro Ltd. The vehicles concerned being listed below:

Volvo B6: 426-31 L426-8XVV, M429/30BNV
Leyland Olympian: 650-53 H650-3VVV; 711/2 K711/2ASC
Bristol VRT: 723 LFJ853W; 725 LFJ854W; 731 FDV809V; 732 FDV838V; 733 LFJ868W; 737 FDV811V; 750 FAO417V; 751 FAO418V; 871 TNH871R; 872 TNH872R; 873 TNH873R;
889 XNV889S; 890 XNV890S; 891 XNV891S; 902 CBD902T; 903 CBD903T; 908 FRP908T;
910 FRP910T; 926 ONH926V; 948 VVV948W; 953 VVV953W; 954 VVV954W; 972 KRU846W

Volvo B6 saloons 423-5 L423-5XVV and Bristol VRT machines 722 (LFJ863W) and 944 (URP944W) were also to be included in the sale, but due to the loss of contracts, the three B6s were transferred to Northampton and the two VRTs were replaced by similar 723 and 948. As a goodwill gesture, United Counties painted 428 (L428XVV) into Premier Buses blue and yellow livery free of charge.

1998

Thirty-four vehicles were taken into stock over the course of 1998. The planned deliveries of new rolling stock for 1998 consisted of ten Volvo Olympians and nine Dennis Dart SLF low-floor single-decks. The remainder of the intake was formed of acquired vehicles from various sources.

The first two new vehicles to arrive during 1998 were the two outstanding Volvo Olympians, 567/8 – R567/8DRP, mentioned under the 1997 heading. Both vehicles were taken into stock during January 1998.

An arrangement was made with sister company Stagecoach Cambus/Viscount operations for the exchange of three coaches for a similar number of vehicles. United Counties had a surplus number of coach-seated vehicles and 168 to 170 – P168-70KBD were transferred to Stagecoach Cambus between April and May 1998. Passing the other way were three Northern Counties bodied Volvo Olympian machines registered P569-571EFL. The vehicles were numbered 703 to 705 by United Counties and were placed in service from Bedford.

To modernise their fleet, Stagecoach London were taking stock of a large number of new vehicles which in turn meant a cascade of older vehicles to Stagecoach's provincial operations. United Counties was allocated seventeen Leyland Titan machines that had been displaced from both the SelKent and East London operations. Prior to entering service, these vehicles were converted to a single-door layout. Only three were taken into stock over the course of 1998, the remainder arrived during 1999. The first arrived registered NUW595Y, and given rolling stock number 800, being acquired in May. The second machine arrived in June, registered NUW588Y. It took up rolling stock number 801, later being renumbered 810. The final Titan to arrive in 1998 was registered B96WUV, numbered 814. Like the Leyland Fleetlines taken into stock in 1995, the Leyland Titans were all allocated to Corby garage.

New rolling stock began to be delivered during October 1998, when the first seven of the ten Volvo Olympians were taken into stock. Carrying Alexander RL bodies, these new vehicles were received by Northampton depot registered S756-62DRP, taking stock numbers 756-762DRP. The final three arrived during December, preceding the October deliveries numbered 753 to 755, S753-5DRP.

United Counties received its first low-floor vehicles during October when a fleet of nine Dennis Dart SLF saloons arrived, again being allocated to Northampton. The batch were allocated rolling stock numbers 453 to 461 and carried matching S-CVV registration marks. Carrying the stylish Alexander ALX200 bodywork, these vehicles wore the Stagecoach stripe livery, complete with the widely used 'Lo-Liner' brand denoting that these vehicles were low-floor machines.

United Counties upgraded the driver training fleet during 1998 when the two remaining Leyland Titan PD3 machines were withdrawn. Over the year, the company was suffering from a staff shortage and extra machines were acquired to help train drivers. Sourced from Busways Travel were a trio of Bristol LH machines which arrived during February. These vehicles took stock numbers 1005 to 1007 and were registered TCL142R, WEX929S and SVL834R. Also to help the cause, a quartet of former Ministry of Defence Dodge Commando saloons were acquired through Eastwood Commercial Motors of Birmingham. Rolling Stock numbers 1008 to 1011 were allocated to these vehicles which were registered C249UNV, E32RNV, D692ENV and C508UNV. These machines were allocated to Kettering, Northampton, Bedford and Corby respectively.

A couple of vehicles were re-registered during 1998. January saw Leyland Olympian 612 revert to its original registration D382XRS, with cherished plate WLT528 being transferred to 559 – R703DNH. Leyland Tiger 116 – VLT255 lost this cherished plate, reverting back to B357KNH. The VLT255 mark being reallocated to 147 – K759FYG, one of the Stagecoach Express X5 coaches.

Four vehicles were decorated with all-over advertisements during 1998. The first was yet another Volvo B6 saloon. 403 (L403JBD) gained a green based livery for Kempston estate agent Waldens, being completed in February. Next to be treated was Kettering based Mercedes-Benz 709D 339 (M339DRP) which received an advert for Kettering and Corby local radio station KCBC. Volvo Olympian 695 (R695DNH) was used to advertise radio station, 'Northants 96'. Leyland Olympian 660 (K660UNH) lost its advertisement for British Petroleum in favour of a blue based livery for Marie Curie Cancer Care Centre. This vehicle wore this advert for a number of years.

United Counties loaned Volvo Olympian 702 (R702DNH) to Stagecoach Cheltenham & Gloucester which required it to operate a private hire commitment. It was exchanged for Leyland Olympian 104 (G104AAD). A vehicle shortage at Kettering led to the hire of a Bristol VRT registered RTH927S from local independent Rodgers Coaches of Weldon.

1999

1999 saw twenty-six vehicles taken into stock by United Counties, with a mere three being new vehicles.

The fourteen outstanding Leyland Titan machines were taken into stock over the March to December period. 801-9/11-3 were registered NUW553/4/6/7/8/69/76/65/84/90Y, A632THV and B99WUV. The final two were numbered 815 and 816, registered B117WUV and A830SUL.

The Stagecoach Group had shares in the Virgin West Coast Main Line train service. The company decided to commence a number of Rail Link services connecting to the service around the country. United Counties was one company to be chosen to operate one of these services. It was set up to operate between Milton Keynes and Luton Airport, with the vehicles being garaged at Bedford. For this service, three Volvo B10M coaches were taken into stock from Thames Transit Ltd. These Berkhof bodied machines were previously used on the Oxford Tube express service between London and Oxford. The three vehicles in question were appropriately registered 6253VC, 9258VC and 9737VC, which took up stock numbers 164 to 166. A special dedicated livery was applied to these vehicles, this being a red and white livery with Virgin Trains logos and route branding applied.

The only new vehicles to enter the fleet were three more Alexander ALX200 bodied Dennis Dart SLF saloons. 462 to 464 arrived in August 1999 registered T462-4ONV. However, these vehicles did not enter service until September so were re-registered V462-4TVV. Joining the nine delivered the previous year on Northampton town services, these vehicles were again branded as 'Lo-Liners'.

The last vehicles to be taken into stock during 1999 were six Volvo B10M coaches, again sourced from Thames Transit Ltd. These machines arrived to replace the 'J' and 'K' registered Volvo B10M coaches employed on the X5 service. During September and October 1999, five Jonckheere Deauville and a Berkhof Excellence were taken into stock for such use. The latter vehicle was registered M105XBW and carried stock number 105. The five Jonckheere coaches were initially numbered 101 – L155LBW; 102 - L157LBW; 103 – L158LBW; 104 – L159LBW and 106 – L156LBW. United Counties took the decision during October to renumber two of these. 101 became L158LBW and 103 – L155LBW. All six were branded for the service, with the major towns and cities displayed on the side windows, complete with a big Stagecoach Express logo on the sides and front.

1999 saw six vehicles receive all-over advertisements. First was Mercedes-Benz 709D 370 (L370JBD) which had its red De Montfort University livery replaced by a purple one for the same University. 422 (L422MVV) lost its advertisement for Bedford Markets in favour of one for Chicago Computers, Bedford. Two Leyland Olympians gained advertisements for Northamptonshire newspapers. 667 (K667UNH) gained one for the *Kettering Evening Telegraph*, whilst 668 (K668UNH) gained one for the *Citizen*. These vehicles replaced similar advertisements that had been applied to VRTs 939 and 940. Interestingly, 939 received the Stagecoach colours for the first time in September 1999, having been used as an advertising bus for a period of fourteen years. The final two vehicles gained advertisements for Autohaus of Kettering. The vehicles chosen were Mercedes minibuses 308 (N308XRP) and 354 (K354ANV), both being completed during December 1999.

At the start of the year, Kettering experienced a minibus shortage. To compensate for this, United Counties hired a Mercedes-Benz 709D from sister company Stagecoach Cambus. They loaned the company 209 (N642VSS) for a period of six days before it was required for use back with Cambus.

In a bid to attract passengers away from the local taxis in Corby, United Counties relaunched the town services under the Corby Magic Mini brand. For this, a livery of black with gold stripes was introduced to a small fleet of Iveco minibuses. 303 – D726YBV was one of a number of these minibuses acquired in 1990 for this operation. It is seen on layover at Corby Bus Station.
D.J. Hancock

One of two coaches taken into stock by United Counties from the Stagecoach Malawi operations was Duple Laser bodied Leyland Tiger 116. It was originally registered B357KNH with the company but later gained cherished registration VLT255. It is seen at Northampton wearing Stagecoach stripes, complete with Coachlinks fleet names.
Gary Seamarks

1991 saw a small batch of Alexander RL bodied Leyland Olympians acquired from Northern Scottish. These were shorter than those purchased by United Counties during the late 1980s. 615 – 685DYE was originally registered D379XRS. It is seen loading at St Pauls Square, Bedford, on town service 107. *Gary Seamarks*

In contrast, 1992 saw the acquisition of the Megadekka F110NES tri-axle Leyland Olympian from Stagecoach East Midlands. This vehicle served Bedford very well over the years and has now been added to the Stagecoach Heritage fleet. Upon entry into the fleet, this vehicle was allotted rolling stock number 600. It is seen departing Bedford Bus Station. *Gary Seamarks*

Between 1992 and 1996, a number of Alexander bodied Mercedes-Benz 709D minibuses entered service at all of United Counties' garages. The initial few batches were used to displace the numerous Iveco minibuses that had been delivered during the late 1980s. Like them, they were branded as 'Street Shuttles', with 357 – K357ANV showing off the branding well whilst sitting at Bedford Bus Station. This batch of 'K' registered machines later replaced the Iveco minibuses on the Corby Magic Mini network. *Gary Seamarks*.

The 709D was modified after the first batch around the destination display as seen above. 319 – N319XRP represents the 1996 cohort of deliveries. It is seen exiting Bedford station heading towards nearby Clapham on town service 109. *Gary Seamarks*

1992 and 1993 proved to be busy years for the intake of new vehicles by United Counties. A number of Northern Counties bodied Olympian machines were taken into stock by the company. Fifteen Leyland Olympians were taken into stock in 1992, represented here by 664 – K664UNH seen at rest in Bedford. *Gary Seamarks*.

Outwardly, there was no physical difference between the Northern Counties bodied Leyland and Volvo Olympians received by United Counties. Representing the intake of fifteen Volvo Olympians is 682 – L682HNV which is seen entering the old Greyfriars Bus Station in Northampton. *D.J. Hancock*

164 • UNITED COUNTIES BUSES

Like the Olympians mentioned previously, the intake of midibuses in 1992 and 1993 also bore no difference in appearance from each other. The initial intake was of a small batch of Alexander Dash bodied Dennis Dart saloons at Northampton. 452 – K106XHG is seen operating a Northampton town service entering Greyfriars Bus Station. *D.J. Hancock*

The mainstay of the 1990s midibus fleet was the Volvo B6, with forty-two being operated at varying times by the company, some for longer than others. One of the longer serving B6 saloons was 418 – L418JBD, a vehicle that operated from Bedford garage for its life with United Counties. The introduction of twenty-one of these vehicles replaced double-deck operation on key town services in Bedford. It is seen loading in Midland Road, Bedford, an area now pedestrianised, bound for the small nearby town of Kempston. *Gary Seamarks*

The third batch of Volvo B6 saloons to operate with United Counties were allocated to Huntingdon garage. 427 – L427XVV is showing off the batch well here as it exits Huntingdon Bus Station. This vehicle later transferred across to Huntingdon & District in 1997. *Gary Seamarks*

Representing the large number of Alexander Dash bodied Volvo B6 saloons which gained all-over advertisements during their careers is 402 – L402JBD. It is seen wearing a multi-coloured advertisement for Bedford based company Michael R. Peters, for which many of the type carried advertisements. It is seen about to cross Bedford's Town Bridge whilst heading out to the Harrowden Road area of Bedford. *Gary Seamarks*

166 • UNITED COUNTIES BUSES

370 – L370JBD carried two advertisements for the now non-existent De Montfort University in Bedford. It is seen here carrying the second, purple version of the livery, about to leave Bedford Bus Station for the nearby village of Pavenham. *Gary Seamarks*

Another Bedford-based vehicle to gain an all-over advertisement was Alexander RL bodied Leyland Olympian 636 – F636YRP. It is seen here arriving at the town's bus station having completed a journey on route 179. This black based livery was the original one it carried for the *Bedford Times and Citizen* newspaper. *Gary Seamarks*

158 – L158JNH was new to United Counties in August 1993 for use on the Coachlinks network. This photograph shows it operating a more mundane local country service passing through Kettering. *Gary Seamarks*

The X5 between Cambridge and Oxford was launched in 1995 using a small batch of Plaxton Premiere bodied Volvo B10M coaches acquired from Roadlease, Sheffield. 146 – K758FYG is seen leaving Bedford for Cambridge, showing off its full branding. A brief comparison between the old and new Plaxton coach styles can be made with the Paramount bodied Tiger in the left of the photograph. *Gary Seamarks*.

168 • UNITED COUNTIES BUSES

The slightly more modern Plaxton Premiere Interurban is seen in this photograph of 171 – P171KBD. It is seen approaching journey's end in Oxford City Centre having just completed a journey on the X5, although it is carrying Coachlinks branding. This vehicle would later be converted to a 70-seater school bus for operation at Bedford garage. *Gary Seamarks*

As a result of school contract gains in the Bedfordshire and Huntingdon areas, a batch of thirteen Leyland Fleetlines machines with varying body styles were taken into stock from various sources. Due to their height, they were all allocated to Corby garage allowing Bristol VRT machines to be cascaded to the area required. Seen at the town's Bus Station is 989 – OCU804R, carrying Alexander bodywork. The Corby Magic Mini livery can be seen on the Iveco on the right. *D.J. Hancock*

A trio of ECW bodied Bristol LH saloons were acquired by United Counties in February 1998 from fellow Stagecoach subsidiary Busways. They were all put to use as driver training vehicles and for this they gained an all-yellow livery. SVL834R was numerically the last of the trio, numbered 1007. It is seen at the rear of Bedford garage. *Roger Warwick Collection*

October 1998 saw the introduction of the first low-floor buses to the United Counties fleet. A batch of nine Alexander ALX200 bodied Dennis Dart SLF saloons were allocated to Northampton, where they were primarily used on town services 15/15A. To promote the low-floor feature, Stagecoach as a group branded the vehicles as 'Lo-Liner' which can be seen applied to 455 (S455CVV) heading toward the Northampton district of Blackthorn. *Roger Warwick Collection*

Six former Oxford Tube coaches were taken into stock in 1999 by United Counties, this time to replace the hired Plaxton coaches on the X5 service. Five of these vehicles were Jonckheere Deauville models and are represented here by 101 – WLT908. *Gary Seamarks*

Along with the five Jonckheere bodied Volvo B10M coaches from Stagecoach Oxford in 1999 came a solitary Berkhof bodied machine for use on the X5. M105XBW was allocated rolling stock number 105 and is seen loading at Milton Keynes Rail Station whilst bound for Cambridge. The Stagecoach Express names and route branding applied is clearly visible in this photograph. *794 Preservation Group*

A new service linking Milton Keynes Station and Luton Airport was introduced in 1999, using a trio of former Oxford Tube coaches. 165 – N45MJO is seen out of service in the rear yard of Bedford garage. The service operated under the Virgin Rail Links brand, and a different livery was applied to the vehicles, which can be seen above. Appropriate branding was also applied to the vehicles. The service later became commercial and was numbered the 99. *David Beddall*

The intake of a number of new, low-floor vehicles by Stagecoach London saw a number of older London buses become obsolete. Many of the provincial Stagecoach operations received examples of these vehicles, with United Counties being no exception. Seventeen Leyland Titan machines were taken into stock at Corby garage. 813 – B99WUV is seen on layover at the former Corby Bus Station. *David Beddall*

2000–2009

2000

A mere eight vehicles were taken into stock by United Counties over the course of 2000, all being second-hand vehicles.

First to arrive were a trio of Alexander Dash bodied Volvo B6 saloons from Stagecoach Midland Red. These vehicles carried registration marks L451 to 453YAC and were allocated stock numbers 426 to 428. Swapped with similar bodied Dennis Dart saloons 450 to 452 (P450-2KRP), these vehicles were initially garaged at Northampton, before joining the remainder of the Volvo B6 fleet at Bedford.

The ancillary fleet gained two new members over the course of the year. The first vehicle was a Reeve Burgess bodied Mercedes-Benz L608D minibus sourced from Stagecoach Cumberland. Registered D560RCK, this vehicle was numbered 1012 and was acquired to replace Bristol LH 1007 – SVL834R on driver training duties in July 2000. It was added to Bedford's allocation. The second vehicle was also acquired for driver training duties, and was the fifth Dodge Commando saloon to be acquired by the company. Arriving into stock in August, this vehicle was allotted rolling stock number 1013 and was registered D780GNV. This vehicle was allocated to Northampton garage.

A fourth Berkhof Excellence was acquired for use on the Virgin Rail Link service between Milton Keynes and Luton Airport. 167 – 3063VC was taken into stock in December from Stagecoach Midland Red and joined the three similar vehicles acquired the previous year at Bedford depot. Unlike the other three, 167 already wore the Virgin Rail Link livery so a change of branding was all that was needed.

The final vehicles to be acquired were a pair of ECW bodied Leyland Olympians which were acquired from sister company Stagecoach Cambus. Allocated to Bedford, these vehicles were allotted fleet numbers 651 and 653, registered A561KWY and A683KDV respectively.

The last Leyland Tiger coach that dominated the United Counties coaching fleet during the 1980s and early 1990s were withdrawn from service. 120 to 122 – C120-2PNV left the fleet over the course of the year.

2001

Stagecoach relaunched its UK bus operations during 2001. This involved the reorganisation of companies into groups, and a new livery introduced replacing the stripes. The new livery was known as the Rolling Ball livery and incorporated the red, orange, blue and white colours of the previous livery. United Counties was placed into a

group with Stagecoach Cambus and Stagecoach Viscount, forming the new Stagecoach East group. Control for the United Counties garages remained at Northampton, with new fleet names 'Stagecoach in Bedford' and 'Stagecoach in Northants' being adopted, replacing the Stagecoach United Counties fleet names on the vehicles.
Thirteen second-hand vehicles were taken into stock over the course of 2001.

Before we take a look at the vehicles taken into United Counties stock, we first consider the loss of seven coaches to fellow Stagecoach East company Stagecoach Viscount, comprising four Plaxton Premieres and three Jonckheeres. The Plaxton coaches lost to Viscount were 153/4 – K153/4DNV and 155/6 – L155/6JNH; whilst 101-3 were the Jonckheere coaches transferred, by which time had been re-registered to WLT908, 647DYE and WLT682. In addition, a solitary Alexander bodied Volvo Olympian was transferred to Stagecoach Viscount. The vehicle in question was Northampton based 762 S762DRP which left the fleet during April. At the same time, Bedford based Jonckheere coach 106 was placed on loan to Stagecoach Viscount.

The first vehicles to be taken into stock by the company were six Leyland Olympians arriving in January. The first carried ECW bodywork and was acquired from Cambus, being part of the same batch as the two acquired in December 2000. The vehicle in question took rolling stock number 652 – A681KDV which joined Bedford's allocation. The remaining five double-deck vehicles were Northern Counties bodied Leyland Olympians, again being sourced from Cambus. They retained the fleet numbers of their previous operator, being numbered 508 to 512, registered F508-12NJE. Bedford was the recipient of these vehicles. The Northern Counties bodywork applied to these vehicles varied from those purchased new by United Counties in the early 1990s, in that the bottom rear window was indented, in a similar style to the Leyland Titan machine.

Northampton's low-floor fleet was increased by a further two acquired from Viscount in June 2001. R356LER and R366JVA were the vehicles concerned, and these two vehicles were allocated rolling stock numbers 448 and 449. These machines were further Alexander ALX200 bodied Dennis Dart SLF saloons.

Yet another ancillary vehicle was taken into stock during August 2001, again from Stagecoach Cumberland which had become part of the Stagecoach North West group. The Mercedes-Benz 609D minibus introduced another new style of bodywork to the company, this being constructed by North West Coach Sales. The minibus was numbered 1015 by United Counties, registered H838GLD. It was put to use as a driver training vehicle from Kettering depot.

The final four vehicles arrived during November. The first was a solitary Volvo B6 saloon, from the L-YAC batch, which United Counties had acquired three of the previous year. L454YAC became numbered 429 and joined the others at Bedford. It entered the fleet from Cambus, which had acquired it from Midland Red at the same time as Northampton acquired the other three.

The remaining three were Alexander RL bodied Volvo Olympians acquired from Viscount. Like the Leyland Olympians acquired earlier in the year, 584 to 586 – R584-6JVA retained the fleet numbers of their previous owner. These three were also added to Bedford's allocation during November.

Corby based Leyland Titan 804 – NUW557Y was withdrawn from service by United Counties during August and was placed on loan to Stagecoach in Cambridge during September.

During the year, United Counties withdrew tree lopper 1002 PRX191B. This vehicle was not replaced by them.

2002

For the third consecutive year, United Counties received no new rolling stock. Second-hand vehicles were again taken into stock, with nine arriving over the year.

The first arrived during January from Stagecoach Cambus in the form of a pair of Northern Counties bodied Volvo Olympians. These vehicles were numbered 526 and 527, registered P526/7EFL. Northampton gained the use of 526, whilst 527 entered service at Bedford.

January also saw the arrival of two ECW bodied Leyland Olympians from Stagecoach Midland Red. The vehicles in question took up rolling stock numbers 521 and 522 and were registered A546/7HAC. Corby and Kettering benefitted from their use.

A surprise acquisition took place in May when a pair of ECW bodied Bristol FLF Lodekka machines were acquired by United Counties from Stagecoach Viscount. These vehicles took stock numbers 952 and 953, and were registered JAH552/3D. Both vehicles were quickly repainted into a purple, white and gold version of the new Stagecoach livery to celebrate Her Majesty the Queen's Golden Jubilee. 952 was an open top vehicle, whilst sister 953 was closed topped. Both vehicles were allocated to Northampton garage.

The amalgamation of the United Counties, Cambus and Viscount fleets led to the better utilisation of the fleet operating with all three companies. Vehicles were swapped internally as required which will be seen throughout this chapter. There were a number of fleet number clashes between vehicles in the United Counties, Cambus and Viscount fleets. To sort this situation, the executives at Stagecoach East took the decision to introduce a single fleet numbering sequence to the group, taking effect from May 2002. In comparison to the other two fleets, United Counties escaped the majority of the renumbering, with just the Dennis Dart SLF saloons, a handful of Olympians and Leyland Titans/Bristol VRTs being renumbered. The vehicles were renumbered as follows:

Dennis Dart SLF: 453 - 464 to 233 - 244; 448/9 to 256, 266
Leyland Olympians: 651 - 653 to 518 - 520; 713 - 716 to 723 - 726; 708 - 710 to 728 - 730
Volvo Olympians: 560 - 568 to 740 – 748; 559 to 749; 701/2 to 751/2
Leyland Titans: 803/5/8/6/7/9/10/11/12/16/14/13/15 to 903 – 910, 912 - 916
Bristol VRT: 849 to 949

June saw three additional Plaxton Premiere bodied Volvo B10Ms leave the United Counties fleet. 157 L157JNH was transferred to sister company Viscount, whilst 158/9 L158/9JNH moved to Cambus.

Three Plaxton Premiere bodied Volvo B10M coaches left the United Counties fleet shortly after purchase in 1996. The vehicles in question were 168 to 170, P168-70KBD. These vehicles returned to United Counties during June when they were allocated to Northampton. They were used there on the newly introduced Stagecoach Express service X7 between Northampton and Leicester. These vehicles, like those used on the X5, were repainted into new livery and branded up for the service.

Alexander bodied Leyland Olympian 647 – G647EVV went on loan to Viscount, operating in the Peterborough area during November.

It is worth a note here that by April 2002, United Counties were operating just two Bristol VRT machines, a type that once dominated the fleet. The two remaining VRTs were numbered 849 and 966. Both were operated from Bedford depot. However, by October these two machines were withdrawn from service, being replaced by two Leyland Olympians on school contracts.

2002 saw the upgrade of vehicles used on the Stagecoach Express X5 service using cascaded Plaxton Premiere bodied Volvo B10M coaches that had previously operated on the Coachlinks network from Kettering. The vehicles concerned were 181 to 186 – R181-6DNH which were reallocated to Bedford where they gained the new Stagecoach livery and appropriate branding.

The application of all-over advertisements slowed down in the new millennium. Alexander ALX200 bodied Dennis Dart SLF saloon 463 – V463TVV gained an advertisement for Autohaus Garage of Northampton and Kettering, similar to that applied to a couple of Mercedes-Benz 709D minibuses. This vehicle was treated to this livery in June.

The repainting of vehicles into the new rolling ball livery had progressed slowly over the course of 2001 and the early part of 2002. The first vehicles to receive this livery were Mercedes-Benz 709D minibus 305 – N305XRP which was the first single-deck in the new livery, the first Dart SLFs. were 256/266, the first Volvo B6 in new livery was 419 L419JBD and the first double-deck was 699 – R699DNH.

August 2002 saw North West Coach Sales bodied Mercedes-Benz 609D 1016 transferred from Stagecoach in Peterborough to Kettering, registered H839GLD. This vehicle was converted into a van.

2003

From January, Stagecoach UK Bus replaced the local fleet numbers applied across the country to a single numbering system where no fleet numbers were duplicated. The main purpose of this change was to allow the easy transfer of vehicles within the Stagecoach group. It also made it easier to fuel Stagecoach buses at any Stagecoach garage in the country, as the fuel logs were computerised. Each vehicle was given a number for life. The United Counties fleet was renumbered as follows:

Leyland Titan
903-16 to 10556/9/65/9/76/84/8/90, 10830, 11034/96/9/117
   (NUW556/9/65/9/76/84/8/90Y, A830SUL, A634THV, B96/9, 117WUV)

Leyland Olympians
600 to 14000 F110NES
601-11 to 14001-11 ARP601-11X
620-49 to 14020-49 F620-33MSL, F634MSP, F635-8YRP, G640-9EVV
654 to 14054 H654VVV
655-70 to 14055-70 K655-70UNH
618/6-7/2-4 to 14472/6/7/9/82-4 C472SSO, GSO6/7V, D379/82/3/4XRS
724-6 to 14493-5 J620-2JCR
508-12 to 14508-12 F508-12NJE
728-30/23 to 14708-10/3 J808WFS, K709/10/3ASC
521/2/18-20 to 14946-50 A546/7HAC, A561KWY, A681/3KDV

Volvo Olympian
749/40-8/51-61 to 16209-232 83CBD, R560-8DRP, S753-62DRP
527/6/69-71 to 16527/55/69-71 P527/6/69-71EFL

584-586 to 16584-6 R584-6JVA
671-685 to 16671-85 L671-84HNV, L685JBD
686-99 to 16688-99 P686-92JBD, R693-9DNH

Bristol FLF
952/3 to 19952/3 JAH552/3D

Volvo B6
401-422 to 30401-22 L401-21JBD, L422MVV
423-425 to 30423-5 L423-5XVV
426-429 to 30551-4 L451-4YAC

Dennis Dart SLF
233-44 to 33453-64 S453-61CVV, V462-4TVV
255/6 to 33396/9 R356LER, R366JVA

Mercedes-Benz 709D
301-326 to 40301-26 N301-26XRP
332/4-49 to 40332/4-49 M332/4-49DRP
350-59 to 40350-9 K350-9ANV
360-83 to 40360-83 L360-80JBD, L381-3NBD

Mercedes-Benz 609D
1015 to 41983 H838GLD

Mercedes-Benz L608D
1012 to 41998 D560RCK

Dodge Commando G13
1008-1014 to 48010/2/43/5/61/2 C249, 508ENV, D682, 780ENV, E32RNV, E36RRP

Volvo B10M
106/4 to 52021/4 L156/9LBW
164-7 to 52032/3/5/6 6253, 3063, 9258, 9737VC
150-4 to 52120-4 K150-4DNV
160-62 to 52160-2 L160-2JNH
168-73 to 52368-73 P168-73KBD
174-86 to 52474-86 R174-86DNH

The United Counties fleet hadn't seen significant investment in new vehicles since 1997/8. This left United Counties with an ageing fleet and one that was becoming more unreliable. Seventy-four vehicles were taken into stock over the course of 2003, with thirty-seven of these vehicles being new. The order for new rolling stock called for eleven Optare Solo midibuses and twenty-six Transbus Dart saloons.

By 2003, Corby had the oldest fleet of all United Counties depots, having a fleet of 'K' and 'L' registered Mercedes-Benz 709D minibuses, Leyland Titans and Leyland Olympians. A start was made in 2003 to modernise the Corby fleet by introducing the eleven Optare Solo machines to this depot. These were the first new vehicles to be taken into stock by United Counties since 1999. Funding for these vehicles partly came from Northamptonshire County Council. Delivered during

May 2003, these vehicles took up rolling stock numbers 47029 to 47039 and carried new registrations KX03KYS-W/Y-Z, KZA-D. These were the first United Counties vehicles to carry the new style registration series and the new Stagecoach interior. The introduction of these new vehicles also saw the introduction of a new livery, two-tone orange with the brand 'Corby Star' applied to them. 47037 KX03KZB was delivered to United Counties as KX03KAB, but this mistake was quickly rectified and was correctly registered KX03KZB.

The twenty-six Transbus Dart/Transbus Pointer machines were taken into stock during November. These vehicles took stock numbers 34419-44 KV53EYU/W-Z, EZA-H/J-P/R/T/U/W/X/Z. These vehicles were put to use on a revised town network in Bedford where they replaced the fleet of Volvo B6 saloons. Six Volvo B6 machines were initially retained by United Counties, these being 30401/3/14/7/8/22, all of which wore all-over advertisements. 30410/5 were placed on loan to Stagecoach Viscount, which was also the destination of 30553 which became a permanent transfer to that company. Major roadworks in Kempston led to the delay in the arrival of these from September to November. These roadworks led to the loan of a number of single-deck vehicles to Bedford which will be explored later in this chapter.

Before taking a look at the number of acquired vehicles from other companies, a number of former United Counties vehicles were taken back into stock during the year. Four were Plaxton Premiere bodied Volvo B10M coaches registered K153/4DNV and L155/6JNH. This quartet were originally numbered 153 to 156 with United Counties but gained new national fleet numbers 52123/4 and 52155/6 whilst at Peterborough. Returning to the company in September, Bedford received 52123/4 whilst the other pair were placed into service from Northampton. Leyland Olympian 647 – G647EVV and Volvo Olympian 762 – S762DRP were also repatriated to United Counties during March, and like the coaches they had been renumbered as 14047 and 16232 respectively. At the same time Bedford lost Northern Counties bodied Volvo Olympian 16527 – P527EFL when it transferred back to Stagecoach Cambus.

Between March and April, United Counties took four Northern Counties bodied Volvo Olympians into stock. Three were sourced from Stagecoach London whilst the last came from Peterborough. The trio of London Olympians were numbered 16113, 16167 and 16174 – R113XNO, R167/74HHK. 16113 was added to Bedford's allocation, whilst Northampton took stock of the latter two machines. The former Peterborough Olympian was registered P528EFL and carried rolling stock number 16528, joining the two London Olympians at Northampton.

Six additional coaches were taken into stock during 2003 in the form of Plaxton Expressliner bodied Volvo B10Ms. The first two arrived from Cambus in April. The vehicles concerned were numbered 52108 and 52109, registered ACZ7490/1 and both were allocated to Northampton depot.

The next four were sourced from Stagecoach North West and were of the slightly remodelled Expressliner 2 model. These vehicles were acquired to replace the Berkhof Excellence bodied B10M coaches on the Virgin Rail Link service between Luton Airport and Milton Keynes. A change in colour was applied to these vehicles, comprising a silver and red based livery with yellow relief on the front of the vehicles. Appropriate branding was also applied to these vehicles. Like the previous Virgin Rail Link vehicles, this batch were allocated to Bedford. These vehicles were numbered 52329 to 52332 and were registered N129-32VAO, being re-registered with the cherished registration plates from the Berkhof coaches. 52330/2 were the first to be taken into stock in August, 52329 in September, with 52331 being the last to arrive in October.

A further Northern Counties bodied Volvo Olympian was taken into stock from Cambus in September. The vehicle concerned was 16527 – P527EFL which re-entered the United Counties fleet after a brief period of operation with Cambus.

The last three months of 2003, October in particular, saw a number of second-hand vehicles arrive with United Counties. First to arrive in October were Alexander Dash bodied Dennis Dart saloons 32772/4-6, registered N772/4-6RVK from Stagecoach Viscount. These vehicles were allocated to Northampton where they were pressed into service on the town network. These vehicles were joined by Plaxton Pointer bodied Dennis Dart 32771 – M771DRG which was acquired from the same source. A similar vehicle registered L756VNL was taken into stock from the same source in December, numbered 32756 it was also allocated to Northampton.

More arrivals in October came in the shape of eleven Northern Counties bodied Volvo Olympian machines from Cambus. Possessing rolling stock numbers 16004-7 and 16431-7, these vehicles were registered P804-7GMU and VLT255, WLT512, WLT528, WLT682, WLT908, 647DYE and 685DYE, the latter seven carrying the cherished registrations previously carried by United Counties Routemasters. All seven were added to Northampton's allocation.

The final four vehicles to be taken into stock by United Counties arrived during December. Three double-deck machines and a solitary coach arrived over the course of the month. The double-deck machines were from the P-EFL batch from Stagecoach Viscount. 16537-9 – P537-9EFL were taken into stock. The coach was registered N451XVA and was another Plaxton Expressliner 2 bodied Volvo B10M model. This vehicle carried stock number 52301. All four vehicles were allocated to Bedford.

Many vehicles gained repaints into the new corporate livery over the course of 2003. One vehicle was chosen for an all-over advertisement during the year. The vehicle concerned was Volvo B6 30414 – L414JBD which gained an advert for KIA Motors, Bromham, replacing the previous advert for the Toyota Garage in Bromham carried by this vehicle, being completed by the end of August.

As mentioned above, the coaches taken into stock for the Virgin Rail Link service were registered prior to entering service. 52329-32 (N129-32VAO) gained new registration marks 3063, 6253, 9258 and 9737VC respectively. This led to 52032/3/5/6 losing these marks in favour of original registrations N46/3/5/2MJO, the latter coaches being added to the ancillary fleet as driver training vehicles. A new, predominantly blue with orange and red stripes livery was adopted for vehicles on such duties.

Volvo B6 30552 – L452YAC was involved in a serious accident whilst in service in Stewartby, a village to the south of Bedford. Severe damage was sustained by this vehicle which led to its withdrawal.

Four vehicles were taken on loan by United Counties during 2003. The first three were Alexander Dash bodied Dennis Dart saloons from Stagecoach Viscount. They were taken into stock to assist United Counties when one of the major trunk roads into Bedford was closed due to roadworks. The division route involved a low bridge, restricting the services to single-decks. The vehicles concerned were numbered 32650-2 – N350-2YFL.

The final vehicle to be taken into stock came from Transbus International and was in the form of a Transbus Dart MPD registered SN03LGA. The vehicle was loaned for demonstration purposes for the upcoming fleet renewal at Bedford. The vehicle wore a blue and white livery and carried Transbus fleet names.

2004

2004 was another good year for the intake of vehicles. No less than eighty-three new and second-hand vehicles entered service with United Counties. Thirty-nine of these vehicles were new stock which United Counties were successful in securing, all being allocated to the Northamptonshire operations.

The first were eleven Transbus Trident/ALX400 machines. These were the first new double-deck machines received by United Counties since 1998 and were the first low-floor double-decks to enter service with United Counties. Delivered between March and May 2004 and joined to Kettering's allocation, these Tridents took rolling stock numbers 18101 to 18111 and carried registrations KX04RDY/Z, REU, RFE/F, RVJ/F/K/C/M/N. These vehicles replaced Volvo Olympians on a revamped service X4. The service was extended from Northampton to Milton Keynes and continued north-east to Peterborough. The vehicles gained branding for the service which was branded 'Cross County X4' in green and white lettering.

Corby was the next to receive new vehicles, further upgrading the fleet. The first batch of vehicles came in the form of five East Lancs bodied Scania OmniDekka machines. Registered KX04RCU/Y/Z, RDU/V these vehicles were numbered 15401 to 15405. They entered the fleet between March and April 2004. Like the Optare Solo minibuses delivered the previous year, these vehicles wore the orange, red and yellow Corby Star livery. These vehicles were the first of their type to be acquired by Stagecoach, with funding coming partially from Northamptonshire County Council.

A further four Optare Solos arrived during March, being allocated to Corby to enhance the Corby Star network. The vehicles were numbered 47042-5 – KX04RBV/Y/Z, RCF. An additional Solo was sourced and arrived during April when it took up stock number 47046 – KX04RCU, joining these others at Corby. An unusual acquisition was of a Renault/Rohill vehicle registered KS03HNL. The vehicle gained the Corby Star livery and was numbered 48203, entering service from Corby.

Eleven Transbus Dart/Pointer machines were taken into stock during June 2004, the first new vehicles for Northampton since 1999. These vehicles were allotted rolling stock numbers 34585 to 34595, registered KX04RUW/Y, RVA/C/E/P, KP04GZL-N/R/S. All eleven saloons entered service on Northampton town service 1 during July, where they displaced seven Volvo Olympian machines.

The final new vehicles to be taken into stock were also allocated to Northampton and were in the form of seven Optare Solo machines. These vehicles were purchased as a result of direct competition between United Counties and First Northampton. The two companies competed on a number of town services in Northampton. The Optare Solo machines were put onto a new service in competition with First's service 4, the United Counties service being numbered 4U. 47123-9 – KN54XYP/R/T/U/V/W/X arrived in November and gained appropriate route branding for this new service.

The first of the second-hand vehicles to be acquired were eight Alexander ALX200 bodied Dennis Dart SLF saloons from Stagecoach Cambus. These vehicles were registered R813-9, 720YUD and took up stock numbers 33813-33820. These vehicles were added to Northampton's allocation where they helped to provide the public with a modern, low-floor fleet on the town network whilst competing with First Northampton which, at the time, had a considerably elderly fleet.

An unusual acquisition took place in August 2004 when a former Hong Kong Citybus Alexander bodied Leyland Olympian was taken into stock. The vehicle concerned was registered H46GBD and took up rolling stock 13626. This vehicle was painted into Megabus.com livery and was garaged at Northampton and acted as a spare vehicle for the Megabus network. Northampton gained this vehicle as it was deemed the closest garage to the M1 motorway in case of a breakdown. This was a low-cost interurban network of services introduced over the course of 2003 and 2004 by Stagecoach using former Hong Kong Leyland Olympians. The vehicle remained with United Counties for only a couple of months before being reallocated to Stagecoach South Midlands' Rugby depot.

Over the course of 2004, United Counties set out to replace its remaining fleet of Volvo B6 saloons. To start the process, two Alexander Dash bodied Dennis Dart saloons arrived from Stagecoach South East. These vehicles were numbered 32542/50 – J542/50GCD and both joined Bedford's allocation.

United Counties encountered an arson attack on 16 September, when eleven vehicles were destroyed at the company's Biggleswade outstation. The vehicles destroyed were Leyland Olympians 14031 F631MSL, 14037 F637YRP, 14039/41/4 G639/41/4EVV and 14065 K665UNH and Volvo Olympians 16211 R561DRP and 16585 R585JVA, Plaxton Pointer bodied Dennis Dart 32756 L756VNL, Alexander bodied Mercedes-Benz 709D 40326 N326XRP and Volvo B10M 52122 K152DNV.

To cover for the loss of these vehicles on a short-term basis, a number of vehicles were drafted in from other Stagecoach East depots and other Stagecoach companies. Local independent Barfordian Coaches also provided a solitary vehicle. Volvo Olympians 16139 – R139EVX, 16582 – R582JVA and 16590 – S590BCE came on loan from Peterborough. Cambridge loaned Leyland Olympians 14525 – H475CEG and Volvo Olympian 16023 – P823GMU. Northampton provided Megabus double-deck 13626 and Transbus Dart 34590. Five Northern Counties bodied Scania double-deck machines were also taken on loan from Stagecoach South East. 15332/51/2/8/62 were in the process of being transferred to Stagecoach Manchester, being diverted to Bedford on the way through. Manchester provided Volvo Olympians 16754/65/71/5. The final vehicle was former United Counties Bristol VRT SNV931W from Barfordian Coaches.

On a more permanent basis, a number of vehicles were taken into stock from various sources. First were three Northern Counties bodied Volvo Olympians from Stagecoach North West. The vehicles concerned were numbered 16243-5 and registered L243-5SDY, all being allocated to Bedford. Alexander bodied Leyland Olympians 14472/6/7/9/83/4 which were already in United Counties ownership were transferred from Corby to Bedford. They were replaced at Corby by six Leyland Olympians. From Stagecoach South Midlands came ECW bodied Olympians 14935/7 – C962/4XVC. Stagecoach North East provided four Leyland Olympians to United Counties, these being Northern Counties bodied 13026 – A26ORJ; ECW bodied 14179 – C179ECK; Leyland bodied 14520 – F41XCS and Alexander RH bodied 14631 – C631LFT. A replacement for Dennis Dart 32756 was sourced from Stagecoach South East. It came in the form of an Alexander Dash bodied Dennis Dart registered K575HNC, numbered 32575. This latter vehicle was allocated to Bedford and arrived a week after the fire.

A pair of Alexander bodied Mercedes-Benz 709D minibuses were acquired from Stagecoach South Midlands. The vehicles were numbered 40137/9 – M337/9LHP and were allocated to Northampton depot. The final vehicle to make its way to United Counties during September was Optare Solo 47050 – KP04HVR. This vehicle was new to Wilsons Coaches and was swapped with them for Renault Rolhill 48203. The Solo joined similar vehicles on the Corby Star network, already being in this livery before acquisition.

A programme to upgrade the coaches on the Stagecoach Express X5 service commenced in October when United Counties acquired eighteen Plaxton Expressliner 2 bodied Volvo B10M coaches from various Stagecoach companies. B10Ms from five different batches were acquired between October and December, these being formerly used by Stagecoach on National Express work. The batches concerned were 52382/7 – P622/7ESO; 52434-9 – R34-9AKV; 52444/5/7 – R454/5/3FCE; 52450-4 R450-4JDF and 52493/4 R663/4TKU. The first two vehicles came from Stagecoach East Scotland, 52434-9, 52444/7 and 52450/1 from Stagecoach South Midlands, 52493/4 from Stagecoach East Midlands and 52445, 52452/3 from Stagecoach North West. 52454 – R554JDF was due to be transferred to United Counties but was caught up in the Carlisle floods of January 2005, in which around eighty Stagecoach vehicles were damaged. 52454 was towed to Bedford for assessment but the decision was taken not to repair the vehicle. All coaches were repainted into the new corporate livery. The X5 service was relaunched, with the Stagecoach Express name being dropped in favour of the new brand 'Cross County' with a red logo and white and yellow writing being applied to vehicles, along with landmarks from Oxford, Milton Keynes and Cambridge. The arrival of these vehicles allowed the withdrawal of Plaxton Premiere bodied B10M coaches 52474-9 which transferred out to Stagecoach South East.

A fourth Alexander Dash bodied Dennis Dart was acquired from Stagecoach South East in October. 32582 - J702YRM joined similar vehicles at Bedford, where it entered service wearing the stripe livery rather than the new corporate livery.

Three United Counties vehicles were involved in accidents during 2004. Firstly, Northampton based Transbus Darts 34585/93 were involved in a collision with each other whilst in service after one came under attack from youths. Both were seriously damaged but were repaired and placed back into service. The third vehicle was Mercedes minibus 40325 – N325XRP which had to be withdrawn from service after suffering severe accident damage.

A replacement was found for 40325, being acquired from Stagecoach South Midlands. The vehicle was numbered 40140 – M340LHP and was allocated to Bedford.

As mentioned above, the intake of the Alexander bodied Dennis Dart saloons led to the demise of the Volvo B6 saloons, with 30418 being the last operated by United Counties.

The driver training fleet was boosted by the addition of Jonckheere bodied Volvo B10M coaches 52021/4. These gained the new corporate driver training livery, similar to that applied to the former Virgin Rail Link coaches.

A solitary vehicle gained an all over advertisement during 2004. Bedford based 34422 – KV53EYY was treated to a predominantly white based livery for Gareth Woodfine Solicitors.

2005

Compared with the previous two years, 2005 proved to be a quiet year for the intake of new vehicles. Seventeen new and second-hand vehicles entered the fleet during the year.

The new vehicles comprised a trio of Alexander Dennis Pointer bodied Darts, all of which were allocated to Northampton. These vehicles were delivered to United Counties during November. They took up stock numbers 34771 to 34773, registered KX55UDB/D/E. They helped to boost the modern image of Stagecoach in the town.

Following further significant investment in the Stagecoach London operation, a number of vehicles were displaced from London service and were put to further use in the provinces. Five Dennis Dart SLF saloons were allocated to United Counties in February 2005 when three with Alexander ALX200 bodies and two Plaxton Pointer MPDs were taken into stock. All five were shorter vehicles than had previously operated with the company. The ALX200 models were numbered 34097/8 and 34102, registered S497/8BWC and S102WHK. The two Plaxtons were numbered 34141 and 34160 – V141/60MVX. All five were allocated to Northampton where they were put to use on yet another service introduced to compete with First Northampton. This time it was numbered the K9 and carried branding for this service between the town centre and Kings Heath.

During August, Bedford lost four dual-purpose Volvo Olympians (16213-5/8 – R563DRP, etc) in favour of four bus-seated Volvo Olympians, these being swapped with Viscount. Northern Counties bodied 16534 – P534EFL and Alexander bodied 16580/2/3 were taken into stock by United Counties.

Stagecoach reacquired a number of the low-floor machines that were involved in the Carlisle flooding during January 2005. The result of the floods saw Carlisle gain a new fleet of vehicles, which led to the re-distribution of the reacquired vehicles around the Stagecoach group. One such vehicle was allocated to United Counties which placed it into service at Bedford garage. The vehicle acquired was a Transbus Pointer Dart saloon 34580 – PX04DSE, taken into stock during August.

Bedfordshire County Council was trying to resolve the congestion in Bedford town centre. Part of the solution came in 2005 when a new Park & Ride site was constructed near the village of Elstow, just to the south of the town. United Counties was chosen to operate the new Elstow Park and Ride scheme which commenced in November. For this service, Bedfordshire County Council had acquired four Alexander ALX200 bodied Dennis Dart SLF saloons from Bharat Travel. These vehicles were allocated rolling stock numbers 33181 to 33184 by Stagecoach, registered VX51RBY/Z, RCF/U. The livery chosen for these vehicles was green and blue with appropriate Park and Ride branding, along with Bedfordshire County Council logos.

On 30 January 2005 the new Cross County X5 service was relaunched. By this time, the coaches that had been acquired the previous year had been refurbished and repainted into new corporate livery, and had branding applied to them.

2006

The lack of new rolling stock taken during 2005 was more than made up for in 2006 when eighty-six new and second-hand vehicles entered the fleet. Seventy of these vehicles were new buses, with a number of them being partly funded by both Northamptonshire and Bedfordshire County Councils. The year also saw a number of United Counties route networks relaunched which led to the introduction of many of the new vehicles.

First to arrive were three second-hand Plaxton Pointer bodied Dennis Dart saloons from Stagecoach Devon. These Darts were exchanged with Devon for Leyland Olympians 14510 to 14512 – F510-2NJE. The Darts were numbered 32139 to 32141 and carried registration plates L139-41VRH. All three were repainted into new corporate livery before arriving with United Counties, and were allocated to Bedford depot.

Another exchange was made, this time with Stagecoach Manchester. They required two double-deck machines, with United Counties sending Volvo Olympians 16004 and 16005 north. United Counties received Alexander PS bodied Volvo B10M saloons

20852/3 – P852/3GND, the first of their type to operate with the company. Both were allocated to Northampton.

The first of the new rolling stock arrived in February in the form of ten Alexander Dennis Dart/Pointer saloons. Registered KX06JYH/J-L/N-P/R-T, these vehicles were numbered 34826 to 34835. They entered service during March on a revamped network of services between Bedford, Biggleswade and Hitchin. All ten were allocated to Bedford where they displaced elderly Leyland Olympians on this group of services. Over the course of the year, the principal country services that operated from Bedford were to be re-branded, given planet names. The above batch of services were branded for Mars, giving the vehicles a smart appearance. Five more arrived during April. They numerically preceded the Mars batch, being numbered 34821 to 34825, KX06JXU/V, JYU, LNU/V. The first four vehicles were allocated to Kettering where they were placed into service on a relaunched service 19 between Kettering and Desborough, for which 34821-3 were branded. 34824 and 34825 were unbranded, the latter vehicle acting as a spare for the Mars network at Bedford.

March and April saw another batch of low-floor double-decks enter the fleet. 18400 to 18410 were registered KX06JXW, JYC-G/T/Y/Z, JYA/B. 18400-6/10 were added to Northampton's allocation where they received branding for service X46 between Northampton, Wellingborough and Raunds, with 18410 remaining unbranded. The missing vehicles, 18407 to 18409, were allocated to Kettering where they were used to enhance the Cross County X4 service for which they gained branding.

The biggest reorganisations of a route network during 2006 was the re-launch of the Kettering and Wellingborough town networks. To operate these services, a batch of eighteen Optare Solo minibuses were taken into stock by United Counties to replace an ageing fleet of Mercedes-Benz minibuses. Over the course of March and April, these vehicles were received by the company numbered 47401 to 47418. Registrations KX55PEO, PFA/D-G/J/K/N/O/U/V/Y/Z, PGE/F/K/O were carried. These vehicles were partly funded by Northamptonshire County Council, and they wore a green livery. 47401-12 gained branding for Connect Kettering, 47413-6 Connect Wellingborough, the final two just simply branded as Connect, acting as spares for the two networks.

The Connect network was expanded further during May and June which required four additional Optare Solo minibuses. These four machines were transferred from Corby to Kettering, these being 47029 to 47032 and repainted from orange to green. The transfer of these vehicles left Corby short of four vehicles. The gap was filled by the arrival of four additional minibuses numbered 47338 to 47341. These vehicles were registered KX06TYF/G/H/K, all being painted orange.

The Bedford minibus network underwent a transformation during October. For this, a third batch of Optare Solos were taken into stock by United Counties. Seven new and one second-hand machine were taken into stock by Bedford. Funded by Bedfordshire County Council, these vehicles wore a light blue version of the new Stagecoach livery, appropriately being branded as the Blue Solo. The vehicles concerned were numbered 47435 to 47442, and were registered YN53SVV, YJ56AOL-P/R/S. 47435 had previously operated with Expresslines of Bedford on a Park & Ride service under the Bedford Dart brand.

Six Alexander Dash bodied Dennis Dart saloons were taken into stock in October 2006. They took up stock numbers 32002-4/6-8 – P102-4HNH and P450-2KRP, being acquired from Stagecoach South Midlands. All six were added to Bedford's allocation.

32006 – 32008 were new to United Counties in 1996 as 450 to 452 before being transferred in 2000 to Midland Red. 32002-4 gained branding for the V1 Venus service between Bedford and Wootton/Cranfield, replacing Volvo Olympians which were not required on these services. 32007/8 gained branding for route 51 between Bedford and Clapham/Oakley, and 32006 remaining unbranded.

The Virgin Rail Link between Milton Keynes and Luton Airport received six new coaches during October 2006. These were in the form of Plaxton Profile bodied Volvo B7R machines registered KX56JZJ-O. These vehicles were garaged at Bedford numbered 53271-6. A livery of red and silver was applied to these vehicles with route branding. 53272 went on loan for a few months at Northampton, remaining in all red. These were the first wheelchair-accessible coaches to operate with the company.

The final new vehicles to be taken into stock during the year were nine Alexander Dennis Pointer Dart machines in November. Allocated to Northampton, these vehicles were put to use on route 16 and gained branding for this service. The vehicles in question took stock numbers 35218 to 35226 – KX56JYY/Z, JZA/C-H.

The final intake of second-hand vehicles was undertaken during December in the form of five Alexander PS bodied Volvo B10M saloons. 20201/6, 20809/14/6 were allocated to Bedford registered M201LHP, N206TDU, N809/14/6DNE. Acquired from Stagecoach South Midlands, 20201/814/6 were reallocated to Northampton, whilst 20206/809 remained at Bedford.

The re-launch of the Bedford country services saw a number of vehicles gain branding for the various services. Volvo Olympian 16672 and 16674 were branded for the Pluto service P1 between Bedford and Northampton, 16677/8/80 gained branding for Mercury M50 service between Bedford, Rushden and Kettering, 16527/8/34/7-9 gained branding for Jupiter services J1/2 to Flitwick and Clophill, 16580/2-4/6 gained branding for Venus service V1 between Bedford, Wootton and Cranfield, and 16243-5 gained branding for Saturn S1 service between Bedford and Luton.

2007

2007 was another quiet year for vehicles entering the United Counties fleet. The first vehicle arrived during February when Alexander PS bodied Volvo B10M 20813 – N813DNE arrived from Stagecoach South Midlands. This vehicle joined Bedford's allocation and gained branding for the Jupiter service, and was joined by similar 20206, 20809/14/6 on the same service where they replaced double-deck machines.

Northern Counties bodied Volvo Olympian 16008 – P808GMU was acquired from Stagecoach Cambus during March 2007. This vehicle was acquired for use on a school contract at Bedford.

April saw four Volvo B10M machines enter the United Counties fleet. Three carried the Alexander PS body style, the fourth being a Jonckheere Mistral bodied coach. The single-deck machines were numbered 20202, 20217/8 – M202LHP and M217/8HBD and were allocated to Northampton. The Jonckheere Mistral bodied Volvo B10M coach arrived from Stagecoach Glasgow. This vehicle was a smart-looking vehicle and was allocated to Bedford, registered KSU461 and numbered 52644.

A plan was put into place to convert the Bedford allocation to single-deck, removing all double-decks from the fleet. A number of Volvo Olympians were transferred to Stagecoach West Scotland with which a deal had been made to swap Volvo B10M saloons for the Volvo Olympians. Alexander PS bodied B10M 20326 – N326VMS was acquired from Stagecoach West Scotland during September 2007. The arrangement was however cancelled so this was the only example to be received by United Counties. 20326 was added to Bedford's allocation.

Stagecoach Red & White Coaches 52402 arrived at Bedford for conversion into a school coach and went on trial from this garage. It was used to see the suitability of seventy-seater coaches on such contracts. This trial was successful and as a result, a programme commenced during May whereby a fleet of surplus coaches stored at Bedford began to be converted to seventy-seater coaches. Over the course of May and November this programme progressed and the coaches were repainted into a yellow version of Stagecoach's livery. The coaches converted were 52155/6/60/1/2, 52368-73, 52482-4 – L155/6/60/1/2JNH, P168/73KBD and R182-4DNH as well as, 52124 – K154DNV and 52486 – R186DNH.

United Counties wished to replace the coaches operating the Cross County X5 service. The company had the idea of replacing coaches with double-deck vehicles. As a result, the company converted a surplus dual-purpose double-decker for use on the X5 service; the conversion was completed in February 2007 when Bedford based Alexander RL bodied Volvo Olympian 16209 – R34TAC emerged branded for the Cross County X5 in a special livery where the front of the top deck was painted red instead of blue in the standard livery. It also had a bike rack fitted to the rear of the lower deck.

Four similar Volvo Olympians were repainted into dedicated school liveries for use on school contracts in the Bedford area. First to be completed was 16228 – S758DRP which received a two-tone blue livery with a yellow front roof dome for the 'Biggleswade & District Bus Users Association' and was used to transport school children to Bedford's independent schools, being completed by July. This was followed by 16223/4 – S753/4DRP which received a two-tone green livery with a yellow roof dome from the 'Shefford & District Bus Users Association'. The final two were 16227 – S757DRP and 16229 – S759DRP which also received the two-tone blue livery during October and November. These vehicles had undergone refurbishment and had seat belts and CCTV cameras installed.

A new scheme was introduced by Stagecoach during November known as 'greenbybus.com'. This saw many of Bedford's Transbus Dart saloons receive branding for this scheme. In addition to this, 34432 – KV53EZJ gained a one-side contra-vision advert for this scheme.

2008

2008 was yet another quiet year in terms of vehicles being taken into stock by the company. Initial vehicle orders for 2008 called for a batch of seven ADL Enviro 200 bodied MAN 14.240 saloons for operation in Northampton.

The seven ADL Enviro 200 machines were the first to arrive with the company. Six of these vehicles were numbered 39694-8/700, these vehicles carried registrations KX08HRA/C/D/E/F/J, all arriving in May 2008. The seventh, 39699, was involved in an accident whilst on delivery so was sent back to ADL for repairs, therefore, this vehicle was re-registered to KX58JZG, arriving with the company in June. All seven were put to use on routes 9 and 9a between Northampton and Duston.

United Counties were seeking a replacement for the Plaxton Expressliner bodied Volvo B10M coaches operating the Cross County X5 service during 2008. June saw the arrival of a Plaxton Panther bodied Volvo B9R coach on loan from Plaxton, Scarborough. It was put to use on the X5 from Bedford to test the suitability of the type on the service. The trial was a success and an order for seventeen of the type was placed. The first two arrived with United Counties during December, registered KX58NBN and KX58NBO respectively. These gained rolling stock numbers 53605 and 53606.

Another route upgrade, this time for the X4 between Peterborough and Milton Keynes, saw ten ADL Enviro 400 bodied Scania N230UD machines taken into stock from Stagecoach Manchester. The first two to arrive were 15452 and 15453 – MX08GHZ, GJE. They made an appearance at Kettering depot in December. The rest followed in the early part of 2009.

A trio of Alexander PS bodied Volvo B10M saloons were branded for the X7 service (Northampton-Leicester). The vehicles concerned were 20201/2 and 20217 respectively.

2009

2009 proved to be a busier year for the intake of vehicles by United Counties, with thirty-seven new and second-hand buses arriving. An order for twelve ADL Enviro 300 machines was placed, again for Northampton.

The remainder of the Plaxton Panther bodied Volvo B9R coaches for the X5 arrived at Bedford during January. They took up stock numbers 53601-4/7-17 and were registered KX58BJ/K/L/M/Y/Z, NCA/C/D/E/F/J/N/O/U. 53614 was badly damaged in a fatal accident when only two weeks old. The impact caused the coach to catch fire.

The remainder of the Scania N230UD double-deck machines arrived from Stagecoach Manchester in January 2009. These vehicles were numbered 15444-9/54/5, and carried registrations MX08GHH/J/K/N/O/U, GJF/G. They joined the two delivered in December the previous year at Kettering, displacing the Transbus Tridents (18101-11) from the service. The Tridents were re-deployed for further use with United Counties.

The new ADL Enviro 300 single-deck machines were taken into stock in April and May, carrying the MAN 18.240 chassis. These vehicles took up rolling stock numbers 22832-43 and were registered KX09BGU/V/Y/Z, BHA/D/E/F/J/K/L/N. They were put to use on route 1 between Northampton Town Centre and Rectory Farm.

Further MAN vehicles to be taken into stock were a pair of Alexander ALX300 bodied MAN 18.220 saloons. 22920 and 22921 were acquired from Stagecoach Oxford in April 2009, registered S920/1CFC. These vehicles were allocated to Northampton depot where they operated route 8 which had been taken over from Northampton Transport.

Three of the Volvo B10M coaches displaced from the X5 service – 52434/5/7 – R34/5/7AKV – were repainted into a red livery and put to use as driver training vehicles.

United Counties gained a pair of publicity vehicles when two Mercedes-Benz 709Ds, 40139 and 40371 (M339LHP, L371JBD), were converted from buses for this use. They also gained a revised Stagecoach livery.

A pair of ECW bodied Leyland Olympians were taken into stock from sister company Cambus in 2000. Representing these two vehicles is A561KWY, originally numbered 651 by United Counties. It is seen on layover at Bedford Bus Station. *David Beddall*

A fourth Berkhof bodied Volvo B10M coach arrived in 2000 from Midland Red South to help cover an increase in the PVR of the VT99 service. Registered 3063VC, this vehicle was allocated fleet number 167. It is seen here in Central Milton Keynes. *David Beddall*

188 • UNITED COUNTIES BUSES

Originally delivered to United Counties in stripes, D560RCK was later repainted into the special Stagecoach training livery. It served the company well, operating from Bedford garage. In 2003, it gained national fleet number 41998 which it is seen carrying in this photograph. *David Beddall*

510 – F510NJE was part of a batch of five Northern Counties bodied Leyland Olympians taken into stock by United Counties from Stagecoach Viscount in 2001. All were allocated to Bedford, where we see 510, and all featured an indented rear lower-deck window similar to that of a Leyland Titan. *Gary Seamarks*

Seen at the now closed Waterden Road, Stratford, garage in London is 19953 – JAH553D. This is one of a pair of Bristol FLF machines taken into stock by United Counties in May 2002. On the day it was put to use on special services around the Stratford and Ilford areas. *David Beddall*

The new order for Bedford town services in 2003 was twenty-six Transbus Dart/Pointer saloons. Representing the batch is 34430 – KV53EZG, seen unloading after completing a trip from the Putnoe area of Bedford. These vehicles gave the Bedford fleet a smart and modern appearance. *David Beddall*

47039 – KX03KZD is seen representing the Corby Star fleet of Optare Solos introduced to the town over the course of 2003 and 2004. The smart orange livery is shown clearly in this photo. It is seen on launch day in Corby town centre. *David Beddall*

The Virgin Rail Link VT99 service introduced in 1999 was upgraded to Plaxton Expressliner 2 bodied Volvo B10M coaches from Stagecoach Cumberland in 2003. A revised livery was also applied to the four vehicles. 52330 is seen in the yard of Bedford garage sporting a cherished registration gained from one of its predecessors. *David Beddall*

An unusual buy by Stagecoach were five Scania OmniDekka machines for the Corby Star network. Partly funded by Northamptonshire County Council, these five vehicles were the only new examples of the type to be taken into stock by Stagecoach. Other second-hand, similar vehicles, were taken into stock by Stagecoach when they acquired the Yorkshire Traction business. 15405 – KX04RDV is seen resting at Corby garage. *David Beddall*

A more traditional double-decker to be taken into stock by Stagecoach was the Transbus Trident/ALX400 model. United Counties received an initial eleven Tridents at Kettering garage to operate the Cross County X4 service between Peterborough and Milton Keynes. 18111 – KX04RVN is seen on layover in Peterborough City Centre complete with appropriate branding for the service. *David Beddall*

Four Alexander Dash bodied Dennis Dart saloons arrived from Stagecoach South East in 2004. In appearance, these vehicles are identical to the Volvo B6 machines previously operated by the company. 32582 – J702YRM is seen at Bedford bus station shortly after a repaint into the new corporate livery. *David Beddall*

Compared to their predecessors, only one Transbus Dart saloon was adorned with an all-over advertisement. 34422 – KV53EYY was the chosen vehicle which advertised Woodfine Batcheldor Solicitors of Bedford. It was treated to this livery in 2004. *David Beddall*

Purchased to operate service 4U in Northampton in direct competition with First Northampton were 47123-47129. 47128 – KN54XYW is seen in Milton Keynes having completed a journey in from Northampton on the X88/X89 'Gold' service. These Solos were put to use on this service after the competition with First Northampton subsided.
David Beddalll

2004 saw the arrival of a number of Plaxton Expressliner 2 bodied Volvo B10M coaches from a number of Stagecoach subsidiaries. They were acquired to upgrade the X5 service from similar vehicles. Representing the type is 52493 – R663TKU seen loading at the old Milton Keynes Coachway bound for Cambridge. The service was relaunched from Stagecoach Express to the 'Cross County' brand, and the branding used can clearly be seen in this photograph.
David Beddall

2005 saw the opening of a Park and Ride site to the south of Bedford. United Counties won the contract for the service and acquired four Alexander ALX200 bodied Dennis Dart SLF saloons with the aid of Bedfordshire County Council. A green and blue livery was applied to the vehicles along with branding for the service. 33183 – VX51RCF shows off the smart livery worn by these vehicles. The service departed from a stop adjacent to the town centre rather than the bus station. *David Beddall*

One of the smarter single-deck types to be operated by United Counties was the Alexander PS bodied Volvo B10M. Over the course of 2005 and 2006, a number arrived with the company from Stagecoach Manchester and Stagecoach Midland Red. 20915 – R915XVM was one of the former Manchester saloons allocated to Bedford garage. *David Beddall*

One of three former London Dennis Darts were taken into stock from Stagecoach Devon in 2006. Corby garage finds 32139 – L139VRH on layover. This vehicle was originally numbered DRL139 with London Buses before transferring to the Stagecoach London operation in September 1994. *David Beddall*

2006 saw the launch of the 'Planets' at Bedford garage. The principal country services gaining branding. The service between Bedford and Luton was branded 'Saturn'. This can be clearly seen in this view of 16245 (L245SDY), a Northern Counties bodied Volvo Olympian transferred to United Counties in September 2004 from Stagecoach North West. This was one of three transferred from this operator to help cover for the loss of a number of vehicles in an arson attack at the Biggleswade outstation. *794 Preservation Group*

The Bedford to Northampton service was re-branded as 'Pluto' using a purple branding. 16674 – L674HNV is seen showing off this branding rather well whilst on layover at Bedford Bus Station. *David Beddall*

Mercury was the branding given to the route operating between Bedford and Kettering. 16678 – L678HNV, a Northern Counties bodied Volvo Olympian, is seen on layover at Bedford Bus Station. *David Beddall*

The Bedford-Flitwick-Dunstable corridor was branded as Jupiter. The service was initially operated by a batch of Northern Counties bodied Volvo Olympians new to Stagecoach Cambus. 16534 – P534EFL looks rather out of place at the Biggleswade outstation. *David Beddall*

The Jupiter route was later cut back to Flitwick and the double-deckers were replaced by former Stagecoach Manchester Alexander PS bodied Volvo B10M saloons. 20816 – N816DNE is seen carrying route branding at Bedford Bus Station. *David Beddall*

The more local county service between Bedford and Cranfield was branded as Venus. For this a small batch of Alexander RL bodied Volvo Olympians were branded. Seen on layover at a foggy Bedford Bus Station is 16580 – R580JVA.
David Beddall

Low passenger numbers meant that the Venus route did not need double-decks to operate. A batch of three Alexander Dash bodied Dennis Darts were soon acquired from Stagecoach Midland Red South and placed into service on this route. 32003 – P103HNH is seen here at Bedford Bus Station carrying appropriate branding for the route.
David Beddall

The Biggleswade and Hitchin routes gained a batch of eleven new single-deckers in 2006 which gained branding for 'Mars'. Representing the batch is 34829 – KX06JYL which is seen parked in the yard of the Biggleswade outstation.
David Beddall

The addition of four ADL Dart/Pointer saloons at Kettering brought the total up to fifteen of the type. 34821 – KX06JXU was numerically the first operated by the company, although the Kettering Darts were delivered after the Bedford batch. it is seen branded for route 19, approaching Kettering town centre.
Liam Farrer-Beddall

The Kettering and Wellingborough town networks gained eighteen Optare Solo machines in 2006. The fleet is represented by 47405- KX55PFF which is branded for Connect Kettering but is seen in Church Street, Wellingborough, operating a Wellingborough town service. *David Beddall*

In 2006, Bedford also received a small batch of Optare Solos to replace the Mercedes-Benz 709D minibus from the town network. The fleet of eight Solos were partly funded by Bedfordshire County Council, with the buses adopting the blue colours of this council. They were branded as the Blue Solo. 47440 – YJ56AOP is seen parked at Bedford bus station. *David Beddall*

The Virgin Rail Link service between Milton Keynes and Luton Airport gained a batch of six new vehicles in 2006. The small batch of Plaxton Profile bodied Volvo B7R coaches received another new livery for the service as shown above. These were the first wheelchair-accessible coaches to operate with United Counties. KX56JZJ was one such vehicle taken into stock, numbered 53271. It is seen loading in Central Milton Keynes bound for Luton Airport. *David Beddall*

In 2007, United Counties refurbished Volvo Olympian 16209 – R34TAC adding in additional luggage racks at the rear of the lower saloon. It was then trialled on the X5 service from Bedford for a number of months. Whilst in this guise it wore a distinctive livery shown above. It is loading at Bedford bus station for a journey to Cambridge. *David Beddall*

The first new MAN vehicles to enter service with United Counties in 2008. Seven were taken into stock to operate the 9/9a services between Northampton town centre and Duston. 39700 – KX08HRJ is seen heading to its terminus on The Drapery. This was the only one that did not carry branding for this service.
Liam Farrer-Beddall

The choice for the X5 replacement was the Plaxton Panther bodied Volvo B9R model. Seventeen were taken into stock over the winter of 2008/9, and the service relaunched in February. 53610 – KX58NCC represent the batch here at Milton Keynes. These coaches were also fitted with wheelchair lifts.
Liam Farrer-Beddall

Former Stagecoach Manchester 15446 – MX08GHK is seen on layover at Milton Keynes Coach Park before operating another journey to Peterborough. These vehicles were acquired to take over from the Transbus Tridents on this service. Unlike their predecessors, these vehicles gained full branding for the service. *David Beddall*

22832 – KX09BGU represents the longer ADL Enviro 300 body style on the MAN 18.220 chassis. Northampton received a batch of these vehicles to operate town service 1. The branding applied to these vehicles can be seen in this photograph. 22832 is seen exiting North Gate bus station in the town. *Liam Farrer-Beddall*

A pair of Alexander ALX300 bodied MAN 18.220 saloons were acquired in 2009 from Stagecoach Oxford. 22920 – S920CFC is seen exiting the old Greyfriars bus station in Northampton branded for route 8. *Liam Farrer-Beddall*

New to East Midland, 52644 – KSU461 was acquired by United Counties from Stagecoach Glasgow. It was predominantly used on the X5 to support the Volvo B9R coaches. This was one of the smartest modern coaches operated by the company. It is seen at rest in Bedford garage. *David Beddall*

THE FINAL YEARS 2010–2014

2010

The 2010 intake saw thirty-eight vehicles enter the United Counties fleet. A small number, nine, of these vehicles were new vehicles, the remainder were vehicles that had been acquired from various sources. Before looking at the intake for the year, it must be noted here that in August, the control of Bedford depot transferred from Northampton to Cambridge. Vehicles continued to operate on the United Counties operators' licence until 2013, and therefore we shall continue to record the vehicle movements until this time. It will be noticeable the number of vehicles that were transferred to Bedford from both Cambus and Viscount.

The first of the new vehicles to be allocated to United Counties consisted of three ADL Enviro 400 bodied Scania N230UD machines similar to those acquired the previous year from Stagecoach Manchester. Registered KX59BBN/O, BCY, these vehicles took up rolling stock numbers 15606 to 15608 respectively. They were allocated to Kettering from where they were placed into service on the X4, with appropriate branding being applied to these vehicles. They arrived with the company in March 2010.

Northampton depot benefitted from the remaining six new vehicles to be taken into stock. This time, these vehicles were integral ADL Enviro 300 single-decks. 27681-6 (KX60AZF/G/J/L/N/O) were delivered to United Counties in October and November 2010.

Sixteen Volvo Olympians were inherited from both Stagecoach East and Stagecoach East Midlands over the course of the year to replace older Leyland Olympians from the fleet. Nine carried Northern Counties bodywork, the remainder the Alexander RL body style.

The Northern Counties bodied Olympians were all former Stagecoach London machines, numbered 16010/3/5/8/20, 16113, 16162/7 and 16174. Registered P810/3/5/8/20GMU, R113XNO and R162/7/74HHK. 16015/8/20, 16113/62/7/74 were all acquired from fellow Stagecoach East garages in May 2010. 16013 arrived in September, and 16010 in October. Bedford took stock of 16010/3 and 16162/7; Corby gained 16015, 16113 and 16174; whilst Northampton was allocated 16018 and 16020.

The Alexander RL bodied Olympians were sourced from Stagecoach East Midlands and were split between Kettering and Corby, with the exception of one which was allocated to Bedford. The vehicles taken into stock were numbered 16454/9/60 – P154KWJ, P159, 460KAK; 16495/6, 16500 – P145/6/50KWJ. 16496 was first to arrive and was the one allocated to Bedford. 16500 arrived in August, followed by 16459/60/90/5 in September. 16454 was last to arrive, taken into stock in December 2010.

Seven Plaxton President bodied Dennis Trident machines were acquired from Stagecoach Viscount in October 2010. Numbered 17691-7 (X701-7JVV), these machines were new to Stagecoach Cambus in 2001 and were the first of their type to operate with the Stagecoach Group. The first three were allocated to Bedford, with the remainder being allocated to Kettering. The latter operated services between Oundle and Peterborough, taken over from Stagecoach Viscount.

Five single-deck machines were taken into stock over the final four months of 2010. The first was Optare Solo machine AE06TWN. Allocated rolling stock number 47354 by Stagecoach, this machine was acquired from Stagecoach East Midlands and allocated to Bedford for use on the local town network.

The remaining four saloons came in the form of Dart machines. September saw the arrival of a pair of Plaxton Pointer bodied Dennis Dart SLF machines at Northampton from Stagecoach East. These vehicles were numbered 33323 and 33324, registered P323/4EFL. The third was an Alexander ALX200 that had previously operated with United Counties in 2005. 34098 – S498BWC re-entered the fleet in October from Stagecoach Midland Red and joined Northampton's allocation. The final example was a more modern ADL Dart/Pointer machine, again acquired from Stagecoach Midland Red. 35176 (KX56KGZ) was new in September 2006 and arrived with United Counties in December 2010 and was allocated to Corby.

The fleet of coaches allocated to Bedford depot for school contracts were repainted in a revised version of the all yellow livery. This time, they received an orange front, yellow sides relieved by a grey skirt.

2011

2011 was a busy year for the intake of vehicles into the United Counties fleet, with fifty-three arriving over the course of the year. Twenty of these vehicles were new rolling stock, whilst the remainder arrived from various sources.

It may be recalled that in 2009, 53614, a new Plaxton Panther coach, was involved in a serious accident which saw the vehicle written off, leaving the X5 allocation a vehicle short. A replacement vehicle was purchased during 2011 when 53618 arrived at Bedford in May. Registered AE11FMF, this was the first vehicle in the United Counties fleet to reflect the Cambus ownership of Bedford depot, represented by the 'A*' registration mark.

The Bedford town network underwent a reorganisation during the year. One of the biggest changes was the renumbering of the Park and Ride service to route 2. This replaced the original service that ran into Kempston, leaving route 1 to cover half of this service. Originally, the service was operated by the original Transbus Dart machines, but due to the increase in passenger numbers on the service, Stagecoach sought some financial help from the local council to purchase some double-deck machines to help ease loadings. These vehicles duly arrived with the company in June 2011, numbered 19888-893. Carrying registration marks AE11FUD/F/G/H/J/M, these vehicles were the first of the AD E40D/ADL Enviro 400 machines to enter service with United Counties. They were soon branded as 'Bedford Bus', similar to the 'Citi' mark adopted by Cambus in Peterborough and Cambridge.

The final batch of new vehicles comprised thirteen ADL Enviro 400 bodied Scania N230UD machines. As with the previous batch of vehicles of this type, they were allocated to Kettering for use on the X4 service. These machines were all delivered in November 2011. This was the first United Counties route to gain 'Gold' status. Fitted with leather seats and to a higher specification, these machines also had a revised version of the Stagecoach livery. Again, these vehicles gained route branding on the sides of the vehicles.

Second-hand vehicles of various types were again taken into stock, including Volvo Olympians, ADL Tridents, Dennis Dart SLF saloons and Optare Solos.

Stagecoach Manchester and Stagecoach East Midlands were the source of the Volvo Olympians, all carrying Alexander RL bodies. East Midlands provided 16492 and 16494 in February and joined others at Kettering depot. Three similar vehicles arrived from Manchester in October and November, numbered 16796 – P726GND and 16755/7 – R755/7DRJ. Again, they were all allocated to Kettering. Two further Olympians were sent to United Counties but were not taken into stock. These were numbered 16786 and 16789 – P716/9GND. In addition to these, Bedford received 16581 – R581JVA in December 2011 from sister company Stagecoach Viscount.

Bedford's double-deck fleet was given a more modern appearance with the arrival of six ADL Trident/ALX400 machines from Stagecoach Viscount. 18411 – 18416 arrived in March 2011 and were registered AE06GZH/J-N respectively.

Seven Wright Crusader bodied Volvo B6BLE saloons were acquired from Stagecoach in the Fens during April 2011. The vehicles concerned were registered R120-6HNK, they were numbered 21160 to 21166 respectively. Allocated to Bedford, these vehicles were very smart in appearance and operated for a number of years with the company. The batch originated with Huntingdon & District and would regularly appear on the once-a-month service between Huntingdon and Bedford.

Various Dennis Dart SLF saloons were taken into stock during the second half of 2011. First to arrive was 33322 – P322EFL, a Plaxton Pointer bodied Dennis Dart SLF. This joined sister vehicles 33323/4 which had arrived the previous year. It was allocated to Corby depot. September saw the arrival of the majority of the single-deck vehicles. Stagecoach Merseyside provided 33132 and 33140/2 – P810/4/9YCW. These vehicles carried Wright bodywork. The first was allocated to Northampton, the other two to Corby. Bedford gained Alexander ALX200 33806 – R706YUD in the same month. Three Pointer bodied machines of varying ages arrived from Stagecoach Midland Red. These were former London 34123 – V175MVX; 34495 – KV53NHM and 35218 – KX56JYY. 34123 was allocated to Corby, whilst Northampton took stock of 34495 and 35218. The final Dart SLF machine was another Alexander ALX200 from the same source. 33356 – P806NJN arrived with United Counties in October 2011 and was allocated to Corby.

The final six vehicles to be taken into stock were five Optare Solos. The first two were numbered 47015 and 47069 – KX51CTV, KN04XKC. Both were acquired from Stagecoach Midland Red in September and joined the Kettering allocation. They were mainly employed on Wellingborough town services. The other three were registered AE06TWV/P/U and were numbered 47351-3. These joined similar 47354 at Bedford.

An all-over advertisement was applied to Bedford based Transbus Dart/Pointer saloon 34421 in January 2011. Based on a pink livery, this vehicle was used to promote the Cancer Research UK campaign.

2012

2012 saw twenty-nine vehicles enter the fleet, with fifteen new vehicles and the remainder being acquired.

Northampton took stock of the fifteen new vehicles, these being Scania K230 saloons complete with ADL Enviro 300 bodywork. 28621-35 – KX12AKY/Z, ALO/U, AMK/O/U/V, ANF/P, AKN/O/P/U/V.

The year started with a pair of Plaxton bodied Volvo B10M coaches from Stagecoach Viscount, arriving in January. 52398 – P108FRS and 52415 – R115OPS were acquired by Bedford depot to replace the driver training fleet.

Five Alexander RL bodied Volvo Olympians were acquired by United Counties in July, with a sixth arriving in September, a seventh arrived in November. 16056, 16070 and 16125 – R156/70VPU, R125EVX all arrived at Bedford from Stagecoach in the Fens. Stagecoach Midland Red provided 16618 and 16619 (S918/9ANH) in July and were allocated to Kettering. 16593 – S593BCE was acquired from Stagecoach in the Fens in September, joining similar vehicles at Bedford. The final Olympian acquired in November also came from Stagecoach Midland Red. 16691 – P691JBD was the vehicle concerned and was one of the original vehicles purchased by United Counties in 1996.

Four Dart SLF saloons arrived with United Counties in 2012. The first arrived in July numbered 34479 – PX53DKF. Like the Volvo Olympians acquired by Bedford, this vehicle came from Stagecoach in the Fens. The remaining three were acquired in November from Stagecoach Midland Red. 34111 to 34113 (V173/12/3MVX) were the vehicles concerned, allocated to Corby.

During the summer of 2012, London hosted the Olympic Games. Prior to this, 27681 went on loan to Stagecoach London for a pre-Olympic event in January 2012. Stagecoach was involved in a large-scale transport operation around the London area, with many of the ADL products operated by the company across the United Kingdom sent down to London. United Counties sent six ADL Enviro 300 saloons, 27681-6, to operate Olympic contracts in London with the newly created Stagecoach UK Bus Events between July and September. However, a number of United Counties vehicles went on loan across the country. Stagecoach Cambus took 15452-5, 15606, 19888-93 and 35218/9 on loan to cover for vehicles seconded to London. 28621 to 28627 were placed on loan with Stagecoach Hampshire Bus. The double-deck machines were loaned between July and September, with the single-deckers being loaned between August and September.

2013

The opening three months of 2013 saw six vehicles enter the United Counties fleet from Cambus, Viscount and Midland Red. From the latter source came Alexander RL bodied Volvo Olympian 16514 – R414XFC. It was sourced in February and was allocated to Northampton. During the same month Bedford was the recipient of a pair of Optare Solo machines from Stagecoach Cambus. 47341 – KX06TYK and 47659 – AJ58RBO were the vehicles in question and were put to use on town services. The first of the pair, 47341, originated with United Counties at Corby.

During February, Bedford was in need of more vehicles fitted with tachographs so that they could be called upon to operate the X5 if needed. Two such vehicles were swapped with Stagecoach Viscount in the form of ADL Enviro 400 machines. 19892 and 19893 moved north to Peterborough whilst 10012/3 – AE12CKD/F were reallocated to Bedford.

The final vehicle to be acquired in February came in the form of a Plaxton Premiere bodied Volvo B10M coach registered R541GSF. This machine came from Cambus and was slotted into Bedford's allocation where it was used as a driver training vehicle.

It may be recalled from earlier in this chapter that the control of Bedford depot moved from Northampton to Cambridge in August 2010. It took until the end of March

2013 before the vehicles were added to the Cambus operators' licence, along with Stagecoach Viscount and Stagecoach in the Fens. The vehicles that transferred across were recently acquired ADL Enviro 400s 10012/3; Leyland Olympian 14000; Volvo Olympians 16221/4-7, 16581/93; Dennis Tridents 17691-3, 18109-11; native Enviro 400s 19888-19891; Volvo B6BLEs 21160-5; Dennis Dart SLFs 33181-4, 34097, 34102; Transbus Darts 34419-35, 34479, 34771/3, 34825-835; Optare Solos 47341, 47351-4; 47435-442, 47659; Volvo B10M coaches 52124, 52155/6/60-2, 52368-73, 52437, 52441, 52482-6, 52644; Volvo B7Rs 53271-4 and Volvo B9Rs 53601-13/5-8.

Between March and December, United Counties took stock of a large number of second hand vehicles. Before we look at these, the company was in receipt of nine ADL Enviro 400 bodied Scania N230UD double-deck vehicles in October. These vehicles were built to the more luxurious Stagecoach Gold specification. The routes chosen were the X46 and X47 between Northampton and Raunds, via Wellingborough and Rushden. Allocated to Northampton, the vehicles concerned were numbered 15935 to 15943, registered YN63BYA-D/F-H/J/K.

The operations of First Northampton were slowly wound down over the course of 2013, with the company finally ceasing to operate in June 2013. United Counties picked up the majority of the routes previously operated by First, with Uno gaining a handful of services. To operate these services, a number of vehicles were taken into stock to help, some on a short-term basis, others operating for a longer period of time.

A number of former Corby and Kettering Solos were the first to be taken into stock. 47034/5/7 (KX03KYY/Z, KZB) and 47402/4/6-8 (KX55PFA/E/G/J/K) arrived over the course of March and April. 47035 and 47037 were taken into stock from Stagecoach Oxfordshire and Stagecoach Midland Red, whilst the remaining vehicles were officially acquired from Northamptonshire County Council, on behalf of which United Counties had previously operated the vehicles.

June saw a busy month for the intake of vehicles, with eleven vehicles arriving from various sources. From Stagecoach Midland Red came former London Trident 17054 – T654KPU and two ADL Enviro 200 bodied MAN 14.240 saloons numbered 39692/3 – KX08LVN/O. Stagecoach Cheltenham & Gloucester provided a quartet of Plaxton Pointer bodied Dennis Dart SLF saloons numbered 33508/9/11/3 – W508/9VDD, X511/3ADF. The final four vehicles were more of the Dennis Dart SLF saloon. 34097, 34102 – S497BWC, S102WHK were bodied by Alexander on the ALX200 model, with 34141/60 – V141/60MVX being Plaxton Pointers.

Two Northern Counties bodied Volvo Olympians arrived at Northampton in August from Midland Red. 16680 – L680HNV and 16873 – P905RYO were the vehicles concerned. 16680 originated with United Counties.

September was another busy month for United Counties with fifteen vehicles entering the fleet. From Stagecoach Yorkshire came a trio of ADL Enviro 400 machines that originated with Stagecoach Manchester. Numbered 19010/2/20, these vehicles were registered MX06XAK/M/V respectively. Two further Alexander ALX300 bodied MAN 18.220 saloons were also taken into stock. 22935 – S935CFC came from Stagecoach Oxford whilst 22459 – S459OFT came from Stagecoach Midland Red. From the same source came Alexander ALX200 bodied Dennis Dart SLFs 33650/2/4 – R150/2/4CRW and Plaxton Pointer bodied 34133 – V133MVX. The remaining five vehicles were sourced from Stagecoach Merseyside. Transbus Dart/Pointer saloons 34473-7 were registered PX53DJV/Y/Z, DKA/D. All fifteen were allocated to Northampton depot. 22935 and 33650/2/4 only lasted in service until November 2013.

Plaxton Pointer bodied Dennis Dart SLF 34122 (V122MVX) and similar Transbus Darts 34625/42/4 – KX54OOY, GX54DWN/P were acquired from Midland Red and were allocated to Northampton. The large intake of single-deck vehicles in the fleet was to help remove the numerous vehicles that did not conform to the Disability Discrimination Act which required all single-deck vehicles to be of a certain specification by the start of 2014.

Over the course of 2012 and 2013, the Corby Star fleet gained a revised version of the livery. The red at the rear of the vehicle was replaced by a dark blue.

2014

2014 saw forty-one vehicles enter service with United Counties, and unlike previous years, the majority of them were new vehicles.

The new vehicles came in the form of thirty-seven AD E20D/Enviro 200 saloons. They were delivered in two batches. January saw the arrival of 37038-51 YX63ZWF/G/H/J/K/L/M/N/P/R/S/T/U/V. These vehicles displaced the 33, 34 and 35 prefixed Dart machines. This removed the last of the non-compliant Dennis Darts from the service fleet. Some of these vehicles were transferred within United Counties to Kettering and Corby depots. The remaining vehicles, 37052-74 YX63YPT/V/W/X/Z, YRA/C, LKP, YRE/F/G/J/L/M/N/O/P/R/S/T/U/V/W, were delivered to the company in February and March. The arrival of these vehicles saw wide-spread branding applied to the batch for various routes. 37038-41 gained purple branding for route 5 (New Duston-Southfields); 37043-5 gained blue branding for route 10 (West Hunsbury-Parklands); 37046/7 had pink branding applied for route 15 between the Town Centre and Kingsthorpe. 37052-7 gained branding for route 8 (Blackthorn-Bicester), again in pink; 37058-62 for route 12 (Camp Hill-Kings Heath). 37063-9 gained red route branding for the Daventry Dart services D1-D3 between Northampton and Daventry.

March saw the arrival of a solitary ADL Dart/Pointer saloon, 35176 – KX56KHB, again being allocated to Northampton. At the same time, another former Corby Optare Solo (47032 – KX03KYV) arrived back with its original operator. Both were acquired from Stagecoach Midlands Red South.

The final four vehicles to arrive in 2014 came in the form of Dennis Trident/Alexander ALX400 double-decks. The first two arrived from Stagecoach Fife Scottish in March. These both originated with Stagecoach London back in 1999 and had operated with a number of operators before arriving with United Counties. The vehicles concerned were numbered 17037 – S837BWC and 17060 – T660KPU. Both were allocated to Kettering. The other two originated with Stagecoach Oxford. 18127 and 18128 – KN04XJA/B arrived at Northampton from Stagecoach Cheltenham & Gloucester in August.

The United Counties story came to an end when the services operated by the company were registered under the Midland Red (South) operators' licence. The change of operator took effect from 12 October 2014. The vehicles were also transferred across to the Midland Red operators' licence. The amalgamation of the two companies formed the new Stagecoach Midlands operation, with the head office for the company remaining at Northampton.

Representing the trio of new Scania N230UDs delivered in 2010 is 15608 – KX59BBO. Initially used on the X4, the arrival of the Gold specification buses for the route saw these three buses reallocated to route 50 between Kettering and Bedford. It is seen stopped at Skinners Hill, Rushden, bound for Kettering. It shows clearly the route branding carried by these vehicles.
David Beddall

Representing the numerous Alexander RL bodied Volvo Olympians acquired by the company from East Midlands is 16459 – P159KAK. It is seen on layover in Peterborough City Centre. The former London Olympians acquired in 2010 are already represented in this book.
David Beddall

The smart Plaxton President body style can be seen in this photograph of 17695 – X705JVV, one of seven Dennis Trident machines acquired from Stagecoach Viscount in 2010. 17695 is seen on layover in Church Street, Wellingborough.
David Beddall

The other six new vehicles to enter the fleet during 2010 were ADL Enviro 300s. During the summer of 2012, these vehicles were used on Olympic contracts in London. 27681 – KX60AZF is seen passing St Pancras in July 2012.
Liam Farrer-Beddall

THE FINAL YEARS 2010–2014 • 213

The final batch of new vehicles to enter service with United Counties during 2011 came in the form of thirteen ADL Enviro 400 bodied Scania N230UD machines built to Gold specification. The smart gold and blue livery applied to these vehicles is shown here. 15751 – KX61DLZ is seen having just started its journey to Corby from Northampton. *Liam Farrer-Beddall*

Under the control of Cambridge, the fleet at Bedford depot began to be modernised. Six ADL Trident/ALX400 machines were taken into stock from Peterborough in 2011 to replace older Volvo Olympian machines. 18411 – AE06GZH is seen parked outside Bedford bus garage in September 2011. *Liam Farrer-Beddall*

The first new double-deckers for Bedford garage since 1998 arrived in June 2011. 19890 – AE11FUG is seen having just completed a journey in from Kempston. The new Bedford Bus logo is displayed clearly in this photograph. *David Beddall*

Seven Wright Renown bodied Volvo B6BLE low-floor saloons were acquired from Stagecoach in the Fens during 2011. Bedford received the full allocation of these vehicles where 21160 – R120HNK is found in between duties. These vehicles were smart in appearance. *David Beddall*

THE FINAL YEARS 2010–2014 • **215**

Midland Red South took stock of the first Optare Solos in the Stagecoach Group. One of this batch, 47015 (KX51CTV), was acquired by United Counties in 2011 and was allocated to Kettering garage from where it was put to use on Wellingborough town services. It is seen parked in Church Street, Wellingborough. *David Beddall*

53618 – AE11FMF was the replacement for accident victim 53614. It is seen loading at Bedford bus station before travelling to Cambridge. The X5 branding can be clearly seen in this photograph. *David Beddall*

The final vehicles to be acquired by Bedford before the fleet transferred across to the Cambus operators' licence were a pair of ADL Enviro 400 machines. 10013 – AE12CKF was swapped with two similar vehicles, arriving from Peterborough. *David Beddall*

The second United Counties route to gold was the X46/X47 in 2013. Nine ADL Enviro 400s were taken into stock. 15937 – YN63BYC is seen loading in Wellingborough heading towards Thrapston. *Liam Farrer-Beddall*

Fifteen ADL Enviro 300 bodied Scania K230 saloons arrived at Northampton during 2012. The batch was split between the X7 and Northampton town services. 28627 – KX12AMU was one of those put to use on route 2 in Northampton. It is seen departing Northampton's North Gate bus station. *Liam Farrer-Beddall*

Three ADL Enviro 400s were taken into stock from Stagecoach Manchester via Stagecoach Yorkshire in 2013. Northampton North Gate bus station provides the background to this photograph of 19012 – MX06XAM operating a town service. *David Beddall*

United Counties took five Transbus Dart/Pointer saloons from Stagecoach Merseyside during 2013. 34474 – PX53DJY is seen rounding Greyfriars bus station heading for the University of Northampton. *Liam Farrer-Beddall*

The final pair of vehicles taken into stock by United Counties came in the form of these former Stagecoach Oxford Tridents. 18127 – KN04XJB is seen parked on The Drapery in Northampton before heading out to Pineham. *David Beddall*

Thirty-seven ADL Enviro 200 saloons arrived during the first two months of 2014 at Northampton. They replaced older single-deck vehicles, some of which were cascaded around United Counties. 37046 – YX63ZWP is seen travelling along The Drapery in Northampton. *Liam Farrer-Beddall*

One of the routes to gain an upgrade to the Enviro 200 saloons was the Daventry Dart network running between Northampton and Daventry. 37069 – YY63YRR is seen heading towards Daventry after loading in The Drapery. *Liam Farrer-Beddall*

INDEX

ADL
    Dart 181, 182, 183, 184, 199, 206, 210
    Enviro 200 185, 202, 209, 210, 219
    Enviro 300 186, 203, 205, 207, 208, 212, 217
    Enviro 400 186, 205, 206, 208, 209, 213, 216, 217
    Pointer 181, 182, 184, 199 206, 210
AEC
    Regal 28, 29, 30, 31, 39
    Regent 30, 39, 40
    Reliance 90, 98
    Routemaster 15, 126, 142, 146, 147, 149, 151, 152, 154
    Swift 70
Albion Lowlander 84, 86, 87, 102
Alexander 86, 93, 94, 98, 124, 127, 129, 143, 150, 152, 168
    ALX200 157, 159, 169, 173, 175, 179, 182, 206, 207, 209
    ALX300 186, 204, 209
    ALX400 210
    Dash 149, 150, 151, 155, 164, 165, 172, 173, 178, 180, 181, 192, 194, 198
    PS 156, 182, 184, 186, 194, 197
    RH 179, 180
    RL 127, 141, 145, 146, 148, 151, 154, 155, 156, 157, 161, 166, 173, 182, 185, 198, 205, 207, 208, 211
    Sprint 151, 162, 180
    T 95, 114

Beadle 41, 42, 43, 47, 50
Bedford (town) 7, 10, 12, 13, 14, 15, 16, 45, 50, 58, 59, 63, 68, 70, 73, 74, 75, 78, 81, 82, 85, 86, 87, 88, 91, 92, 94, 95, 96, 97, 98, 99, 104, 105, 111, 112, 115, 116, 117, 118, 123, 124, 125, 126, 127, 128, 129, 130, 132, 139, 141, 142, 143, 145, 146, 147, 148, 149, 150, 151, 152, 153, 154, 155, 156, 157, 158, 159, 161, 162, 163, 164, 165, 166, 167, 168, 169, 171, 172, 173, 174, 175, 177, 178, 180, 181, 182, 183, 184, 185, 186, 187, 188, 189, 190, 192, 194, 195, 196, 197, 198, 199, 200, 201, 204, 205, 206, 207, 208, 211, 213, 214, 215, 216
Bedford
    CFL 94
    OB 41, 43, 46, 49, 50
    OWB 46
    SBO 71, 77
    WLB 28, 29
    WLG 27
    WTB 48
    YMQ 118, 132
    YRQ 89, 91, 92, 93, 95, 96, 97, 110, 117, 119
    YRT 92, 95, 109, 114
Birch Bros. 13, 72, 81, 82, 85, 90, 92, 93
Bristol
    FLF6B 52, 67, 68, 69, 71, 78, 88, 90, 99, 174, 176, 189
    FS6B 67, 68, 69, 70, 73, 74, 98, 100
    FS6G 70, 76, 86, 90, 117, 119
    FSF6G 89, 92
    GO5G 39
    JO5G 16, 30, 35, 41, 42, 45, 46, 51, 52
    K5G 30, 32, 36, 38, 39, 40, 41, 42, 43, 46, 47, 49, 58, 68, 94
    K6B 43
    KS5G 44, 48
    KSW5G 48, 59, 60, 62
    KSW6B 45, 49, 50, 60, 61, 62, 63, 86, 88
    L5G 31, 32, 37, 41, 44, 45, 46, 50, 51, 55, 57, 59, 68
    L6B 41, 44, 46, 55
    LD6B 49, 50, 51, 52, 66, 86, 87, 107
    LD6G 86, 89, 90, 94, 95, 96, 101
    LH 71, 95, 97, 158
    LH6L 72, 72, 83, 98, 105, 169, 172

INDEX

LHS6P 84
LL5G 44, 46, 47, 56
LL6B 45, 71, 80
LS5G 49, 50, 51, 52, 57, 65, 67, 68, 70, 72, 75, 81
LS6B 49, 50, 64, 68, 88
LS6G 52, 64, 70, 71, 75, 80, 92
LWL5G 46, 47
LWL6B 45, 61, 71
MW6G 52, 66, 67, 68, 70, 71, 72, 73, 79, 86, 87, 89, 93, 98
RELH6G 69, 71, 72, 74, 85, 87, 89, 93, 95, 96, 98, 104, 118, 122
RELH6L 111, 122, 123
RELL6G 71, 72, 79, 82, 84, 85, 87, 92, 96, 99, 103, 104, 106
RESL6G 86, 89, 92, 106, 117
SC4LK 51, 65, 68, 69
SUL4A 70, 76, 78
VRT 71, 72, 83, 85, 87, 89, 90, 91, 93, 95, 96, 97, 99, 105, 109, 112, 116, 117, 118, 119, 121, 122, 123, 124, 125, 126, 127, 129, 130, 135, 145, 146, 147, 148, 149, 150, 152, 153, 154, 155, 157, 158, 168, 174, 180
Burlingham 30, 31, 39

Cambridge 11, 16, 29, 73, 124, 134, 144, 153, 167, 170, 173, 180, 181, 193, 201, 205, 206, 208, 213, 215
Cambus 15, 16, 156, 157, 159, 172, 173, 174, 177, 178, 179, 184, 187, 197, 205, 206, 208, 209, 216
Carlyle 137
Charter Way 96, 113
Chevrolet 27, 28, 29
Coachlinks 15, 73, 124, 125, 126, 129, 134, 136, 140, 141, 144, 149, 150, 151, 153, 155, 156, 160, 167, 168, 175
Connect Kettering / Wellingborough 183, 200
Corby 10, 11, 12, 13, 14, 15, 16, 29, 60, 85, 90, 91, 96, 97, 98, 99, 117, 118, 121, 123, 125, 126, 128, 131, 142, 145, 146, 147, 148, 151, 152, 153, 154, 155, 157, 158, 160, 162, 168, 171, 173, 174, 176, 177, 179, 180, 183, 190, 191, 195, 205, 206, 207, 208, 209, 210, 213
Corby Star 177, 179, 180, 190, 191, 210
Court Line Coaches 13, 92, 94, 99, 108, 110
Crossley 29
Crosville 88, 94, 98, 107

Daimler
   CF6 28
   CVG6 92
   Fleetline 124, 138, 147
   Y 21
Daventry 9, 10, 12, 13, 14, 210, 219
Deansgate 94, 113, 133
Dennis
   Dart 149, 150, 154, 155, 164, 172, 178, 180, 181, 182, 183, 192, 195, 198
   Dart SLF 157, 158, 159, 169, 173, 174, 175, 176, 179, 182, 194, 206, 207, 208, 209, 210
   Lance 39, 46
   Lancet 28, 31, 39, 45, 46
   Loline 84, 86, 101, 102
   Trident 206, 210, 212
Devon General 127, 129, 150
Dodge 126, 147, 150, 158, 172, 176
Duple 28, 29, 32, 39, 46, 48, 50, 146
Dominant 94, 95, 97, 112, 118, 120, 134, 137
   Laser 146, 149, 160
   Super Vega 71, 77

East Lancs 84, 85, 101, 102, 179
East Yorkshire Motor Services Limited, 88, 103
Eastern Counties 11, 27, 29, 30, 33, 48, 84, 87, 88, 98, 117, 118
Eastern National 10, 11, 12, 13, 28, 29, 31, 32, 43, 45, 46, 48, 49, 50, 51, 54, 55, 57, 58, 59, 60, 62, 68, 69, 70, 75, 87, 89, 90, 99
ECOC 33, 34, 46, 47, 48
ECW 30, 31, 32, 33, 35, 36, 37, 38, 40, 41, 42, 44, 45, 46, 47, 48, 49, 50, 51, 52, 56, 57, 58, 60, 61, 62, 63, 65, 66, 67, 68, 70, 73, 75, 76, 78, 79, 80, 81, 82, 83, 86, 89, 103, 104, 105, 106, 112, 118, 119, 125, 134, 135, 149, 169, 172, 173, 174, 180, 187

FAP Famos 129, 144, 146
First Northampton 179, 182, 193, 209
Fife Scottish 146, 147, 151, 161, 210
Ford
   A 94, 96, 98, 129, 143
   R192 92, 98, 110
   R1014 94, 95, 108, 112, 117, 128
   Transit 97, 116, 118, 121, 122, 124, 127, 128, 133, 137

Gilford 28, 29, 30, 31
Grose 21
Guy 29, 39

Arab 39, 50
B 28, 29

Huntingdon 11, 12, 14, 15, 31, 45, 86, 89, 95, 97, 99, 108, 121, 122, 123, 141, 144, 145, 146, 148, 149, 151, 154, 156, 165, 168, 207

Iveco A49.10 124, 125, 126, 127, 128, 129, 130, 138, 139, 145, 146, 147, 148, 149, 150, 151, 153, 154, 160, 162, 168

Jonckheere
    Deauville 159, 170, 173, 181
    Mistral 184, 204, 209

Kettering 7, 8, 9, 10, 11, 13, 14, 15, 16, 18, 19, 26, 28, 29, 31, 32, 40, 45, 62, 65, 75, 77, 85, 86, 87, 88, 89, 90, 91, 93, 94, 95, 96, 97, 98, 99, 112, 114, 116, 117, 118, 119, 121, 123, 124, 125, 126, 127, 128, 129, 130, 131, 134, 136, 139, 145, 147, 149, 150, 151, 152, 154, 155, 156, 158, 159, 167, 173, 174, 175, 183, 184, 186, 191, 196, 199, 200, 205, 206, 207, 208, 209, 210, 211, 215

Lancia 21, 28, 29, 31
Leighton Buzzard 10, 52, 70, 76, 82, 94, 96, 98, 117, 118, 123, 132
Lex 118, 132
Leyland
    36HP 17, 22, 24
    C7 19
    Cub 29, 31, 48, 117
    Fleetline 152, 154, 157, 168
    GH7 19
    Leopard 72, 81, 82, 92, 93, 94, 95, 97, 98, 99, 114, 115, 116, 117, 118, 119, 120, 121, 122, 123, 124, 125, 129, 131, 132, 134, 135, 137, 144, 145, 146, 151
    Lion 20, 21, 25, 26, 28, 31, 32, 38, 39, 40, 41, 42, 46, 49, 50
    Lioness 29
    National 87, 88, 89, 91, 93, 94, 95, 96, 97, 98, 99, 111, 115, 116, 117, 119, 122, 123, 128, 130, 148, 149, 150, 152
    Olympian 117, 118, 119, 124, 125, 127, 129, 134, 135, 141, 145, 146, 148, 149, 150, 151, 152, 153, 154, 156, 157, 158, 159, 161, 163, 166, 172, 173, 174, 175, 176, 177, 179, 180, 182, 183, 187, 188, 205, 209
    RAF 18, 19, 24

SG7 20
SG11 20
ST 17, 22, 23
Tiger 46, 120, 121, 124, 130, 136, 140, 146, 147, 149, 150, 151, 153, 154, 156, 158, 160, 172
Tiger Cub 88, 90, 107
Tiger TS3 28, 32
Tiger TS7 29
Tiger TS8 31
Titan 128, 129, 157, 158, 171, 173, 174, 175, 176, 188
Titan PD1 47
Titan PD2 84, 85, 100
Titan PD3 143, 151, 153, 158
Titan TD1 21, 26, 28, 40, 46, 47
Titan TD2 27, 33, 39, 47
Titan TD3 47
Titan TD4 29, 47
Titan TD5 47
Z5 19
London 7, 10, 11, 29, 31, 34, 45, 72, 79, 85, 91, 93, 106, 111, 126, 130, 150, 159, 189, 208, 212
London Buses Limited 126, 142, 147
London Country Bus Services 120, 135, 137
London Transport 38, 39, 40, 41, 42
London United 154
Luton 12, 13, 14, 43, 45, 50, 56, 57, 59, 60, 76, 79, 81, 84, 85, 86, 87, 88, 89, 90, 91, 94, 95, 96, 97, 98, 99, 100, 101, 102, 103, 104, 106, 108, 110, 116, 117, 118, 119, 120, 121, 122, 123, 125, 128, 130, 132, 137, 141, 159, 171, 172, 177, 184, 195, 201
Luton Corporation Transport 13, 84, 85, 86, 88, 89, 100, 101, 102, 103, 104

Magicbus, Glasgow 129, 145
Maidstone & District 90
MAN
    14.240 185, 209
    18.220 186, 203, 204, 209
Marshall 72, 81
Maudslay 26, 28, 30
MCW 154
MCCW 84, 88, 100, 107
Mercedes-Benz
    309D 96, 113
    609D 173, 175, 176
    709D 127, 148, 150, 151, 154, 155, 158, 159, 162, 175, 176, 180, 186, 200
    L406D 94, 113

L608D 172, 176
O302 71
Milton Keynes 13, 14, 15, 93, 94, 95, 96, 97, 98, 99, 100, 113, 120, 121, 122, 123, 124, 131, 153, 156, 159, 170, 171, 172, 177, 179, 181, 184, 186, 187, 191, 193, 201, 202, 203

National Bus Company 13, 15, 17, 72, 76, 86, 87, 88, 89, 90, 92, 93, 94, 95, 99, 100, 118, 121, 123
Northampton 7, 8, 9, 10, 11, 12, 13, 14, 15, 16, 18, 21, 23, 28, 29, 31, 32, 34, 35, 38, 40, 45, 51, 55, 56, 65, 68, 70, 71, 73, 76, 85, 86, 87, 88, 89, 90, 91, 92, 93, 94, 95, 96, 97, 98, 99, 115, 116, 117, 118, 119, 120, 122, 123, 124, 127, 128, 129, 130, 131, 134, 140, 141, 143, 144, 145, 147, 148, 149, 150, 153, 154, 155, 156, 157, 158, 159, 163, 164, 169, 172, 173, 174, 175, 177, 178, 179, 180, 181, 182, 183, 184, 185, 186, 193, 196, 202, 203, 204, 205, 206, 207, 208, 209, 210, 213, 217, 218, 219
Northampton Omnibus Company 9, 10, 21
Northampton Transport 92, 93, 149, 150, 186
Northern Counties 143, 148, 150, 152, 155, 157, 163, 173, 174, 177, 178, 180, 182, 184, 188, 195, 196, 197, 205, 209
Northern Scottish 146

Optare Solo 176, 179, 180, 183, 190, 200, 206, 207, 208, 209, 210, 215
Oxford 10, 11, 29, 31, 40, 45, 77, 153, 159, 167, 168, 170, 171, 181, 186, 204, 209, 210, 218

Park Royal 72, 82
Plaxton 91, 108, 110, 128, 131, 140
   Elite 92, 111, 117
   Expressliner 177, 178, 181, 185, 190, 193
   Panorama 97
   Panther 186, 202, 206
   Paramount 120, 124, 126, 136, 145, 148, 153, 154, 155
   Pointer 178, 180, 182, 206, 207, 209, 210
   Premiere 149, 150, 153, 154, 156, 167, 168, 173, 174, 175, 177, 181, 208
   President 206, 212
   Profile 184, 201
   Supreme 115, 129, 140, 144

Renault 130, 179, 180
Reo Pullman 27, 28, 30
Ribble 120, 137, 145, 146, 147, 148, 149, 150
Robin Hood 125, 127, 129, 139, 146, 147

Rushden 7, 8, 9, 10, 12, 13, 14, 18, 29, 45, 72, 76, 80, 82, 85, 86, 88, 89, 91, 92, 93, 95, 97, 152, 184, 209, 211

Scania 180
   K230 207, 217
   N230UD 186, 205, 206, 209, 211, 213
   Omnidekka 179, 191
Scottish Bus Group 90, 101
South Midland 45
Southern Vectis 71, 77, 90, 94
Stagecoach
   Express 153, 158, 159, 170, 174, 175, 181, 193
   Gold 206, 209, 211, 213, 216
   In the Fens 16, 207, 208, 209, 214
   London 157, 171, 177, 181, 195, 205, 207, 209, 210, 211
   South Midlands 180, 181, 183, 184
Stamford 9, 13, 14, 61, 83, 89, 109
Strachen 21
Studebaker 28

Thornycroft 21, 27
Tilling Group 11, 12, 29, 39, 63, 101
Tilling Stevens 26, 29, 31, 38
Transbus
   ALX400 179, 186, 191
   Dart 176, 177, 178, 179, 180, 181, 182, 185, 189, 192, 206, 207, 208, 209, 210, 218
   Pointer 177, 179, 182, 189, 207, 209
   Trident 179, 186, 191, 203

Virgin Rail Link 159, 171, 172, 177, 178, 181, 184, 190, 201
Viscount 15, 16, 157, 173, 174, 177, 178, 182, 188, 205, 206, 207, 208, 209, 212
Volvo
   B6 150, 151, 152, 153, 154, 155, 156, 157, 158, 164, 165, 172, 173, 175, 176, 177, 178, 180, 181, 192
   B6BLE 207, 209, 214
   B7R 184, 201, 209
   B9R 186, 202, 204, 209
   B10M 126, 127, 140, 145, 147, 148, 149, 150, 153, 154, 155, 156, 159, 167, 170, 174, 175, 176, 177, 178, 180, 181, 182, 184, 185, 186, 187, 190, 193, 194, 197, 208, 209
   Olympian 150, 153, 154, 155, 156, 157, 158, 163, 173, 174, 175, 177, 178, 179, 182, 184, 185, 195, 196, 197, 198, 201, 205, 207, 208, 209, 211, 213

Welford 9, 11, 27, 51, 70, 76
Wellingborough 7, 8, 9, 10, 11, 12, 14, 15, 17, 18, 21, 32, 39, 40, 45, 78, 85, 88, 94, 96, 97, 98, 99, 117, 118, 119, 123, 127, 129, 140, 147, 183, 200, 207, 209, 212, 215, 216
Wellingborough Motor Omnibus Company 7, 17, 18, 22, 23, 24
West Yorkshire Roadcar 89, 90, 92
Weymann 47, 50, 84, 100

Willowbrook 27, 28, 40, 41, 46, 49, 70, 72, 89, 92, 93, 95, 109, 110, 114, 116, 131

X5 153, 156, 158, 159, 167, 168, 170, 174, 175, 181, 182, 185, 186, 193, 201, 202, 204, 206, 208, 215

York Brothers / Coaches 14, 15, 128, 140
Yorkshire Traction 89, 191
Yorkshire Wollen District Transport 124